The Business of Ethnography

The Business of Ethnography

Strategic Exchanges, People and Organizations

Brian Moeran

Oxford • New York

56686403

English edition
First published in 2005 by
Berg
Editorial offices:
First Floor, Angel Court, 81 St Clements Street, Oxford OX4 1AW, UK
175 Fifth Avenue, New York, NY 10010, USA

Berg is the imprint of Oxford International Publishers Ltd.

Library of Congress Cataloging-in-Publication Data
Moeran, Brian, 1944-
    The business of ethnography : strategic exchanges,
people, and organizations / Brian Moeran. — English ed.
        p.   cm
    Includes bibliographical references and index.
    ISBN 1-84520-194-9 (hardback)—
    ISBN 1-84520-195-7 (pbk.)
1.   Business anthropology—Japan. 2.   Corporate
culture—Japan. 3.   Ethnology—Japan—Field work.
4.   Japan—Social life and customs. I.   Title.

GN635.J2M64 2005
302.3′5—dc   2004023153

British Library Cataloguing-in-Publication Data
A catalogue record for this book is available from the British Library.

ISBN-13 978 1 84520 194 4 (hardback)
          978 1 84520 195 1 (paperback)
ISBN-10 1 84520 194 9 (hardback)
          1 84520 195 7 (paperback)

Typeset by Avocet Typeset, Chilton, Aylesbury, Bucks
Printed in the United Kingdom by Biddles Ltd, King's Lynn.

www.bergpublishers.com

Dedication

For the Fox and the Wolf
who in their very different ways helped make this book possible
with great love and affection

Contents

Acknowledgements

It is customary to frame a book like this with acknowledgements.

The various periods of fieldwork which provide much of the material appearing in this book were funded for the following purposes by the following institutions: (1) 'The production, marketing and aesthetic appraisal of Japanese folk craft pottery' by the Social Science Research Council of Great Britain (April 1977 through March 1978) and Japan Foundation (April 1978 through March 1979); (2) 'Pottery as an art form in Japan' by the Economic and Social Research Council of Great Britain (April through September, 1981) and the School of Oriental and African Studies, University of London (October 1981 through March 1982); (3) 'The social processes of advertising production' by the Japan Foundation (January through December, 1990); (4) 'Economy, culture and self-identity: a comparative study of international women's magazines' by the Danish Centre for Advanced Studies in the Humanities (September 2000 through August 2001) and the Danish Research Agency (September 2001 through December 2002). I really do thank them all for putting their faith in me and for providing the necessary funds to enable the research to get done.

An immense number of people have helped me in Japan over the years, and I cannot begin to thank them all here for everything that they have taught me. I would like to mention, though, the following for their very special input into my fieldwork investigations: Gotō Eisuke, Ikuma Katsuhiro, Kajiwara Jirō, Miyamoto Fusa, Miyamoto Reisuke, Naganuma Kōichirō, Nakamura Kin'ichi, Sakamoto Shigeki, Sakamoto Fumiko, Sakamoto Isae, and Sano Yoshihide. Kuroishi Kōyū, Kanetake Mariko and Ted von Holst have always been there to provide moral (and oenological) support when needed. Others in the world who have helped the cause of fieldwork include Katie Breen, Sandy Brown, Pamela Lam, Joseph Newland, Sekiji Toshio, Kim Shuefftan, and Yasuda Takeshi. Those old – and, alas, getting older – friends who have provided much needed sanity over the decades include Katerina Aggelaki, Diana Hume, David and Maya Kennedy, Vito Orlando, Sarah and Philip Ramp, and Rodney Rooke, while those two loving boys of mine, Alyosha and Maya, are wonderful support to have in my dotage. For her part, Ursula does her best to keep me young.

Among those whose work I have found directly or indirectly inspiring in the writing of this book are Howard Becker, Richard Caves, Clifford Geertz, Ulf

Hannerz, Chie Nakane, Walter Powell, Lise Skov, John Van Maanen and Tony Watson. Some I am fortunate enough to know and their company greatly to enjoy; others I have never met, but hope to one day. With yet others – especially Erving Goffman and Pierre Bourdieu – it is, alas, too late. Thank you all.

And then there are those who have so generously and forbearingly put up with me as an academic colleague, and provided ideas and support, over the years. I think in particular of Lionel Caplan, Audrie Cantlie, Richard Fardon, Mark Hobart, Stefan Kaiser, Adrian Mayer and David Parkin, at S.O.A.S.; Burton Benedict, Beth Berry, Alan Dundes, Nelson Graburn, Irv Scheiner and Don ('Kanjirō') Shively, at the University of California, Berkeley; Arne Kalland at the Nordic Institute of Asian Studies; Jonathan Grant, Michael Martin, Kirsten Refsing, Antony Tatlow and Wong Heung Wah, at the University of Hong Kong; Suzanne Beckmann, Sven Bislev, Fabian Csaba, Eric Guthie, Dorte Salskov-Iversen, Majken Schulz, Anne-Marie Söderberg, Ole Stromgren and Charlie Tackney at the Copenhagen Business School; and Otto Due, Lisa Hannestad, Philippe Provençal, and Vladimir Stolba at the (now defunct) Danish Institute of Advanced Studies in the Humanities. The anthropologist Michael Jackson, though never – alas! – a colleague, has provided over the years a rare combination of friendship and intellectual stimulation for which I am extremely grateful. I am acutely aware of, and slightly embarrassed by, the male-dominated content of this list.

And now that I have set my research within the activities of various funding bodies, revealed my partial networks of friends and colleagues, and framed the academic field to which I owe allegiance, I will move you on to the substance of this book …

Preface

Writing this book has been a delight. I don't know whether it had something to do with the late autumn air in Aigina, the unfashionable Greek island where I am fortunate enough to have a home, or the fact that a fast approaching sixtieth birthday enabled me to bring this cycle of writing to a close, but the words have flowed ever since I first put pen to paper (OK, opened a computer file) six weeks ago.

A couple of days after I arrived, Yiorgos, the baker, greeted me with his customary ironic smile. 'What! Holidays again?' he asked. 'You *do* have it easy as a professor, don't you!'

I explained that I was here to write a book.

'A book?' He nodded, more serious now. 'And what kind of book are you writing?'

'One about ethnography.'

'Ethnography?' Yiorgos pursed his lips thoughtfully. 'As in anthropology, you mean? Now that's a very interesting subject. What exactly are you writing about anthropology?' he asked with that blend of curiosity and intelligent interest that makes a lot of ordinary Greeks such fun to be with.

'Well,' I drew a deep breath, not sure if my knowledge of the language would extend to a technical explanation of frames, networks and fields, 'it's about all the different kinds of exchanges that take place among people and organizations. What I want to argue is that anthropological fieldwork is a really useful way to help us understand how and why people behave in the ways they do – especially in business. And I illustrate my argument by talking about my research in Japan and how people interact in Japanese society.'

'*Japanese* society?' Yiorgos raised both eyebrows to indicate a certain admiration. 'I didn't know you wrote about the Japanese. Now they're a people who interest me *very* much, even though I know very little about them. What is it that makes them tick? How did they get to be where they are now? Are you explaining their history?'

No, I replied. I was keeping to contemporary Japan, although one aim of the book was comparison. I wanted to show how ultimately the Japanese weren't all that different from people here in Europe – English, Greeks, Danes, and so on – in the ways they behaved.

'Is that so? Are they really so similar? That goes against the grain of all you hear and read, doesn't it?' he mused, nodding at what I'd said. And then, 'Will I be able to read your book?'

He was already smiling again as he anticipated my reply.

'Probably not', I admitted.

Yiorgos's question continued to haunt me every time I sat down at my portable computer and gazed out at the unsurpassable view of Methana, Poros, the Pelepponesos and, when the air was clear, a distant Hydra. I felt his sparkling eyes boring into me as I wrote and I've done my best to produce something that can be read fairly easily by an intelligent human being like my baker friend. Of course, such reader friendliness will doubtless alienate me from my academic colleagues who, like the potters I often talk about in these pages, produce works for themselves, rather than for a general public. In a classic repetition of the economic 'disavowal' that characterizes Japan's ceramic-art world, fellow academics tend to persuade themselves that 'good books don't sell' and that books that sell cannot by definition be good.

Whether this book will sell or not, I don't know. To judge by earlier attempts, it probably won't. But I firmly believe that it should be possible for us academics to present complex theoretical ideas in a simple and intelligent manner so that they can be readily understood by those who sit in our classrooms, attend our seminar presentations and skim through our works. Goffman clearly thought so and knew how to do it (which is why his books are published now by Penguin and other popular paperback publishers). Bourdieu – alas! – did not.

'Books', Yiorgos said, as he popped my cheese pie into a bag, 'are meant to be read, not written in the head.'

Brian Moeran
Kleidí

Introduction: Strategic Exchanges

One of the interesting things about life is precisely . . . things. Things bring people together. They oblige them to interact, and to enter into exchanges of one sort or another. Everyday organizations and institutions of all sorts – from ministries to museums, offices to opium dens, and factories to farms – are formed around things. Things create social situations that, in some cases, their participants are no more than dimly aware of and, in others, use ruthlessly to their advantage. People weave, dispute and negotiate meanings in and around things. In the process, they give them their 'social lives'.[1]

Things thus take on a 'social density'.[2] They contribute to and reinforce *certain kinds* of social relationship and exchange. Take weapons of mass destruction (WMD), for instance. They sustain, among other things, the coupling of military with political power, and the prominence of men – usually older men – in public affairs and global politics. They foreground the existence and deployment of specialists in detecting and defusing WMD. They provide a living for hundreds of thousands of young men and their families who are trained, disciplined, kept in readiness and ordered to fight – as and when deemed necessary, with or without their own WMD – an enemy (or, in the meantime, rescue stranded mountaineers, help dam rising flood waters, put out forest fires, and contribute to the spread of venereal diseases). WMD underlie publicized ideological divisions between 'good' and 'evil', between a Christian West and Muslim Arab world, between human beings and their gods. They encourage endless flows of media 'news', (dis)information, speculation, half-truths and gossip with little immediate or systematic analysis – news that is read at breakfast tables, discussed in restaurants during lunch, argued over in pubs and bars all around the world and, eventually, disputed in parliaments and on television chat shows. They also contribute to the linguistic, political and social harassment of immigrants that resurfaces and strengthens its grip on people everywhere. In short, in numerous different ways, not all of them by any means friendly, WMD link people. They maintain the existence of old organizations and institutions, create new associations, form, influence and change opinions and beliefs, and generally affect our everyday lives.[3]

As a social anthropologist, I have spent the last quarter of a century pursuing things, and through them people. An initial interest in pots (more of that later) took me from the seaside town of St Ives in Cornwall, England, to a rural community

1

of potters, farmers, stonemasons and carpenters in a remote mountain valley in northern Kyushu, Japan. Once there, I found myself following pots into local souvenir shops, not-so-local galleries, museums and department stores, talking to different people who were interested in the pots in one way or another as craftsmen, retailers, dealers, auctioneers, critics, academics, bureaucrats, aesthetes, collectors, *aficionados*, and members of the general public. And, as they made them, sold them, passed them on, auctioned them, praised or damned them, gave them histories, administered them, collected them, and used them, all these people talked about pots – and talked about them in such a way that I found myself being drawn across space to another country and back in time to other people, like William Morris and the eighteenth-century Arts and Crafts Movement in Britain. That is the power of things.

And so it proved with other lines of anthropological research. Whether whales or advertising, ceramic art or fashion magazines, things have the power to create and sustain their own social worlds. When things disappear for one reason or another, as they have done for Japan's small-time coastal whalers, the social worlds surrounding them disintegrate.[4] This we know from corporations' decisions to lay off workers and close down factories all over the world, as well as from frequent media stories of 'once vibrant communities' in a country's former coal, steel, shipbuilding or other industry. People's decisions to get involved, or not to get involved, with things have foreseen as well as unforeseen consequences. Two skyscrapers in New York can attract the admiring attention of tens of thousands of visitors to the city over the years (as well as the bustle of 50,000 commuters who went to work there every weekday) until, for reasons of their own, some other people decide that the buildings might be put to 'better' use. Two airplanes and thousands of casualties later, the 'war on terror' is launched – with frightening results. Here, indeed, is the ongoing (anti-)social development of one particular 'empire of things'.[5]

This book is about the *exchanges* that are formed between people and things. It is also about the exchanges that take place among people in their dealings with the things – pots, advertising, art and fashion magazines – that they produce, discuss, distribute, sell or otherwise have an interest in. Since most of these people work in organizations of one sort or another, however, the book also examines the exchanges that take place between them and their organizations, on the one hand, and among organizations themselves, on the other. And because, for the most part, both people and organizations are trying to get something out of these various forms of interaction, the focus is on the *strategic* inputs and outcomes of such exchanges.

The 'strategic exchange perspective' is a way of coming to terms with the old sociological problem of the tension between individual and group, or agency and structure. Put in slightly different terms, we may see it as a tension between creativity and constraint, even – to be philosophical – between free will and determinism. It is a way of looking at how individuals act as agents in initiating, choosing and shaping the social worlds in which they live their lives, while at the same time being constrained and shaped by external social, political and economic forces that themselves affect those social worlds.[6]

The method that I use to describe, isolate and analyse the numerous strategic exchanges outlined in this book is that of anthropological fieldwork, or what outside the narrow confines of academia is commonly called 'ethnography'. Ethnography requires a long-term involvement with and study of the everyday lives, thoughts and practices of a particular collectivity of people. Its results (or lack of them) are founded on the communication that takes place between fieldworker and his or her 'informants' during the period of study, so that ethnography, too, consists of a number of strategic exchanges. It is these that I have sought to highlight in the first chapter of each part of this book.

As the title makes clear, this book is about the business of ethnography: in particular about its fieldwork practices and the things that, as a practising anthropologist, I've learned during the course of several periods of fieldwork in Japan. This does *not* mean that it is a book – yet another book – on 'the Japanese' or 'Japanese culture'. Rather it is about how ordinary people in a contemporary, (post-)industrialized society carry on particular kinds of business and make sense of the social worlds they find there. As such it is a lesson to all of us who at one stage or another need to or already work in a business environment. One part of the business of ethnography is the ethnography of business.

There is, of course, a *double entendre* in the title of *The Business of Ethnography* for I am here making an, albeit understated, critique of what I see as an inadequate discussion in two areas of academic discourse. One is the almost total failure on the part of cultural anthropologists and those closely following the postmodern turn to engage in an analysis of social relations and social organization. The other is an apparent infatuation on the part of those in what may loosely be termed 'management studies' with a generally static concept of 'culture' when writing about business organizations around the world. These two strands of academic discourse are not unrelated: partly because both areas of intellectual endeavour are dominated by American and US-based academics; partly because there appears to be an almost 'cultural predisposition' for 'things cultural' in the United States (as well as in those countries which, like Japan, have been strongly influenced by the United States).

So, in trying to find a satisfactory way of using the ethnographic method to talk about the strategic exchanges between people and things, and within and between organizations in different kinds of business activity, I have taken up three sociological concepts: frames, networks and fields. Broadly spanning micro- and macro-levels of sociological analysis, these concepts all have strategic exchanges at their heart. They were also all developed to cope with the tensions between structure and agency mentioned above. To many of my colleagues, however, these may seem at first glance to be unusual terms to espouse. Of what practical use, after all, are concepts like frame and network, both of which predate the latest trends in postmodern theory by 20 or 30 years and take us back to the oft maligned era of structural functionalism in anthropology? To this a scholar disillusioned with the latest twists and turns in theoretical fashions in anthropology might retort: of what *practical* use is postmodern theory? But such mutual accusations won't get us very far. So let me just say here that I still think it is worth pursuing these concepts a little further and ask you, my readers, to suspend judgement until you've read through the rest of this book. If you're paying proper attention, you will notice that I've added a new dimension to the concept of field, and that I do not always use either frame or network in exactly the way each was developed theoretically back in the 1960s.

So why do I choose *these* terms? And what do I hope to get out of their application? Well, for a start, they *make sense*. One of the problems for all anthropologists who spend long periods of time doing fieldwork of one kind or another is how best to present and analyse the myriad informative bits and confusing pieces that they gather as data.[7] Some, and I tend to fall into this school of thought, prefer to work from ethnographic 'ground zero' up to higher levels of theory and, in the process, let the data 'speak for themselves'. Others, however, find it easier or more intellectually stimulating to tackle a grand theory or two and see how their fieldwork material (what there is of it) fits into the overall argument. There is nothing wrong with either of these approaches provided it is carried out rigorously and, hopefully, written in a language that most of us can understand without having to rush to the latest dictionary of neologisms. But facts and theories – like a married couple, perhaps, or parent-child relationship – should always fit and complement each other.

Over the years, my own fieldwork experience in Japan has led me to believe that the three concepts of frame, network and field also make sense to Japanese themselves. As we shall see during the course of this book, they are acutely aware of particular social situations and have their own words *ba* (setting) and *waku* (frame) to describe them. They pay a lot of attention, too, to the personal connections (*tsukiai*) and social networks (*jinmyaku*, or 'human arteries') that underpin individual and organizational behaviour. They frequently refer to all of these in the broader context of the social worlds (*sekai*) or fields (more later on the difference between them) in which participants find themselves and interact. This is how they see and analyse their society, from micro- to macro-levels of social organization. What is good enough for those I study, then, is good enough for me.

But, my imaginary critics might not unreasonably break in, anthropology thrives on *comparison*. By suggesting that what's good enough for my informants is good enough for me, aren't I merely confining the study of Japanese society and culture to yet more scholarly isolation? The question is: do frame, network and field make sense to *other* people? Yes, is my answer – a resounding yes. Everyone everywhere in the world finds him- or herself acting in frames of one sort or another, involved in networks and making connections, struggling with all kinds of forces and power, and looking for a way through the constraints of 'the system' in which he or she finds him- or herself. That much is common to all our lives. Indeed, these kinds of strategic exchange are as universal as the biological functions that keep us alive. The Japanese, in this respect at least, are no different from anyone else, anywhere else, and the sooner those writing about them swallow this bitter anti-Orientalist pill, the better.

To say that everyone is involved in strategic exchanges taking place in these overlapping social co-ordinates of frames, networks and fields, however, does not mean that all are equally involved in the same way or to the same extent. There are differences in emphases. In some places, on some occasions, frames are very important; in others, and on others, not. Some people *have* to network and make connections if they are to survive in society; others do so only when they *need* to. Power, and the consequent struggle for power, is exercised in different ways in different fields – in the privacy of corporate boardrooms or in the very public eye of the media, by means of quick managerial decisions or endless debate between interested parties. But whatever their emphases, however they function, frames, networks and fields are always there. They never go away.

Frames[8]

All societies consist of people doing things. So we can see social life as consisting of the actions of separate individuals, collectivities whose members act together in a common cause (for example, a pop-music group or baseball team), or organizations acting on behalf of a constituency (a business corporation or professional association).[9] This means that everybody everywhere 'impinges' on other people. The problem is who impinges on whom, when, where and why,[10] and how to study such impinging processes.

One formidable proponent of the study of face-to-face situational interaction and public behaviour was the sociologist Erving Goffman. Impression management, performance, face work, front and back stage or region are just some of the micro-sociological terms that he introduced and made stick in anthropological theory.[11] Borrowing the idea of 'frame' from Gregory Bateson, he applied it to what he called an examination of the organization of *experience*.[12] In frame analysis, as elsewhere, Goffman ended up telling us a lot about the ground rules (including, as we shall see, keys and keying, laminations, breaking frame, out-of-frame activity and so on) that surround the ritual order of everyday life, but rather little about what participants hope or aim to get out of whom, when and why. We thus learn more about strangers and acquaintances than about long-term relationships.[13] In this book I want to use frame analysis to look at different aspects of ongoing *social organization* among people who often know one another quite well (even though Goffman himself said that the latter has been and can continue to be studied quite nicely without any reference at all to frame).[14]

Goffman's work is particularly pertinent here because of the way in which frame has been used to analyse Japanese society, albeit more in terms of space than of performance.[15] In a classic work, Chie Nakane started her discussion of the nature of Japanese society by distinguishing between attribute and frame (*ba*)[16] – initially used to refer to a concrete social group (such as a team, section, department, division, or whole company) – and proceeded to argue that, while most Westerners value persisting, context-independent attributes in social interaction, the Japanese prefer to emphasize contextual social relationships. Thus she regarded frame (*ba*) as of 'primary importance' in small-group identification, while attribute was of a 'secondary matter'.[17]

As Nakane intimated, Japanese *are* very aware of the ways in which each frame affects their social behaviour. They know instinctively where to take up a position in a room full of people, what bodily posture to adopt, what level of language to use when talking to others and what kind of things may be said when. Indeed, they consciously mould both time and space to fit in with the performance of these frames – in the office, in meetings, at school, during formal drinking parties, and so on – and they adapt their (body) language to each frame and stage of action therein.[18] It is this constantly shifting aspect of Japanese social behaviour, therefore, that I believe Nakane was quite right to emphasize by means of the concept of frame.

There is more to frames than this, however. Wherever we live, frames *enable networks*. By examining personal relations operating in a continuous interplay of cause and effect through a series of frames, we can begin to work out the paths taken by informal networks and formal organizations in the various different fields of ceramic art, advertising and fashion-magazine publishing discussed in this book. But frames also *enable organizations*. By participating in work-related frames, participants make sense of an advertising agency, magazine publisher or department store, as well as of clients, advertisers, customers and their roles and actions in the fields of advertising, fashion or art marketing as a whole. The fact that they often use these understandings to their own short- or long-term advantage shows how frames contribute to strategic exchanges.

Those who participate in more frames with a greater variety of people tend to have more opportunity to develop personal ties with other participants. People's behaviour in each frame, therefore, is affected by the presence of other participants (as well as by the absence of those who might have been there). It also tends to influence what comes next and to be influenced by what has gone before. Business frames thus socialise participants in certain patterns of behaviour and, over time, project or work teams of various kinds develop a certain dynamic among themselves, as well as in the presence of outsiders. This dynamic enables individual members to reveal more or less of their 'selves' in an ongoing continuity of frames that ultimately contributes towards the maintenance and strengthening of networks.

Networks

Most of this book is concerned with the organization of different kinds of business in what have been called the 'creative industries'.[19] Without networks to help them, it seems, businessmen wouldn't know where or how to begin going about their tasks. Indeed, their world would probably fall apart. This is because the successful conduct of business matters partly depends on the effective use of personal connections, and partly on the fact that the organizations they work for are in certain important respects themselves social networks.[20]

So the concept of social network helps us understand the linkages existing in a field between different institutional spheres, as well as between different systems of groups and categories.[21] The positions of actors in a network of relationships explain their actions, which both shape and are constrained by that particular network. It is the network characteristics of an organization that enable a comparative analysis of all organizations operating in a field.[22] But networks also ramify in all directions and stretch out seemingly indefinitely – which makes the ways in which people use, maintain and activate them very difficult to study and talk about coherently. At the same time, they also intersect, running parallel with each other for a while before branching off on their separate paths, so that a field – like a city or the 'world system'[23] – becomes a *network of networks*.

Network analysis faces another difficult task. How best can we analyse and properly integrate relationships between *individuals*, on the one hand, and *collectivities* like business corporations, on the other? The concept of network was first developed by anthropologists like John Barnes and Clyde Mitchell, when they became involved in the study of 'complex', rather than 'simple', societies.[24] It seemed like a useful way of moving analytically beyond the kind of enduring relationships in a social institutional framework that they had analysed hitherto.[25] In contrast to such anthropological studies of networks, which have for the most part focused on individuals, however, scholars interested in business and bureaucratic organizations in one way or another have tended to look at both formal and informal inter-firm relationships that together create a complex web of organizational ties.

This two-stranded nature of network analysis is particularly obvious in scholarly accounts of the organization of Japanese society. On the one hand, there is work that looks at different types of actors in exchange transactions, the norms of reci-procity that apply therein, and the strategies that individuals adopt, in terms of the instrumentality and expressiveness found in their social exchanges.[26] On the other, there are studies of the institutionalized relationships among firms (particularly, but not exclusively, among those involved in outsourcing and sub-contracting rela-tionships). Such clusters of companies are marked by ties of affiliation, long-term relationships, multiplexity, extended networks and symbolic signification which effectively help them adjust to external shocks and fluctuations in the economy, promote high rates of capital investment, and often lead to preferential trading. This kind of network organization has been called 'alliance capitalism'.[27] One Japanese scholar has gone further and, well ahead of Manuel Castells, called Japan a 'network society'.[28]

The challenge for network analysis, it seems to me, is in its simultaneous appli-cation to *both* individuals *and* organizations, and that is something I take up in Chapters 5 and 6. Although we tend to think of networking in (Japanese) business in terms of individuals lubricating the wheels of social interaction at an interper-sonal level, we must also realize that such networking is carried on at an institu-tional level. Networking thus creates and sustains an ongoing dialectical relation between individual employees and organizational units in all societies. It, too, encourages strategic exchanges and contributes to the arrangement of power and struggles in a field.

Fields

The concept of field has been around for some time. Victor Turner, for example, argued that '"fields" are the abstract cultural domains where paradigms are for-mulated, established, and come into conflict'.[29] Every individual operates in a number of different fields, and his or her relationships with others therein can influence events that take place in other fields.[30] But Turner was more concerned with social drama and it was left to the French anthropologist-cum-sociologist, Pierre Bourdieu, to develop systematically the idea of field – in particular vis-à-vis art, literature and cultural production more generally.

Bourdieu argued that a social field of any kind provides its participants with 'a space of possibles',[31] which itself defines the universe of problems, challenges, references, benchmarks and everything else they must know and keep in the backs of their minds if they want to take part in 'the game' – a game that involves playing, for example, the politician, businessman, consultant, academic, or writer (and occasionally all five parts simultaneously). The field is structured into posi-tions which are taken up and fought over by people and organizations whose own dispositions (in the case of companies, we may talk of 'corporate cultures') have some effect on the 'ensemble of relations'[32] that ensue. Whenever one of them forces another out of place and takes over his or its position, the field as a whole reverberates.

Although I may well be treading on dangerous ground here, let me cite as an example an academic field – that of the field of Japanese Studies in Britain during the latter half of the 1980s, when, as a social scientist, I was appointed chair professor in a humanities department. This was unprecedented at the time. University departments of Japanese taught language, literature, history, art and 'culture', not economics, politics, sociology or whatever. The accepted norm was that social scientists interested in Japan took up positions in social science departments (as I had done in anthropology), while humanities experts were employed in departments of Japanese or Japanese Studies. No social scientist was ever, *ever* thought respectable or 'proper' enough a scholar for his or her appointment in a Japanese department to be dreamed of, let alone made. But once a selection committee decided to ignore 'precedent' (it helped that my first degree had been in Japanese at the same institution), it opened up a crack in the positions made available. The whole structure of the field of Japanese Studies was displaced and knock-on effects quickly followed. Within a few years, half a dozen other universities had appointed other social scientists as professors of Japanese. This encouraged departments in the 'old' universities to take up entrenched ideological positions, (re)assert their 'pedigree' and claim educational and symbolic capital. Clearly, the newly appointed professors at 'upstart' academic institutions had no idea what they were doing when it came to the teaching of Japanese language, literature, history, art and culture. They couldn't speak, read or write Japanese properly. Etcetera, etcetera. As the purists would hold, 'the rot' had set in.

All kinds of fields operate simultaneously and people and organizations can slip back and forth between, or elide, them. Academics in the field of Japanese Studies in Britain in the late 1980s, for example, found themselves interacting with businessmen (who wanted to take advantage of the Japanese market which was still buoyant at the time), politicians (who wanted to lure Japanese companies to set up factories and offices in Britain), diplomats and administrators (who wanted to be in control of foundation monies, as well as be seen as au fait with Japanese language and culture, and thus legitimately justified in interfering with university courses and the occasional academic appointment), and a bevy of Japan culture vultures (who were mainly there for free food and drink at the various receptions held around town). For their part, academics wanted to impress businessmen and politicians with their expertise (consultancy offered a parallel, money-making career), and the diplomats and administrators with the practical nature of the courses they ran (in order to gain access to available research, teaching and other funds). Academics could also use this external interest in their Japanese specialization as 'political capital' to influence decisions made within their institutions, and they were invariably extremely polite to all the Japanese businessmen, politicians, diplomats, administrators, and cultural practitioners they met (and with whom they could claim social equality on the basis of a shared 'cultural capital').

In all this to and fro, it became very clear that these overlapping fields were hierarchically structured and that different actors had access to and command of different kinds of resources. These could be material, cultural, social, symbolic or ideological and how they were distributed was what made the field of Japanese Studies the way it was. Politicians and businessmen controlled what Bourdieu called 'political' and 'economic capital'; diplomats and administrators, mainly because of hands-on experience in Japan over the years, had 'cultural capital'; and academics had their 'educational capital'. But the last was contested by those businessmen and diplomats who spoke fluent Japanese and delighted in telling academics how 'out-of-touch' with the business or diplomatic world they were. So businessmen converted their economic into cultural capital, while diplomats managed to convert their cultural into economic capital by being appointed to the board of a merchant bank here, by writing a coffee-table book there, or by being invited to give overly well-paid lectures back in Japan (something that academics, too, occasionally managed to do and so convert their educational into economic capital). And *every*one, *all* the time, kept in touch with one another – on the telephone, at receptions, at art exhibition opening ceremonies, and special lectures of one sort or another – where they exchanged information and gossip and tried their utmost to enhance and use to good effect their 'social capital'.

Because such overlapping fields exist in all realms of social action – advertising, for example, overlaps with fields of fashion, music, media, and entertainment among others – we may talk of a *field of fields*. Each field comprises both the interactions between individuals and the structural relations between social positions occupied and manipulated by social actors (who may be individuals, groups or institutions). A field is thus also a network of strategic exchanges consisting both of forces and of struggles,[33] and it is Bourdieu's ideas that I have picked up and used at some length later on in this book to describe the fields of ceramic art and advertising in Japan and international fashion magazine publishing more globally.

Fieldwork

Two concerns underpin the title of this book, *The Business of Ethnography*. First, ethnography – or more strictly speaking, fieldwork – is an immensely practical skill, although few realize quite how to put its findings to good use outside the academic field. Secondly, over the years, ethnography has been championed primarily by anthropologists who have come to see it as their methodological trademark in the study of 'primitive' or, at least, less-developed cultures, but who have for the most part failed to apply it critically to the study of their own ways in contemporary industrialized societies.[34] These two concerns suggest a differentiation between practical and academic forms of fieldwork.

Strictly speaking, ethnography should refer to the *writing* of results obtained during the course of participant-observation fieldwork investigations. Nowadays, however, the word is interpreted in all sorts of different ways by those in the private sector who have come to recognize its potential value. It has thus become a buzz-word that covers virtually every kind of data collection available to market researchers, from telephone surveys to focus groups, by way of exploratory, tactical, depth and 'ethnographic' interviews.[35] This is why ethnography has been incorporated into this book's title, although from now on I am going to distinguish between fieldwork as a method of doing research and ethnography as a means of presenting the results of that research.

Practical fieldwork is an essential skill that enables us to understand and analyse our own lives and workplaces, families, networks of friends, and so on. All of us most of the time are engaged in the practices of participant-observation-style fieldwork and make use of our observations and findings to come to terms with or criticize different values and the people who hold them, to analyse social situations, and to engage in the kind of planning, persuasion, promotion, profit, and prestige and power games that characterize our everyday affairs. As Tony Watson says:

> Ethnographic research involves feeling one's way in confusing circumstances, struggling to make sense of ambiguous messages, reading signals, looking around, listening all the time, coping with conflicts and struggling to achieve tasks through establishing and maintaining a network of relationships. But this is what we all do all the time as human beings.[36]

The only real difference between this kind of activity and the more formalized academic practices advocated by social scientists is that most of us tend not to make such everyday fieldwork into a conscious endeavour. If we were to do so, however, we would soon realize that we need, indeed have, to be adept fieldworkers who can understand – that is, see behind the façades of – the organizations we work for and use that knowledge appropriately for our own ends. It is this sort of social awareness arising out of the strategic exchanges encountered in practical fieldwork, I believe, that contributes most to the making of a successful businessman or woman.

Fieldwork can be practical in another sense. Those who understand its premises and have experience of its practice should be able to put their knowledge and skills to good use with private-sector employers. After all,

> Every year companies spend thousands of man-hours and millions of dollars struggling to understand, evaluate and predict human behaviour, beliefs, values, and attitudes – the

very heart and soul of applied social science. And every year academic institutions produce thousands of social science graduates, many more than can ever be absorbed into teaching, most of whom will take jobs that make little use of the skills they worked so hard to acquire.[37]

This is where academic fieldwork comes in. Ideally, academic fieldwork should not only help improve the quality of private-sector research practices by training social scientists who can then find rewarding careers making use of their skills. It should also focus more than it has hitherto done perhaps on the study of business organizations; workplace relations; gender, age, race and class structures; corporate cultures, and so on. There are notable exceptions, of course – one thinks of the so-called Hawthorne Studies conducted in one of the supply organizations for Western Electric Company in Chicago from the late 1920s, and the numerous studies conducted by graduate students in sociology at the University of Chicago during the decades following the end of the Second World War – but still there is a tendency for mainstream anthropologists to ignore what is going on in the world of business about them and most of the interesting books get written by other social scientists.[38]

Of course, the study of business organizations itself is fraught with difficulties. Most companies are understandably reluctant to allow researchers free access to their premises, employees, or written records. If they do permit an outsider into their midst, they may well demand and obtain the signing of a confidentiality clause that effectively prevents dissemination of a researcher's more insightful findings. They will almost certainly place restrictions on the amount of time he or she may spend in a particular company or organization. Consequently, while there are, of course, in-depth studies of business organizations of various kinds throughout the world, a considerable part of what passes for business or management studies is based on structured interviews that do not usually allow for more than a scratching on the surface of corporate organization. As a result, there is comparatively little reflection on the actual mechanisms of the social organization of business. This is a pity because corporations are a kind of sociological laboratory with histories, cultures, structures, hierarchies and values to observe and analyse.[39]

It is this lacuna that the book you are reading tries to address. In the chapters that follow, material from four different periods of fieldwork is interwoven into the ongoing argument about strategic exchanges in frames, networks and fields. The first of these is the classic type of anthropological fieldwork, in that it focused on an isolated rural community of potters, located in the southernmost main island of Japan, a couple of thousand kilometres away from Tokyo and a good two-hour drive from the nearest big city. Because potters lived and worked in the same house, it was very easy to study them. All I needed to do was walk from one household to the next, step into a workshop and start talking to the potter (and sometimes his son) who was more or less rooted to his wheel for the best part of the day during the two-month cycle between kiln firings. As the story told in Chapter 1 reveals, it was this kind of fieldwork situation that invited reflection on frames as a means of analysis. Work proceeded according to the different separated processes of production (clay preparation, forming at the wheel, drying, decorating, loading, firing and unloading the kiln), and entertainment, too, had its clearly demarcated frames – primarily in *sake* drinking, but also in singing lessons, softball games, the occasional archery competition, and sports days of one sort or another.

The difference between this and similar kinds of ethnographic studies of isolated communities was that the work made by the potters I was studying had been incorporated into the ongoing aesthetic ideology of the Japanese folk art (or *mingei*) movement. This meant three things. First, the potters' community of Sarayama would be visited by a fairly incessant trickle of tourists (a trickle that turned to a stream, and occasional flood, on fine spring and autumn weekends) who made potters aware of their varied tastes (almost all influenced in some way by the folk-art boom). This plurality of aesthetic choices was added to, secondly, by pottery dealers who came from as far away as Kamakura, just south of Tokyo, to give advice, comment on and buy potters' work on the basis of their marketing savvy. And thirdly, Sarayama would receive the occasional visit from one of the folk-art movement's leaders who would try to reconcile to potters' satisfaction the seemingly contradictory principles of beauty and commerce. (They were never successful in their attempts.)

The result of this external interest was that my fieldwork also took me out of Sarayama, as I followed the paths taken by its pots and found myself moving through a network of connected people all interested in and holding varied opinions about what made them 'good', 'bad', 'beautiful', 'ugly' and so on. It was this network of things that formed the foundation of my second period of fieldwork (also of two years' duration), when I conducted research on the ceramic art market in Japan and found myself following pots from workshops to galleries, department stores and collectors' homes. Because of the way in which I was lucky enough to form a close relationship with one dealer, Eisuke Minamoto (described in Chapter 7), this fieldwork located me very firmly in a network of people. As a result, the nearest I ever got to a physical location for my research, apart from numerous department-store gallery exhibitions, was Eisuke's car, since it was in this that we discussed the ceramic art world and moved around the countryside to visit potters whose work he bought and sold.

This kind of fieldwork was extremely fluid compared with the more static nature of my research in Sarayama since it was based on networks. All I could do as a result was to make sure that whoever I was interviewing passed me on to someone new, follow whatever leads came up, and generally hope for the best. Like all field-work, of course, sometimes things worked well; at other times, they didn't. But I had very little control over what went on and, of course – unlike my time in Sarayama – those I was studying had very little control over what I did. We circled endlessly around one another as we all followed the trajectories of pots, like a flock of seagulls gliding, soaring, dipping and occasionally flapping their wings in the wake of a ship.

The third period of fieldwork, in a Japanese advertising agency, was rather remarkable. Here I had my physical frame again (although the agency was located in five different buildings at the time), but at the same time – as I soon discovered – everyone spent a lot of his or her time outside the office, networking with clients, media organizations, freelance creatives and so on. Even so, whether at home in one of the agency's buildings or abroad in the streets of the capital, most employees found themselves spending almost all of their time in meetings of one sort or another. There they carried out transactions, negotiated, and adopted all kinds of strategies as they tried to achieve their specific aims, influenced all the while by reflections on what it meant to be both 'Japanese' (influenced in part, no doubt, by my 'foreign' presence) and a member of the agency or other organiza-tion. Meetings, then, were frames in which participants made sense of their organ-izations and their actions therein.[40] This period of fieldwork neatly combined the frame and network emphases of my two earlier studies of Japanese pots (by what-ever name) and helped me understand the 'field' as a whole.

What made it rather remarkable was the fact that, before I arrived to start my research, the agency drew up a formal schedule, placing me initially in the Presi-dent's Office, and then, one month at a time, in Media Buying, Marketing, Account Services, Creative, Promotions, International Division, Personnel and so on. This was both an immense relief and a source of worry. It was a relief because starting fieldwork – or, rather, knowing *where* to start – is one of the most difficult things facing a fieldworker, mainly because, having no certain knowledge (though perhaps a clue or two) of what is or is not important to whom among those he or she is studying, he or she wants to make sure of not starting off on the wrong foot and treading on people's toes before the first step of the participant-observation waltz has been taken. In Sarayama, I was lucky. The fact that I had heard that potters didn't take on apprentices (and the fact that I had hoped to become a pottery apprentice myself in order to understand, at first hand, issues related to pro-duction) made me intuitively avoid asking people anything about pottery and the folk-art movement. Instead, I asked them about their family histories – a tactic that paid dividends during the first couple of months of my stay and probably saved me from being thrown out of the community (more on this in Chapter 1).

In the advertising agency, however, I didn't have to worry about where or how to start. Everything was done for me. For the best part of the first week, I was given daily lectures on the overall state of Japan's advertising industry, together with various bits of background information that my self-appointed 'teacher' in the President's Office felt I should know. Soon after, I found myself transferred to the Magazine Department of Media Buying and was, on the first day, given four solid hours of lectures about the ins and outs of this particular part of the advertising business, followed by two more hours the next morning. 'And now', said the department head, 'We're off to the publisher Kodansha to put into practice everything you've heard. Sit quietly, listen to what goes on, make notes, but don't say anything till the end. We'll answer your questions then.' And so it went on, for a whole year. The stuff of ethnography!

As I said, the fact that the agency drew up a schedule for my research before I arrived also got me worried. Was I being directed to examine certain features of its business and not others? Were there secrets that were being withheld from me? If so, why? How important might these be to an overall grasp of the way in which the agency worked and of the field of advertising as a whole? The schedule itself, though, seemed to be comprehensive and included stints in both the computer mainframe section and the Finance Office. If I was being allowed a look into the agency's knowledge database and money matters, surely there was not that much being hidden?

In point of fact, the schedule turned out to be a movable feast, and I was free to extend my stay in one department and curtail it in another as fieldwork developed. I was also able to follow a case study in Account Services while simultaneously being formally placed in the Promotions and Creative divisions. All I needed to do was make sure that the person nominally in charge of my research during my fieldwork in the agency was kept abreast of where I was and whom I was with. All in all, I was incredibly fortunate in my choice of fieldwork site. Never was I asked to sign any confidentiality agreement. Only once was something I wrote 'censored'.[41] Now, I have been told by the new CEO (a personal friend), I may always use the agency's name: ADK (or Asatsu, as it then was). And so that is what I've done.

The final lengthy period of fieldwork in which I have been involved, and which features only spasmodically in the chapters that follow, has been a very different kettle of ethnographic fish to boil into successful research results. The thing at the centre of my study this time is the fashion magazine – in particular those which, like *Vogue, Elle,* and *Marie Claire,* are published in numerous international editions. One research aim has been to find out how and why the contents of these titles do or do not change in five different parts of the world – France, Hong Kong, Japan, the UK and the USA – and how this affects and is affected by gender identities in these places. Another has been to work out why particular countries are chosen to launch a title, and what are the various factors that come into play in the decision to do so. A third has been to find out more about the paradoxes arising from the fact that – like many products of the creative industries – fashion magazines are simultaneously both cultural products (featuring fashion, beauty, travel, women's stories, and so on) and commodities (driven by advertising), and thus heavily implicated in the development of capitalism as a whole.[42]

To put it mildly, this has been an ambitious project on a number of counts: the need ideally to talk to editors, publishers and readers of magazines in five different parts of the world, on the one hand; a massive comparative cross-cultural content analysis of more than 300 magazine editions, on another; the felt necessity to participate in and observe one cycle at least of one magazine's production, in order to get some idea of how different forces come into play and work themselves out in the magazine's cultural content, on yet another. I have carried out dozens of interviews in France, Hong Kong, Japan, the UK and the USA on the first count; wrestled with content analysis, on the second; and more or less failed in my objective on the third.

And yet, what I've been doing over the course of these past two years is what George Marcus has called 'multi-sited research'.[43] Multi-sited fieldwork, he says, presents new challenges to ways of doing and writing about fieldwork, because of the fact that people are no longer rooted in particular spaces and that we need to follow them around. But, upon reflection, I find that *all* my fieldwork experiences have been multi-sited. Even in a pottery village I found myself following people down the local valley to sports gatherings and drinking parties, following searches for raw materials and the distribution of orders to retail outlets. In the advertising agency, ADK, I was placed in one structural division after another and followed individual employees around both within and outside the agency as they interacted with clients, media organizations of one sort and another, marketing consultants, their own creative, PR, SP and other divisions, and so on and so forth. But this 'multi-sited' fieldwork was firmly anchored in the framework of a business corporation. Neither my informants nor I lived in the kind of 'borderless world' in which we had to 'remake' the basic understandings of our fieldwork practices, as Marcus claims more generally.[44] Nor could this be said of my fieldwork among fashion-magazine publishers since, even though editors, 'creatives', and publishers were all in immediate contact with one another around the world, they also all worked within particular organizational frames that defined their patterns of behaviour. In short, these 'new and more complicated research locations' did *not*, so far as I can judge, give rise to 'shifts in the character of both fieldwork and fieldworker'.[45]

On the basis of past and current experience, therefore, I am not yet convinced that there is a significant difference between, on the one hand, the *methodology* of fieldwork – frame-based fieldwork in easily identified physical locations like a pottery community or advertising agency, and network-based fieldwork through department stores and media organizations – and, on the other, the *object* of fieldwork (pots and pans or ads and magazines). What *is* significant is that it is virtually impossible, when conducting the kind of transnational, multi-sited fieldwork that Marcus espouses, and in the limited time available, to get to grips with organizations, networks, frames and fields in such a way that we can learn to see beyond the 'front' to the 'back' stages of what is going on (more on that in Chapters 1, 4, and 7) and so become anthropologists, rather than mere in-depth journalists, or the kind of cultural – and one might add, management – studies 'ethnographers' criticized by Marcus.[46]

But maybe this is an issue that I should leave for now and come back to in my Conclusion, when you have had a chance to 'read, mark, learn and inwardly digest' (as one of my primary school teachers used to say) a number of tales from the field. It always helps to have a few examples to argue with.

Notes

1. Arjun Appadurai (ed.) *The Social Life of Things*, 1986.
2. Annette Weiner, 'Cultural difference and the density of objects', *American Ethnologist* Volume 21, Number 2, 1994, pp. 391–403. As I understand it, Weiner's concept of density is a little different from that used here, since she refers to the density of an object while I am applying the idea to social relations.
3. It is not the correctness or incorrectness of this presentation of the effects of WMD that matters. It is the fact that there is scope for such an interpretation in the first place. This is the general function and end result of people's interaction with things.
4. Arne Kalland and Brian Moeran, *Japanese Whaling: End of an era?* 1992.
5. Fred Myers (ed.), *The Empire of Thing: Regimes of value and material culture*, 2001.
6. Tony Watson, *In Search of Management: Culture, chaos and control in managerial work* (rev. edn), 2001, p. 25.
7. This is the problem of what Clifford Geertz, following the philosopher Gilbert Ryle, has famously called 'an elaborate venture in ... thick description' (Geertz, *The Interpretation of Cultures*, 1973, p. 6).
8. Some of the material appearing in the following three sections has already been published in the journal *Global Networks*, Volume 3, Number 3. See Brian Moeran, 'Fields, networks and frames: Advertising social organization in Japan', 2003a.
9. Herbert Blumer, *Symbolic Interactionism: Perspective and method*, 1986, p. 85.
10. John Barnes, 'Networks and political processes', in J. Clyde Mitchell (ed.) *Social Networks in Urban Situations*, 1969, pp. 51–76.
11. Erving Goffman, *The Presentation of Self in Everyday Life*, 1959; Ulf Hannerz provides a very useful summary of Goffman's work in Chapter 6 of

his *Exploring the City: Inquiries toward an urban anthropology*, 1980.

12. Gregory Bateson, *Steps to an Ecology of the Mind*, 1972, pp. 177–93; Erving Goffman, *Frame Analysis: An essay on the organization of experience*, 1986 (1974), pp. 10-11.

13. Hannerz, *Exploring the City*, p. 214.

14. Goffman, *Frame Analysis*, p. 13.

15. Takie Sugiyama Lebra, 'The spatial layout of hierarchy: residential style of the modern Japanese nobility', in her edited *Japanese Social Organization*, 1992, pp. 49–78.

16. I will address the problems of Nakane's use of terminology and the translation of *ba* into *frame* in the English version of her book in Chapter 2.

17. Chie Nakane, *Japanese Society*, 1970, p. 3.

18. Joy Hendry, *Wrapping Culture: Politeness, presentation, and power in Japan and other societies*, 1993, pp. 123–32.

19. Richard Caves, *Creative Industries: Contracts between art and commerce*, 2000.

20. Wayne E. Baker, 'The network organization in theory and practice', in W. Richard Scott (ed.), *Organizations: Rational, natural, and open systems*, 1987, pp. 397–429.

21. Cf. M.N. Srinivas and André Beteille, 'Networks in Indian social structure', *Man*, Volume 64, 1964, pp. 165–8.

22. Nitin Nohria, 'Is a network perspective a useful way of studying organizations?' in N. Nitin and R. Eccles (eds), *Networks and Organizations: Structure, form and action*, 1992, pp. 4–8.

23. Hannerz, *Exploring the City*; and 'The global ecumene as a network of networks', in A. Kuper (ed.), *Conceptualizing Society*, 1992, pp. 34–56.

24. John Barnes, 'Networks and political processes'; J. Clyde Mitchell, 'The concept and use of social networks', in his (ed.), *Social Networks in Urban Situations*, 1969.

25. Hannerz, *Exploring the City*, pp. 172–3.

26. E.g. Harumi Befu, 'A theory of social exchange as applied to Japan', in Y. Sugimoto and R. Mouer (eds), *Constructs for Understanding Japan*, 1989, pp. 39–66.

27. Michael Gerlach, *Alliance Capitalism: The social organization of Japanese business*, 1992.

28. Shumpei Kumon, 'Japan as a network society', in S. Kumon and H. Rosovsky (eds), *The Political Economy of Japan*, Volume 3, *Cultural and Social Dynamics*, 2002 [1996], pp. 109–141; Manuel Castells, *The Rise of the Network Society*, 1992.

29. Victor Turner, *Dramas, Fields, and Metaphors: Symbolic action in human society*, 1974, p. 17.

30. Turner, *Dramas, Fields, and Metaphors*, p. 131.
31. Pierre Bourdieu, *The Field of Cultural Production: Essays on art and literature*, 1993, p. 176.
32. Ibid., p. 119.
33. Ibid., pp. 29–30.
34. George Marcus and Michael Fisher, *Anthropology as Cultural Critique*, 1986, p. 1.
35. Marilyn Mitchell, *Employing Qualitative Methods in the Private Sector*, 1998.
36. Tony Watson, *In Search of Management*, p. 8.
37. Mitchell, *Employing Qualitative Methods*, p. 1.
38. For example, Watson, *In Search of Management*; John Van Maanen, *Tales of the Field*, 1988; and Walter Powell, *Getting into Print*, 1986.
39. Mitchell, *Employing Qualitative Methods*, p. 34.
40. Helen Schwartzman, *Ethnography in Organizations*, 1993, p. 40.
41. On this matter, connected with frequent attempts by an advertising client to use its advertising agency to erase or modify newspaper articles that adversely reported its activities, I took legal advice. In the end, I decided to ignore the single individual opposing me in the agency and say what evidence suggested needed to be said.
42. Margaret Beetham, *A Magazine of Her Own*, 1996, pp. 1–5.
43. George Marcus, *Ethnography Through Thick and Thin*, 1998.
44. George Marcus, *Critical Anthropology Now: Unexpected contexts, shifting constituencies, changing agendas*, 1999, p. 5.
45. Ibid., p. 7.
46. Ibid., p. 20.

Part I
Frames

–1–

Baptized by Fire

I want to start this discussion of fieldwork experience and sociological analysis with the kind of fieldwork tale that is fairly typical nowadays because of its confessional nature. This does not mean, however, that I intend to indulge in endless self-conscious reflections that typify what John Van Maanen has referred to as 'vanity ethnography'. There are enough examples of those in print already.[1] Rather, my aim is to explain why I was studying what I was studying, how I got into 'the field', how I then participated in some of the activities of those I was studying as a means of collecting research data, the kind of relationship I began to have with my 'informants' and how they responded to my presence.[2] This will enable me at the end of the chapter to come up with an interpretation of the events that occurred and to provide an analytical tool for the understanding of other fieldwork 'happenings' encountered further along in this book.

The ways in which people all over the world share food and drink, as well as what they do or do not eat and drink, tell us a lot about a society's norms and expectations and are the stuff of anthropology.[3] It has often been noted about the Japanese, for example, that they like to drink together and that, when they do so, they may well exhibit various kinds of behaviour that they keep pent up during the course of their everyday lives. Drinking occasions and their accompanying inebriation thus give ordinary Japanese 'salarymen', for instance, the opportunity to slag off their CEO, department or section chief (and occasionally all three) for not doing 'the right thing' in the office environment. They also allow people to engage in various kinds of physical contact – from a quick tap of the hand on a fellow drinker's arm to (as is more customary with men in the company of women) an intrusive groping of the more private parts of a companion's anatomy – that are taboo in the workplace and other more or less public spaces. The standard analysis of such behaviour suggests that drinking occasions allow participants to vent frustrations caused by the formalities of everyday life and that all is then forgiven and forgotten the following day.

Besides illustrating my argument about the importance of social frames to fieldwork understandings, the tale that I am about to tell here questions the analysis that all that occurs during a drinking session is 'forgiven and forgotten'. Although the protagonists of this story may seem a little unlikely – who, these days at least, is likely to find him- or herself spending four years conducting research in a remote mountain community of ten pottery and four other rural households? – the way that they choose to mix business with pleasure is clearly not. Any of us who has had occasion to engage in business activities knows how important socializing can be to the success or failure of an enterprise. The lessons to be learned from this tale, then, are not as particular as its circumstances.

But, first, let me fill in some background detail. The community where I carried out two years of fieldwork for my PhD thesis and where I quickly returned to live for another two years while carrying out post-doctoral research was (and still is, of course) called Sarayama. This name is commonly given to pottery-making communities in Kyushu, the southernmost main island of Japan. Literally meaning 'plate mountain' because of its location on or near clay deposits, each Sarayama needs to be distinguished from the other pottery-producing communities of the same name. So the pottery made in the Sarayama where I did fieldwork was called Onta ware,[4] after the name of the neighbouring hamlet over the mountain pass once crossed by Sōetsu Yanagi, leading light and founding father of a folk arts and crafts (or *mingei*) movement who 'discovered' the rather unusual handmade slip-ware made by Sarayama's potters back in 1927.[5]

Although Onta ware has become extremely famous throughout Japan as a result of its pottery and the commercialization of the *mingei* arts and crafts movement, Sarayama as a community is unusual because its members refuse to modernize the various techniques they use to prepare clay for the kick wheel and fire pots in wood-fired climbing kilns. This means that it has maintained a somewhat classical form of family or household structure rather typical of what is thought of as 'traditional' in Japanese society. At the same time, it was – and still is – the fact that potters have refused to modernize their methods of production that has endeared them to *mingei* leaders. As a result, the latter idealize Onta pottery which they regard as a very close approximation to the aesthetic ideals of Sōetsu Yanagi, in that it is functional rather than decorative, hand-made on a kick wheel, made from local clay, glazed with natural materials and fired in a wood-fired climbing kiln. *Ergo* it must be beautiful. It was this relation between ecology and rural community structure, on the one hand, and its transformation by urban aesthetes into an aesthetic ideology, on the other, that was the focus of my fieldwork investigations.[6]

It is events leading up to the beginning of fieldwork that often put a stamp on how research itself will, or will not, proceed. In many ways, this is the most difficult and worrying time for a fieldworker who usually does not know the people he or she is going to study and, as a result, can suffer from acute and prolonged bouts of self-questioning, anxiety and occasional panic. After all, it takes quite a lot of courage to step out of your own fairly predictable world of family, friends, colleagues, lover(s), pets and what-have-you, and immerse yourself instead in a totally new and unknown environment, where you have nobody to fall back on for help when you need it and yet where you are very aware of the fact that *everyone* is watching your every move and judging whether you ever *will* have anyone to fall back on for help during your time in the field.

The first practical problem facing any fieldworker, therefore, is how to get accepted as a researcher by members of the community that he or she wishes to study. Here a lot depends on the fieldworker's personality and the 'human chemistry' that he or she is able to engender with those who may – through a combination of outward friendliness, skilful manipulation, and sheer luck of the draw – become 'informants'. But another important thing to consider is how the fieldworker actually gets to the chosen fieldwork site in the first place. In other words, fieldwork *entry* is crucial to the research enterprise as a whole.[7]

In the case of Sarayama, I obtained two rather different lines of entry. The first was academic and, in this particular instance, turned out to be ineffective (although on other occasions, my academic status and scholarly credentials have had a rather remarkable effect on the course of the fieldwork I was undertaking). I was registered for a PhD in the Department of Anthropology and Sociology at the School of Oriental and African Studies, which is part of the University of London. Because, in days of yore (in other words, in the 1960s), a Japanese anthropologist called Chie Nakane had held a joint-position there before returning to Japan to become Tokyo University's first woman professor, it had become department practice to refer to her any PhD student who went to Japan to do fieldwork. (Fortunately for her, as well perhaps as for myself, they numbered no more than a handful.) Over the years, therefore, Professor Nakane had found herself obliged not just to give help and advice to the very occasional would-be anthropologist of Japan, but also to find them suitable fieldwork sites. It seems that, having completed a research proposal in the manner expected in the department, some students had no idea about where or how they could observe in practice all the things that they had written about theoretically.

When it was my turn to go and do fieldwork in Japan, therefore, I was immediately pointed in the direction of Professor Nakane and, a day or two after my arrival in Tokyo, duly made my way into the presence of a diminutive and formidable woman who sat at an untidy desk in her office in the Institute of Oriental Studies at Tokyo University and, rather expressionlessly, listened to me explaining to her in my best Japanese what I wished to study, why I wished to do so, and where I intended to do fieldwork to find out the answers to my questions. When I finished my stumbling presentation at the end of about ten to fifteen minutes, she turned and said to me coolly in English: 'I think you may proceed to the field.'[8]

With that, she took a name card from a plastic box on her desk and wrote on it a phrase requesting that all assistance possible be given to Brian Moeran. She then brought out a *hankō* red seal with her name on it and stamped it firmly at the end of this phrase, before advising me to present it to those I was going to meet in Sarayama and the neighbouring town of Hita. By this act, Professor Nakane publicly legitimated my fieldwork by endorsing it with her own name, itself known extremely widely throughout Japan, and, as the card itself showed, with the name of the country's most prestigious university. In short, I had in my hands a name card that provided me with entry into Japanese society.

My second line of entry was entirely different. In many ways, I have to thank the former Grace Kelly for providing me with the inspiration to study a pottery community at all. Although I had enrolled as a somewhat 'mature' undergraduate student in Japanese at the School of Oriental and African Studies (I was almost 29 years old when I first registered), I was planning to take up anthropology once I graduated and was already looking around for a suitable topic of research. In order to supplement a rather meagre student grant, I used to do the occasional inter-preting work to help feed, clothe and house my family. One such job was working for Tokyo 12 Channel television company, which in those days was running a weekly interview series called something like *Famous People of the World*. Every so often the TV channel's attention would turn to famous people in England and the rest of Europe and I then found myself being flown to all sorts of exotic loca-tions to meet such celebrities as James Hunt, the grand prix driver, Andrew Grima, the jeweller, and Grace Kelly, Princess of Monaco.

Usually, the woman interviewer for the documentary series worked independ-ently of the television film crew (a habit that did not endear her to her Japanese colleagues) and very often arranged meetings with the chosen famous person prior to the crew's arrival. When it came to the Grace Kelly interview, however, she com-mitted a serious breach of principality etiquette (history does not relate exactly what happened) and the film crew and I arrived to find that the planned interview had been summarily cancelled by the palace. In desperation, my employers turned to me for help. By chance, I knew of another interpreter who sometimes worked with the television channel, but who was also a potter, and I remembered her having once mentioned another English potter, Bernard Leach, now very old, who was extremely famous in Japan because of the part he had played in the very early days in building up support for the Japanese arts and crafts movement.

So, even though I knew nothing at all about him, I suggested the name 'Bernard Leach' to the film crew. Much to my surprise, they all beamed with delight and told me what a wonderful choice I had made. Could I please arrange an interview? A few phone calls later, I was in touch with Janet Leach, Bernard's wife, and three days after that we had left the warmth and wealth of Monte Carlo for the some-what cooler and less classy tourist town of St Ives in Cornwall, England. It was as I walked into Bernard Leach's pottery and saw his pots – in particular, a Pilgrim plate – that, like Paul on his journey to Damascus, I had my revelation and decided there and then to study a pottery community for my PhD in anthropology.[9]

It was the Bernard Leach link that was my second point of entry into Sarayama. After the television interview was over, I went back to talk to Bernard a couple of times about his role in the Japanese arts and crafts movement and his visits to pottery communities there, including Sarayama. He was very supportive of my proposed research – even though he was generally, and understandably, sceptical of academics – and suggested that I get in touch with his editor at Kodansha International, Kim Schuefftan, when I reached Tokyo, since it had been some decades since he had had any real contact with the potters. This, of course, I did and soon found myself talking to Kim and a Japanese friend, Toshio Sekiji, who – to bring us full circle back to where I began this story – had just finished working as interpreter for a Canadian film-maker, Marty Gross, during the making of a documentary about Onta ware for a Western audience. It was Toshio who warned me that Sarayama's traditional household system was so strictly exclusive that potters would not tolerate outside apprentices, and who advised me against even thinking of becoming a pottery apprentice, as I was then planning as part of the 'participation' side of my fieldwork's observations. It was Kim and Toshio who told me about one of Sarayama's potters, Inoshige Sakakura, and who then telephoned him to advise him that I was coming to Sarayama at the end of the following week, and asked him to 'take care' of me.

It was, in practice, the second line of entry that proved the more helpful and ensured that, initially at least, I was permitted to carry out fieldwork research in Sarayama. I went straight to Inoshige when I arrived and explained to him what I wanted to do. He arranged for me to stay in the local *sake* shop and an hour or so later came by for a few drinks. Later on in the evening, when neither of us was that steady on his feet, he took me to meet a group of other potters who had just finished their weekly *utai* singing lesson and were also sharing a few *tokkuri* jars of warmed *sake*. Once more I found myself explaining why I was there and what I wanted to do, but it was only when I mentioned Bernard Leach that everyone broke immediately into smiles and began asking me how he was, whether he was in good health, still making pots, and so on. They then proceeded to tell me some of the things they themselves remembered of his visit to Sarayama some 25 years previously. The ice was broken.[10]

Mention of drink brings me to the point of this chapter. One thing I very quickly found out during the first few weeks in Sarayama was that people living there – especially men – loved to drink, whether it be in the local noodle store, someone's private house, or the 'community hall' (*kōminkan*). Indeed, I soon realized that my room on the first floor of the *sake* shop was an extremely strategic vantage point from which to overhear drunken conversations among potters and other community and valley residents – although inebriation, I also quickly realized, affected not only *how* people talked, but *what* they said. A combination of local dialect and grammatically incorrect sentences that tailed off without completion was often enough to defeat these early attempts of mine to listen in on the kind of things my 'informants' talked about when I was not in their presence.

One evening, about a month after my arrival, I was invited to attend a community gathering to celebrate Akiyasama who, as the fire goddess, was clearly an important deity for people who made their living by firing their pots in kilns, and who lived in a densely-wooded mountainous region. This was the first community 'ritual' that I had attended and I looked forward with anticipation to the occasion when two members from each household in the community gathered together in one of the houses to share some food and drink. At the time I was on a high. As I have learned in later research projects, fieldwork can intoxicate the newcomer who is charmed by the people he or she meets, by the ways they behave, and by the seemingly unstoppable flood of stories that they have to tell. It had been an exhilarating first few weeks in Sarayama. Faced with the usual problem, after having finally got to the fieldwork site, of how to start research and *what* exactly I would do next and what questions to ask of those who had agreed to my 'being there', I had decided to ask people about their household and family relations. This proved to be an inspired move. Hitherto, *everyone* visiting Sarayama – from *mingei* critic to inquisitive tourist, by way of newspaper journalist or television announcer – had focused on Onta pottery and the techniques that the potters used to make their wares. Although these outside visitors occasionally asked some general questions about the community as a whole, nobody – it seemed – had ever bothered to conduct detailed enquiries about their household system. This in itself might have meant nothing so far as my own research was concerned, except that for the people of Sarayama the way in which their household system had developed depended in large part on the methods they used to prepare clay. They were thus very involved in their families, were proud of the relations they maintained through kinship, and firmly believed that these were of paramount importance to the structure of the rural society in which they lived and worked.

Although I had been focusing my attention on Sarayama's household structure – if only as a way of getting to know each of the 82 people who lived in the community – I had also been asking one or two questions about pottery as I went along. In reality, of course, the two could hardly be divorced from each other. The Japanese household system has usually been analysed as an economic, rather than mere residential, unit,[11] so that what the potters did for a living and how they made that living were of crucial importance to an understanding of their family ties. Moreover, while preparing my research proposal in London during the six months leading up to my arrival in Sarayama, I had been in touch with Richard Beardsley, an eminent professor of Japanese anthropology at the University of Michigan, who had advised me to make sure that I got details of every pottery household's financial situation.[12] This was no bad advice. After all, to get to the root of any set of social relations, you usually needed to 'follow the money'. The way in which I set about following that advice, however, left a lot to be desired – as I was soon to find out to my cost.

During the course of my fairly leisurely visits to Sarayama's fourteen households, at each of which, as I tried to trace ancestors, in-laws and adoption practices, I was offered seemingly limitless supplies of green tea and sweet bean cakes of one sort or another, I found myself talking to the extremely shy mother of a young potter, Takayoshi, who was in the process of loading his climbing kiln. At one point, clearly anxious to get back to work, she suggested that I ask him for the answer to one of my questions.[13] As it was clear that her son needed every helping hand he could get – he wanted to start firing early the following morning and the kiln was only half filled by early afternoon when I arrived – I decided to make the most of the opportunity. During the course of the next five hours, therefore, I helped load the kiln and occasionally found enough breath to ask about why big pots were always placed on the top shelf of a kiln chamber, why he stacked smaller pots inside bigger ones, why some glazes were on pots at the front of a kiln shelf while others were on those at the back, and so on and so forth.

That evening, as we sealed the last kiln chamber entrance with bricks and mud, I asked Takayoshi if I could help him with the firing next day. He made a non-committal noise that didn't seem to be 'no', although it didn't sound like as clear and resounding a 'yes' as I might have expected, either. Still, in my enthusiasm, I decided to go ahead and the next morning began helping with the firing of a four-chambered climbing kiln. I say 'help', but in fact in the early stages there was virtually nothing to do because the fire had to be built up slowly at the main mouth. By late afternoon, however, when it was time to fire each chamber one by one, I could be of assistance and I found myself carrying bundle after bundle of two-metre-long cedar strips from a nearby shed to the point we had reached in the firing. In the interim, I asked a lot of technical – and probably rather annoying – questions about where the wood came from, who had built Takayoshi's climbing kiln when, what temperature he fired to (and, in the absence of pyrometers or other measuring device, how he knew that he'd reached the right temperature), and so on, and generally engaged in non-committal conversation about the pleasantness of spring in Japan, craft pottery in England, tourism in Sarayama and – to keep the list short – drunken driving. Takayoshi, I was quick to realize, wasn't one of the more communicative members of the community at the best of times, so that by the time it was two in the morning and we had spent the best part of 20 hours gazing into flames that could easily singe the hairs on our arms or eyebrows if we got too close to them, neither of us had very much to say to the other. What words we exchanged were designed more to help us stay awake, therefore, than to communicate matters of import. By the time we closed the fourth chamber at six in the morning, we were both dead tired and, after a lukewarm bath back in the *sake* shop, I collapsed onto my *futon* and went sound asleep for the next ten hours – thereby missing a whole day of fieldwork. Tut, tut.

Having got so far, of course, I couldn't really *not* help Takayoshi when it was time to open and unload his kiln some 48 hours later. So I walked up the hill to his house in the middle of the morning, when I knew he would be well into his work, and asked him how the firing had gone. He gave a non-committal half-smile and grunt. Would he like me to help? I ignored his 'But you're probably busy yourself', and carried a couple of jars from the kiln with him, to show my willingness. Then all the rest of the morning and well into the afternoon, I took armloads of plates and dishes from kiln entrance to workshop, as well as basket-loads of cups, saucers, *sake* bottles, soy-sauce containers, teapots, lidded jars, flower vases and all the other kinds of functional ware for which Sarayama's potters were famous. This, too, was exhausting work, but – mindful of Richard Beardsley's advice – toward the end I also began counting all the different kinds of pots that had come out of Takayoshi's kiln and noting down how much of each he had fired. There was method in my apparent madness. (I had little idea, for instance, of the variety of sizes in which plates were made; nor was I yet fully conversant with the names of the different kinds of pots made in Sarayama.) I already knew that all potters sold their wares at prices that were fixed by their cooperative, and I was reasonably sure of being able to get access to those prices through Inoshige who was proving to be a wonderful informant and, even, friend. This meant that, if I could successfully calculate how much came out of Takayoshi's kiln, and if I then multiplied this figure by the number of times he fired his kiln every year, I would be able to put a rough figure on his household's annual income. Moreover, since most potters' kilns in Sarayama were more or less the same size and since they fired them more or less the same number of times every year, I would be able to get a rough idea about how much the community as a whole earned from its pottery. Clever me!

The Akiyasama fire goddess gathering came the day after I had helped Takayoshi unload his kiln. Still excited at all the progress I seemed to be making in my fieldwork, I joined Moriyuki, the carpenter-builder whose mother-in-law (by a strange combination of marriage and adoption exchanges, she was also his sister- and aunt-in-law) ran the *sake* shop where I was living and walked down the road with him to where we were all to meet. We arrived more or less on time, stepped out of our shoes up into the house and then went straight to the *butsudan* ancestral shrine to pay our respects to the dead (as a mark of respect for the household as a continuing entity). It was only after we had done this that we turned to exchange greeting bows with our host, Yōjirō, and his family. The living owe their existence to the dead, as I knew from what people had already told me, and everyday social relations now were always embedded in the past.

Once everyone was assembled we began to take our places at a U-shaped layout of low tables set with food, chopsticks, dishes and *sake* cups (which seemed to out-number by far the number of those present in the room). There was a brief hiatus, though, as Inoshige wondered aloud where I should sit. 'We sit by age', he explained, before asking me how old I was. When I told him, another potter, Masao, quickly told me to sit beside him. 'I'm 34,' he grinned, 'and Takumi here is 32 so, if you're 33, you sit here between us.' He motioned to a *zabuton* cushion on the floor and I knelt down between the two men who were over the next two years to be my immediate drinking companions. We were ordered by age and by gender. Men sat in the upper half of the room and the women present sat below the youngest men, although they did not seem to adhere so strictly to age order.

Once we had arranged ourselves, Yōjirō greeted us by thanking us all for coming when we were so busy. He then added that we were gathered to celebrate Akiyasama, something that we did three times a year, and that it was his household's turn to act as host, since last time the festival had been held at Rikizō's place, the next house up the hill.[14] He apologized for the poverty of the dishes set before us, but hoped that we would enjoy ourselves nonetheless. This short greeting was followed by a few words from Tanuki – the eldest man present sitting at the top of the tables with his back to the *tokonoma* alcove and ancestral shrine – who thanked Yōjirō and his household for its hospitality and all the trouble those concerned had taken on our behalves. Then, raising his *sake* cup which had been filled by one of three women moving from place to place along the inside of the U-shaped tables, Tanuki loudly called '*Kanpai!*'[15] We all chorused '*Kanpai!*' and took a sip from our cups before beginning to pick at the food in front of us as we entered into polite conversation hampered in its fluency only by sobriety.

Since I had Masao on one side and Takumi on the other, and since I was the newcomer, the three of us started chatting about our families. My own questions over the past few weeks prompted them to comment favourably on my attempts to trace the genealogy of each household. Not unnaturally, they asked me about my own family and ancestors and I did my best to satisfy their curiosity and explain why we *didn't* have any ancestors, as they nodded their heads in commiseration and refilled my *sake* cup a number of times.

Before long, Inoshige who was sitting above Masao called my name as he passed me his empty cup and filled it. A quick glance around the room made me realize that others, too, were exchanging cups, so I drank down the warm liquid and returned Inoshige his cup, which I then filled. This was a cue for Masao to offer me his cup and before I knew where I was, everyone around me seemed to be passing their cups up and down the table, drinking their contents once filled, and getting pretty red-faced and happy in the process. One or two men had got up from where they were sitting, stepped across the low table in front of them and gone across the intervening space to exchange cups with those sitting at the next row of tables. There was a lot of merriment and laughter and quite a few men were becoming quite boisterous. Clearly, now was the time for all good men to join the party!

By this stage – about 20 minutes from the initial speeches – the room had been transformed from an orderly line of people seated by age and gender into a haphazard arrangement where there was one knot of people around Tanuki at the top of the tables, another around me, and a third at the bottom of the room comprising two or three of the youngest men and most of the women. (One or two of the latter had already withdrawn to a different room.) Just as I was beginning to feel the effect of the alcohol and wondering how these potters managed to hold their drink so well when most Japanese would have been flat out on the floor by now,[16] Takumi's uncle, Rikizō, who was sitting on the other side of the table in front of me, suddenly said in a loud voice:

'Tell me, Mr Moeran, why you were counting all the pots Takayoshi fired in his kiln yesterday?'

Slightly taken aback, I did my best to give a disarming smile. 'Well, I was interested in what kind of pots you make here and in how big those climbing kilns are.'

'I'm sure you were!' Rikizō continued in a voice loud enough to attract people's attention. 'But who gave you permission to count them?'

By now the whole room was silent and everybody had turned to listen to what was going on.

'Well, I asked Takayoshi if it was all right', I said, glancing at Takayoshi for help, but he was staring steadfastly at the table in front of him and didn't make any attempt to catch my glance.

'And did he say it *was* all right?'

'Well, I thought –'

'You *thought*,' Rikizō mimicked me mockingly, 'What do you mean by interfering in our private affairs?'

'I wasn't interfering –' I began.

'Then what were you doing? Eh? What gives you the right to look into our financial affairs?' Rikizō knew he had a captive audience. 'Why are you here anyway? Nobody asked you to come here, did they? But you turned up out of the blue, spinning us some story about Bernard Leach introducing you. How do we know that's true? Eh?'

'But I *do* know Bernard Leach,' I protested lamely. 'You can ask people in Tokyo if you don't believe me.'

'How can we believe them, when we can't believe you?' Rikizō pounced again, with all the unanswerable logic that inebriation can effortlessly induce.

'I can write to Bernard and ask him to write to you, if it would help', I said, feeling rather helpless and wondering if, or hopefully when, Inoshige would come to my rescue. But Inoshige, who was sitting beside Rikizō, remained impassive.

'That's not the point. The point is, you came here on some pretext or other and we said OK, you can stay here for a month or two and we'll see what happens.'

'Thank you,' I murmured, bowing to Rikizō. 'I'm very grateful and apologize for the inconvenience I've caused you all.'

'Yes, it is an inconvenience,' Rikizō persisted, his face still red and his words slightly slurred by drink. 'It may seem all right if you ask us some questions about our families. But remember, these are personal matters, too, you know.'

'I understand,' I said, recalling vividly how Takumi's eyes had become wet with tears when, in an attempt to resolve the issue of just how many generations had lived in his household since his family had first founded Sarayama, he had taken all the memorial tablets of the dead from out of the back of his ancestral shrine and laid them very gently, as if they were alive, on the *tatami* matted floor where we were sitting.

'No, you don't. If you did understand, you'd never have forced yourself on Takayoshi during his kiln firing. And then you go around behaving like a tax inspector, trying to work out how much money he earns. That just won't do. You're really rude, you know. Who do you think you are, anyway?'

'I'm sorry, I won't do it again', I said, surprised though mortified at being likened to a tax inspector.[17]

'How are we to know *that*?' Rikizō asked rhetorically. 'How can we *trust* you? You're a foreigner. You *say* you're doing research. You *say* you know Bernard Leach. You *say* you've got a Japanese wife and children living near Nagoya. But how do we know if that's all true or not? *You* can see us here in Sarayama. You can see our houses, our families, the way we work. You can ask your questions, get your answers, and form opinions about us. But *we*'ve got nothing at all on you. Your life's an empty space, so far as *we're* concerned.'

'You're right, Rikizō. We don't know anything about Būchan here.' In coming to my rescue, Inoshige decided to use the nickname that we had all agreed upon my first evening in Sarayama after the *utai* lesson.[17] 'But everything I've heard so far suggests he's telling the truth about Bernard Leach, his research and family. Still,' he continued, turning to me, 'that doesn't mean he should pry into our private affairs when we don't want him to.'

'Definitely not,' said Rikizō defiantly, though slightly mollified. 'He's got absolutely no right –'

'So maybe,' Inoshige interrupted firmly, 'the best thing to do right now is to make sure we don't tell Būchan anything we don't want to tell him, and tell him clearly not to ask questions that we don't want to be asked when he does ask them.'

'And that means not trying to find out anything about our financial affairs.'

'Precisely,' interpolated Yōjirō with a sharp glance at me before adopting the role of a perfect host. 'But still, Rikizō-san, why don't we leave things at that for now, and have another drink?'

As he poured some *sake* into a still grumbling Rikizō's cup, people started talking to one another in low voices that gradually gained momentum. I myself was ignored for what seemed like an age until Inoshige began telling me a story about how, as a young man, he and Takumi had been taught by Bernard Leach to make pitcher handles by pulling the clay between thumb and forefinger. Bernard had come by his workshop every evening during his stay in Sarayama and pointed to line after line of clay handles, saying '*Dame! Dame!* No good! No good!' until, eventually, he found one that passed the test. Takumi, cleverly brought into the conversation in this way, added his recollections and soon it seemed as if Rikizō's outburst had never happened except in my own head.

But, of course, it *had* happened, and I spent a restless night wondering whether I might be forced to leave Sarayama. I cursed my short-sightedness, my stupidity, and an excess of enthusiasm that had failed to see the implications of my – as it transpired, rather inept – counting of Takayoshi's kiln contents. The next morning, in trepidation, I went to see Inoshige. As I stepped into his workshop, Ayako, his wife, looked up from where she was putting spouts onto a tray of tea pots, and said smilingly:

'That was a tough time you had last night, wasn't it? Don't worry. Rikizō often gets like that when he's had too much to drink.'

I hardly knew what to say, but just looked anxiously at Inoshige who was rubbing a huge coil of clay between the palms of his two hands. 'Ayako's right,' he nodded. 'Rikizō tends to get a bit outspoken when he's in his cups. People will remember what was said all right, but in a few days they'll go around as if they've forgotten. Just be careful, is my advice. *I* understand you've got to ask all sorts of questions, even though I often don't understand *why* you ask them – at least, not immediately. But some of the others find it a bit difficult. I've already talked to Takayoshi, Takumi and Masao, though, and we've agreed to help you as much as we can, whatever the older potters like Rikizō say. And if you need to find out about money,' Inoshige added with a grin, 'then start by asking me. We've got nothing to hide, have we, Ayachan?'

Framing Behaviour

As I said at the beginning of this chapter, *Baptized by Fire* is a confessional tale. But it is told with a purpose other than to reveal the kind of mistake any field-worker can make, especially during the early days of his research when he has not yet grasped many – any? – of the nuances of social behaviour among the people he is studying. So, what is this purpose? What is this narrative's 'grand scheme'?

I started my story by pointing out that people in Japan like to drink and that, when they do so, they often exhibit the kind of behaviour that is frowned upon during the course of their everyday working lives. In other words, leisure and work activities give rise to different ways of talking and interacting with others. This is immediately apparent in the account of my seeking Takayoshi's approval to help him load, fire and unload his kiln, on the one hand, and Rikizō's taking me to task during the Akiyasama celebration, on the other. These exchanges were in complete contrast to each other: on the one hand, a series of mumbled words, polite set phrases and other evasive forms of verbal and non-verbal communication; on the other, a string of very direct questions and challenging accusations. With

Takayoshi there was very little eye contact between us and a smile would often be the only answer to a question I asked. With Rikizō, I could feel his eyes bore through me as, red faced and angry, he twisted me this way and that with his own especially sharpened knife of inebriated logic.

What I soon discovered from participation in other drinking occasions was that the kind of behaviour Rikizō had exhibited at the Akiyasama celebration was the norm, rather than the exception, among men when they drank. In other words, *sake*-drinking provided men with a licensed *frame* for letting off the steam that built up, for one reason or another, during the daytime. So people would be polite and mild-mannered during the daylight hours as they went about their daily business, but sometimes hit the roof over their cups in the evenings when they felt that someone had slighted them, pulled a fast one, or generally misbehaved.

But there was something else that caught my attention. The morning after, in advising me to proceed carefully, Inoshige had said that everyone in Sarayama would go around *as if* they'd forgotten what had happened the previous evening. He very carefully did not say that they *would* forget Rikizō's outburst. This suggested that there were two discourses at play in the complex working-out of people's lives in Sarayama. One was a daytime discourse, where people followed the rules of accepted etiquette and behaved in an 'appropriate' manner to those with whom they communicated. The other was a night-time discourse, where those with a grudge would give vent to their feelings and say what they liked to whomever they liked, regardless of the other's age, social role or status in the community's hierarchy. Although often apparently personal, the arguments that broke out during drinking sessions were ultimately almost always concerned, directly or indirectly, with the welfare of the community as a whole. As a result, as I was soon to learn from further experience, the night-time discourse tended to inflect the daytime discourse, since those who drank together *knew* who had said what to whom, when, why, and with what results, even though they feigned to have 'forgotten' what had happened. To put it in a nutshell, the daytime discourse upheld the authority of the community's social structure, while the night-time discourse displayed the power of particular individuals to question and undermine that authority. Those who did not participate in Sarayama's drinking sessions did not have power.[19]

Of course, it would be blatantly dishonest, and stretch my readers' credibility to the limit, were I to claim that I managed to work all this out after a single night's drinking with my 'informants'. That would be to attribute to Japanese *sake* miraculous powers that, alas, it does not possess. It was probably more than a dozen hangovers later, therefore, before I finally began to put all the pieces of the social puzzle into place. But what I did realize at once was the power of *frames* – in the sense here of particular settings in which people came together for a particular purpose – to influence and co-ordinate participants' social behaviour in a number of different, often overlapping, ways. Frames, though, are multifaceted. They are not demarcated simply by their *instrumental* nature (in the sense of occasion). That is, my drawing a distinction between leisure and work and proceeding to analyse a drinking occasion as a series of oppositions between two discourses – of daytime and night-time, authority and power – focusing on the age-grade seniority system that characterized Sarayama's social structure, is not sufficient an analysis in itself. We need also to consider each frame's spatial and temporal aspects.

Let me deal with the spatial aspect first, since it is the *setting* that is the most obvious and easily observable part of frame analysis – something all of us can, and do, observe subconsciously every time we step into a classroom, office, home, café or museum.[20] Of course, some places (a classroom) are more obviously 'framed' (blackboard, teacher's desk or podium, students' benches or chairs) than others (a café), but, even so, we recognize that certain parts of a space (a window seat in a café, for example) are more desirable than others (a table by the door to the toilets) and behave accordingly.[21] In the case of a university classroom, the frame requires that the teacher stand and talk without interruption for some length of time about a particular topic, and that the students sit still and listen (ideally, taking notes of the more interesting things that are being said). These days, this sort of frame would hardly be complete without a PowerPoint presentation – a kind of idiot's guide to the contents of the lecture – so that the spatial frame in many ways influences and renders acceptable certain kinds of behaviour.

In the case of the tale that I have called *Baptism by Fire*, it was the *zashiki* guest room in which we gathered for the Akiyasama festival that provided the spatial frame for how participants would be situated and interact vis-à-vis one another. The existence at one end of the room of the *tokonoma* raised alcove – commonly thought of as the most sacred part of any house – was sufficient to make that the 'top' of the room,[22] and it was there that Tanuki, defined as the most senior participant by his age and gender, sat. Other men then took their places in descending order of age, before the women sat at the 'bottom' of the room, so that the initial spatial frame clearly defined who would sit where. At the same time, the spatial frame also made a distinction between insider (host) and outsiders (guests), for while the representatives of each of Sarayama's fourteen households were arrayed along the top and down the sides of the *zashiki*, Yōjirō – who, at the age of 58, should have been sitting near the top of the room – placed himself at the very bottom of the guest room, facing the senior guest, Tanuki.

If the spatial frame initiates such behaviour while formally classifying its participants into men and women, old and young, outsiders and insiders, and the instrumental frame – together with participants' appearance and manner[23] – influences the kind of communication that can allowably take place during the course of a drinking session, what is the function of temporal frames? Practically, temporal frames may be divided into numerous *strips of activity* that are isolated from the ongoing stream of activity.[24] So how did *they* work during the course of the Akiyasama gathering? In the first place, when we arrived at Yōjirō's house, Moriyuki and I took off our shoes and walked wordlessly to the *butsudan* ancestral shrine where we knelt and bowed our heads in respect. This marked a meeting of outside and inside, present and past history and can be seen as the first strip in the frame as a whole. But the next strip also reinforced this distinction between insider and outsider as Yōjirō (the host) gave his opening speech, in which he thanked us for coming and reminded us of the purpose of our being in his house. A response was then made by Tanuki as the senior outsider, and then the distinction between inside and outside was effectively erased in the next strip when everyone joined in the toast and drank their first cup of *sake* together.

The following strip of the frame occurred simultaneously among groups of two or three men and women sitting beside each other at the line of tables, and consisted of slightly formal conversation as participants warmed to their rice wine. During the course of this interaction, people poured *sake* for each other, but did not exchange cups. A new strip began when cups were exchanged for the first time. As people started talking and laughing in louder voices, exchanging cups with neighbours on either side of them and with those on the far side of each neighbour (that is, with about five men in all), almost all traces of the formality marking the previous frame strip disappeared. The next strip was initiated when one of the men stood up and walked up, down or across the room to exchange cups with people he could not easily reach in the previous strip. It was marked by a redistribution of people spatially, with all participants ending up in one of three or four groups that formed in various places between the top and the bottom of the *zashiki*.

It was during the course of this strip that Rikizō staged his 'mini strip' with opening, development and closure, and – as I was later to find out – it was at this stage in drinking generally that arguments broke out, grew heated and, hopefully, were provisionally resolved. In order to avoid being involved in what on occasion would end in fisticuffs (yes, even the Japanese punch one another when pissed and pissed off), some of the older men and the women would at this point leave the room for the family room with its *kotatsu* sunken pit brazier, and there drink tea to help the effects of the alcohol they had imbibed wear off. In other words, this alternative strip of activity also involved a change in setting. The two together inevitably affected their behaviour and boisterous rowdiness would soon be replaced by polite conversation, moroseness or sleep.[25]

The other thing that I learned immediately, although I was aware of it from previous experience in Japan, was the importance of distinguishing – as the Japanese themselves so clearly do – between 'front' (*omote*) and 'back' (*ura*) behaviour. This is something we are going to encounter time and time again in other tales from the field described in this book. The daytime and night-time discourses discussed above were examples of this distinction. But the distinction also typifies a challenge facing those of us studying organizations of various kinds. How do we *know* that what we observe is 'for real' and that the interpretations that we then provide to 'explain' what we see are adequate? How do we *know* that someone is telling us the truth, the whole truth and nothing but the truth, rather than a bunch of platitudes designed to pull the wool over a researcher's unsuspecting eyes (as we will discover in my third fieldwork tale)? The argument presented in this book is that participant-observation-style fieldwork provides the researcher with an extremely useful – but not the only – clue to what is going on in organizations all over the world. It helps us distinguish front- from back-stage behaviour and helps us get to the heart of social relations, from micro-level frames to macro-level fields.

Notes

1. I will refrain from citing such works. After all, we wouldn't want their authors to take advantage of their possible mention in the citation index to seek promotion in the academic hierarchy, would we?
2. John Van Maanen, *Tales of the Field*, 1988, pp. 93–4.
3. E.g. Charles Frake, 'How to ask for a drink in Subanun', 1964; Thomas Wilson (ed.), *Drinking Culture: Alcohol and the expression of identity, class and nation*, forthcoming.
4. Just to complicate matters slightly, those who named 'my' Sarayama gave Onta a standardized Tokyo pronunciation so that it is often referred to as Onda.
5. The fact that a number of tourists used to visit the hamlet of Onta to look for pots and go away empty-handed and confused (because pots are not, and never have been, made in Onta) was a source of amusement to many local people. Indeed, I myself only arrived in Sarayama, rather than Onta, because a sympathetic young man who gave me a lift in his car from the foot of the valley (there was a rail strike and I had had to hitchhike from Nagoya to my fieldwork village) realized that I was interested in pottery and not farming and dropped me in Sarayama. It took me two days and a very confusing conversation with my landlady, after I had been for a walk over the pass and down to Onta, to realize where I was . . . and wasn't.
6. Brian Moeran, *Folk Art Potters of Japan: Beyond an anthropology of aesthetics*, 1997 [1984].
7. Cf. Helen Schwartzman, *Ethnography in Organizations*, 1993, pp. 48–51; W.F. Whyte, *Learning from the Field*, 1984; David Gellner and Eric Hirsch, *Inside Organizations: Anthropologists at work*, 2001, pp. 4–6.
8. Although I have to admit to being somewhat chagrined at the time at what appeared to be her apparently dismissive tone, Professor Nakane soon became an extremely helpful field advisor and, later, collegial friend. Much of what I

have learned about Japanese society and culture over the years has benefited from conversations with her over lunches and dinners where she has displayed a thought-provoking combination of acute observation and trenchant criticism.

9. I actually used the £100 that I was paid as my interpreting fee to buy the last Pilgrim plate still for sale in Bernard Leach's workshop. Six months later I went to Tokyo and met the cameraman I had worked with. He asked whether I still had the plate and, on hearing that I had, offered me £1,000 for it. I have it on my desk as I write.

10. It was only some weeks later that I found an occasion to bring out Professor Nakane's name card and show it to Inoshige, who examined it closely and made appropriate noises of admiration at my knowing such a famous person of whom he had never heard. Then he gave it back to me with a slightly embarrassed laugh, and quickly changed the subject.

11. Chie Nakane, *Economic and Kinship Organization in Rural Japan*, 1967a.

12. One of his students who had conducted fieldwork in a folk-art pottery village near Kyoto had apparently failed to do this.

13. He did not, of course, know it. Women are always much better than men at being able to trace genealogies, remember which ancestor came before which, and who was married to whom – perhaps because they are themselves outsiders who marry in and have to learn all they can in order to become accepted as full members of their husbands' households.

14. Keen on on classificatory possibilities, my ears pricked up at this piece of information which got me making enquiries along classical anthropological lines during the next few weeks. Fire moved upwards in the kiln from one chamber to the next, and yet the fire goddess herself was celebrated in descending order for households down the valley through which two streams of water flowed. These streams powered the wooden clay crushers that prepared the clay that was then formed into pots at the wheel, but the kick-wheel, I found out, moved in an anti-clockwise direction and so was 'left turning' (*hidari mawari*), while Akiyasama herself – like women in general – was associated with the left side. At the same time, women marrying into Sarayama were said to come 'up' from the valley below. So what? So there seemed to be a direct link between Akiyasama, the continuity of the household system, gender relations, and pottery production. The descending order of households matched the descent of water which potentially extinguished fire and the danger of outside women marrying in, while permitting the cycle of pottery production from raw clay to fired stoneware pot to contine in an endless cycle. Since everyone in Sarayama thought I was over-exerting my imagination when I tried this theory out, however, I never bothered to pursue it further. After all, the 'theory' did not explain why women prepared clay (did

the water they used make them less dangerous?) and men made and fired pots. It certainly failed to take account of such pragmatic matters as the equitable distribution of labour in what was, after all, a family business.

15. *Kanpai* may most accurately be translated as 'Bottoms up!', since it literally means 'dry cup'.

16. The answer was quite simple, although it took me another two or three drinking sessions to work it out. Almost everyone made sure to sit with a large ash tray planted between their crossed legs. When offered a cup, a potter would drink a mouthful of the *sake* before pouring the rest into the ash tray and returning the cup to the original donor. In this way, he fended off the inevitable onset of inebriation and premitted the party to go on much longer than might otherwise have been the case. Needless to say, as soon as I had managed to put two and two together, I followed the maxim of 'When in Rome . . .' (*Gō ni ireba . . .*)

17. A year or so later, my next door neighbour in a neighbouring community to which I had moved with my wife and children down the Ono valley accused me of being a government spy! Such accusations are not infrequently made against anthropologists all round the world.

18. *Chan* is a diminutive form used primarily for children in Japan, but also for grown men and women in rural areas where first, rather than family, names tend to be used in social interaction. The 'Bū' bit comes from Japanese inability to string two consonants together without separating a vowel, and is a lengthening of the first syllable of my name as it is usually pronounced by Japanese: *Bu-rai-an*. Because *bu* is also short for *buta* meaning 'pig', my nickname may be best translated as 'Piglet' – a source of great merriment among my Japanese friends and family.

19. This did not mean that a man had to drink alcohol. At one stage during field-work, for example, Inoshige – who drank far too much for his own good – was advised by his doctor to go on the wagon. He used to turn up at every community drinking occasion, though, armed with two cans of tomato juice which he drank out of *sake* cups passed to him. He then feigned inebriation (he claimed others put *sake* into his tomato juice when he wasn't looking) in order to participate in political discussions and the occasional argument with his fellow villagers. See Brian Moeran, 'One over the seven: *sake* drinking in a Japanese pottery community', in J. Hendry (ed.), *Interpreting Japanese Society*, 1998 [1986], pp. 243–58.

20. Erving Goffman, *The Presentation of Self in Everyday Life*, 1959, pp. 32–4.

21. There may be additional reasons for the desirability of restaurant window seats. In *Spy Hook*, for example, Len Deighton has his spy protagonist comment: 'When we were kids we all firmly believed that the people in the window seats got bigger portions to attract passers-by' (p. 58).

22. The Japanese house is generally divided into public 'front' (*omote*) and private 'back' (*ura*) areas, with the *zashiki* in front and the kitchen at the back. A married woman is called 'Madam of the back' (*okusama*) in standard Japanese, so that spatial architecture implies a gendered division of space. See Takie Lebra, 'The spatial layout of hierarchy: residential style of the modern Japanese nobility', in her edited *Japanese Social Organization*, 1992, pp. 49–78.

23. Goffman, *The Presentation of Self*, pp. 34–36.

24. Goffman, *Frame Analysis*, 1986, [1974], p. 10.

25. Especially vivacious gatherings might sometimes extend to a sixth frame (with various sub-frames) as the 'happier' of the men decided to drive (!) down to the bottom of the Ono valley for a night in the neighbouring town's panoply of bars, with their accompanying cast of simpering hostesses and forthright 'madams'.

–2–

Analysing Frames

Examining social behaviour in terms of *frames* is one useful way to get to grips with what goes on in our everyday lives at the micro-level of sociological analysis. Frames organize social behaviour. The contents of people's activities become themselves frames (like the layout of a fashion magazine, or the structure of an academic book). Frames also organize organizations, collectivities and network behaviour. In our ordinary, everyday activities, all of us find ourselves going through a series of, often quickly, framed episodes, in which we tend to have different realm statuses or attributes. To each of these frames (a telephone call, a casual greeting in the street, a lecture or a goodnight story) we bring different attributes (as friend, neighbour, teacher or parent). In each of them we adopt different kinds of behaviour (informal, ritual, formal or intimate, and so on) as we communicate with different sets of people. In this respect, our lives are like a long reel of film, made up of dozens and dozens of laminated celluloid frames that are projected onto our own and others' consciousness as 'life'. Each frame can be analysed according to its channel of activity, the 'laminations' given to that activity (to make it seem other than it purports to be), and the status of its participants.[1] As fieldworkers, in particular, we need to be aware of this if we are to unpack, unravel and grasp the meanings that are openly revealed, merely implied, and/or concealed by participants in social actions.

I want here to take up the concept of frame, therefore, and discuss it in the light of the work of two rather different and separate scholars. One of these is Erving Goffman, a formidable proponent of the study of face-to-face situational interaction and public behaviour, who not only introduced such micro-sociological terms as impression management, performance, face work, front and back stages, but made them stick in anthropological theory.[2] The other is Chie Nakane, the Tokyo University professor who provided me with her name card as a mode of entry into Sarayama, but who – much more importantly – initiated a structural analysis of Japanese social behaviour in terms of frame.[3] As a result, one focus of anthropological attention in the study of Japanese society has been what is called 'situationalism'.[4]

Focus on the analysis and explanation of the workings of *Japanese* society is important because Japan is still the world's second-largest economy and, for a handful of years more at least, the world's only non-Western superpower.[5] What the Japanese do, therefore, how and why they do what they do when and where, and with what results, should be of concern to others seeking to learn from their example. Unfortunately, however, there has been a strong tendency among scholars of 'things Japanese', as well as among Japanese themselves, to explain the workings of Japanese society according to strictly cultural principles that ultimately suggest that the Japanese are, at worst, unique and, at best, very different from ourselves.[6] This can be seen, for example, in analytical terminology and the use of indigenous phrases – starting, perhaps, with *on* (obligation), *giri* (repayment of obligation) and *haji* (shame),[7] continuing through *amae* (dependence) and *wa* (harmony),[8] and ending up with such classificatory paired terms as *tatemae* 'public attitude' and *honne* 'private reflection', and *omote* 'front' and *ura* 'back' regions.[9] My own take in this not-fully-worked-out discussion of comparative studies is that, not only *can* many Japanese terms be translated quite simply and effectively into another language, but – in the context of frame analysis – they may for the most part usefully be elided with terms used by Goffman. This will help us avoid cultural relativism and make discussions of *Japanese* organization sensibly relevant to our discussion of social organization as a whole.[10]

Frame Analysis

In his Foreword to a second edition of *Frame Analysis*, Bennett Berger points out that *frame* refers to the inevitably relational dimensions of meaning – dimensions that Goffman puts to great effect at the end of his masterly Introduction where he reveals the possibility of frames existing within frames within frames within frames, seemingly – given Goffman's own observational powers – ad infinitum.[11] This possibility in itself depends on participants' ability to control and alter each frame through interactive skills involving stratagems, ruses, manoeuvres and other 'moves'.[12] At the same time, we should recognize that the practice of frame analysis itself depends on the observer's ability to observe these interactive skills and to realize which of participants' moves is in fact a stratagem, ruse or manoeuvre, or whatever.

Without doubt, Goffman himself was *the* master at this game of games. As John Van Maanen has admitted:

> When I try, for example, to do a frame analysis as I imagine Goffman ... might, my results feel and look rather awkward and stilted, if not downright stupid. While this is surely partly my own doing, I suspect part of it also lies with the fact that Goffman knew more than he could say to the rest of us.[13]

Anyone, therefore, who attempts an analysis of frames risks being accused of insufficient powers of observation and of reducing complex behaviour to overly simple, even banal, explanations. It is, nevertheless, a risk we are going to have to take since it is the social *form*, as well as the cultural and communicative content, that is at stake in this methodological discussion.

My focus on the *social* form of frames, however, is almost immediately undermined by Goffman himself who forewarns his readers in his Introduction that *Frame Analysis* is about the organization of experience and *not* about 'the core matters of sociology – social organization and social structure'. The latter, he adds, 'can continue to be quite nicely studied without reference to frame at all'.[14] This means that he pays hardly any attention at all to the power of durable institutional structures to influence framing rules in such a way that participants' 'moves' are limited, or at least affected in some way.

And yet, in the same breath, Goffman adds that he personally believes 'society to be first in every way and any individual's current involvements to be second; this report deals only with matters that are second'.[15] For reasons that will become a little clearer during my discussion of the work of Chie Nakane, I believe that frame analysis *can* and *should* be conducted in relation to those 'core matters of sociology'. I will, therefore, attempt to make use of a number of Goffman's insights and reframe them in the contexts of social organization and social structure.

Is this blatant hubris or a reasonable attempt to extend an analytical frame? One of the difficulties in Goffman's work in general is that he tends to invent, and with each new book reinvent, his own specialist terms – many of which, in spite of their apparent particularism, continue to be used in sociological and anthropological theory (as we noted at the beginning of the chapter). But terminology is itself subject to the same relational dimensions of meaning as are frames on at least two counts. First, as Goffman himself pointed out:

> Once a term is introduced (this occurring at the point at which it is first needed), it begins to have too much bearing, not merely applying to what comes later, but reapplying in each chapter to what it has already applied to. Thus each succeeding section of the study becomes more entangled, until a step can hardly be made because of what must be carried along with it. The process closely follows the horrors of repetition songs, as if – in the case of frame analysis – what Old MacDonald had on his farm were partridge and juniper trees.[16]

Secondly, terms may very well take on lives of their own as they are interpreted and used in ways somewhat different from that originally intended. In this respect, they may be likened to children. Neither turns out quite in the way their progenitors imagined.[17]

What, then, is this terminology and how relevant is it to our discussion? For Goffman himself, *frame* refers to basic elements of organization that govern social events, but also to the organization of involvement as well as of meaning.[18] For its part, *frame analysis* refers to 'the examination in these terms of the organization of experience'.[19] Such experience can be of any kind and include even 'the merely cerebral'.[20] Within each frame it is possible to isolate strips of activity. A *strip* refers to 'any arbitrary slice or cut from the stream of ongoing activity . . . any raw batch of occurrences (of whatever status in reality) that one wants to draw attention to as a starting point of analysis'.[21] In many ways, these strips of activity – such as those I isolated in my analysis of the Akiyasama drinking frame – can be seen as 'mini frames' in themselves.

Primary frameworks

A primary framework is 'one that is seen as rendering what would otherwise be a meaningless aspect of the scene into something that is meaningful'.[22] Although varying in degree of organization, 'each primary framework allows its user to locate, perceive, identify, and label a seemingly infinite number of concrete occurrences defined in its own terms',[23] and it is precisely because of the acceptance of the existence of primary frameworks that acts of daily living are understandable. In other words, drinking sessions are an example of a primary framework for people living in Sarayama and the neighbouring Ono valley; what goes on there – from drinking to singing and dancing, by way of arguments and the occasional punch-up – is immediately recognizable as understandable behaviour by participants and by others living there.

Other frameworks that are primary for Sarayama's inhabitants include family meals, kiln firings, rice transplanting, archery contests, softball games, *shigin* and *utai* lessons, wedding parties, and so on.[24] In the art, advertising and fashion worlds, which we will be looking at in later chapters, primary frames include exhibitions, local pottery association gatherings, auctions, client orientations, (competitive) presentations, account team meetings, studio (and location) shoots, fashion shows, editorial meetings, and so forth. In other words, primary frameworks are those that are seen to be relevant and important to the tasks undertaken by members of a social world, and differ according to the particular business that each social world conducts and is formed around.

According to Goffman, primary frameworks can be *natural* or *social*. Natural frameworks are 'purely physical' unguided events that occur solely as a result of natural causes (the weather as reported in the weather forecast). Social frameworks, on the other hand, 'incorporate the will, aim, and controlling effort of an intelligence, a live agency, the chief one being the human being.'[25] What we find in a social framework are the 'guided doings' of individuals – guided because they are subject to certain standards, norms, expectations and social appraisal. As we have seen, certain kinds of behaviour are expected at certain stages during the course of a drinking occasion in Sarayama and people behave according to those norms and expectations because they know that, to do otherwise (like Rikizō speaking out, for example, immediately after the initial toast) would invite criticism and possibly social sanctions of one sort or another.

A fashion magazine itself constitutes a framework that is part physical, part social. It is of fixed dimensions, generally standardised among all other fashion magazines in a particular country. Its contents, too, are standardised and are mainly and invariably devoted to feature stories (generally to do with women), fashion, beauty and health, with additional material on celebrities, fashion and related commodity news, food, interior and horoscope. Its cover almost invariably depicts a photograph of a young, smiling woman who is either celebrity or model, and the magazine's title is imprinted just above, over or behind her head. Around this photograph are deployed eye-catching headlines in various colours and font sizes to attract potential readers' attention (and the strategic importance of headlines at the top or to the left of the cover depends in large part on the display method adopted in retail outlets). The cover is followed by at least one two-page advertisement spread (and generally five or six), followed by the Table of Contents which is almost invariably spread across two consecutive pages, facing and separated by advertising. After the Contents come the Masthead pages, on which publishing and editorial staff names are credited. This is followed by a brief introduction by the Editor-in-Chief, whose personalised signature appears at the bottom of the page. All these pages are separated by ads. Then follow up-to-date information sections like *In Vogue*, *First Look*, *First Word* and so on, items relating to the fields of fashion, beauty and entertainment, a celebrity interview and/or first feature. In the U.S. only the first page of a feature or interview is ever on the right-hand page; all other editorial matter is on the left, facing advertisements which continue to predominate on the easy-to-note right page of the magazine. Advertisements only stop when the magazine reaches the 'fashion well', approximately 50 pages of uninterrupted full-colour photographs that come approximately two-thirds to three-quarters of the way through the magazine. Thereafter come beauty and health sections, followed by food, interior and horoscope, all placed on left-hand pages facing advertisements. The magazine is completed by the back cover, itself almost invariably an advertisement.[26]

Competitive presentations are the primary framework in which an advertising agency tries to persuade a would-be client that it is better qualified than its rivals to carry out a particular sales-related task. In making a presentation to a potential client, an advertising agency will ensure that it follows a strictly adhered to pattern of exchange that builds to a crescendo approximately three quarters of the way through before gently falling away. Thus a presentation will start with opening speeches by senior members of the agency (who then remain silent during the presentation and ensuing question and answer period, and only speak again during the closing salutations). It then continues with the appointed speaker's summary of points made at the client's orientation with the agency, the agency's own marketing analysis of issues raised at the orientation, and its resulting creative strategy. At this point a creative director may speak to the story boards and commercial video mock-ups that are shown to the client to illustrate the market analysis, or the appointed speaker (an account executive) will continue to do so. After this climax (creative work is what the client *really* wants to see), the agency's presentation will return to more humdrum matters such as media placement and expenditure, before the client is invited to ask questions relating to the presentation as a whole.[27]

A presentation is only one primary framework recognized by members of an advertising agency. Others include the client's orientation, other client meetings, agency account team meetings, separate creative team meetings, pre-presentations, studio photography, filming of commercials, and other activities directly connected with the production of advertising campaigns. But they also include regular section, department, division and board of directors meetings, as well as various other activities (like the CEO's monthly address) that contribute to and maintain the internal organization of an advertising agency. When taken all together, these primary frameworks make up a central element of an advertising agency's culture and we can in this way talk of a social group's 'framework of frameworks'.[28] It is these social frameworks that are of interest to us here.

So far as Goffman was concerned, the real reason for developing frame analysis was in order to be able to point to and explain certain transformations that take place in primary frameworks,[29] rather than the frameworks themselves. It was with this aim in mind that he developed a whole range of other terms to deal with these transformations. Among the most important of these for our purposes are the following: brackets, keying, fabrication, theatrical frame, out-of-frame behaviour and frame breaking.

Brackets

Brackets are conventionalized boundary markers, in time and/or space, designed to set something apart from – and thus to *anchor* it in – the ongoing flow of surrounding events.[30]

> An inset like this, purporting to illustrate, describe, analyse or comment on an argument presented in the main body of the text, is a bracket.

An example of spatial brackets here would be the initial greeting at the ancestral altar by those arriving at Yōjirō's house for the Akiyasama gathering; and of temporal brackets the host's opening speech and senior guest's reply.[31] On some occasions these opening brackets may also be repeated at the end of an event – such as school sports' day, valley 'marathon' race or community archery contest – to mark closure of the primary frame in question. Moreover, each speech given may itself be structured with opening and closing temporal brackets, as a speaker starts by welcoming people to an event at a time when they are so busy, states what the occasion is that has caused them all to be present, and then moves into a more general monologue before finishing up by thanking everyone for attending the occasion at which they are present, when they are so busy.[32]

Brackets can apply to physical objects, too. Let us take up fashion magazines once more as an example. We have noted how the primary framework of a magazine consists of Cover–Ads–Contents–Masthead–Letters (editor's page)–News Items–Interview–Feature and so on. However, if we follow editorial staff's own understandings of the contents of their work, the primary frame of a fashion magazine is in fact the 'fashion well' – those four dozen and more pages of colour photography (divided into 6, 8, 10 or 12 page 'stories') uninterrupted by ads. Of course, there are territorial battles to be fought here. A features editor may regard her work as more important because it has 'content'; a beauty editor may point to the fact that the section for which she is responsible is always advertised in 'prime position' as the leading cover headline (in the top left corner under the magazine title). The Masthead page, however, establishes a clear hierarchy of positions, of which first and foremost is the fashion department. If this is accepted, we may say that the fashion well is the fashion magazine, and that everything else – from front to back covers, from Contents to Horoscope – are bracketing devices.

So brackets are not limited to greetings and speeches of various kinds. They can be seen in the way in which Japanese exchange name cards – presenting and receiving cards with two hands, while simultaneously bowing and repeating their name, before examining them and making use of the information printed there to engage in enquiry and initial conversation. Television quiz and chat shows are bracketed by the appearance and introductory words of the announcer; and again when a song is sung or music played; and, at regular intervals, when we are told that we will now hear 'a word from our sponsor'.

During the course of a studio photography session, brackets are used every time the model is in position on set and the photographer is ready to shoot a particular picture. Either the photographer himself or the stylist/art director (of the magazine fashion story or advertising campaign) will command silence of the assortment of people present. Up to two dozen people (including hair stylist and assistant, make-up artist and assistant, model agency manager, client personnel, studio stage hands and ethnographer) will sit or stand motionless watching the scene as the photographer takes shot after Polaroid shot of the model, while giving instructions for minor adjustments in pose, smile or facial angle, and so on. The bracket is closed by a final loudly-spoken phrase like 'Right!' or 'Thank you', whereupon the model is ushered back to the make-up room by the make-up artist, while an assistant quickly develops the Polaroids. Once these are ready, a new bracket is opened as photographer and art director converge at a particular point in the studio where a table or stand of some sort has been set up for them to examine work in progress. They are quickly surrounded by the rest of the studio crew – including, a little later, the model – all of whom await instructions based on the ensuing discussion between stylist/art director and photographer about what precisely they are looking for in the finished photograph. The photographer then closes the bracket by telling his assistant and stage hands what needs to be done by way of camera positioning, background, props and so on, while an art director may call over client personnel to show them the Polaroids and advise them of the creative team's intentions. A new bracket begins as the work cycle is repeated until all are satisfied with the results.

Keying

A key may be seen as a kind of staging by which an activity meaningfully carried on by participants in a primary framework is suddenly transformed into something patterned on this activity, but seen by those concerned as something else. In this way, keying 'performs a crucial role in determining what it is we think is really going on'.[33] For example, when Rikizō decided to take me to task, he very quickly transformed a strip of activity in which participants were supposed to be playful and entertain one another by means of jokes and singing into one in which an extremely serious community matter could be discussed. Because it was commonly understood among participants that certain things could *only* be broached during *sake*-drinking sessions, since formal etiquette forbade their frank discussion during daytime activities, Rikizō's keying was acceptable and quickly understood behaviour. But the example shows how vulnerable any activity is.[34]

Another example of keying is participant-observation fieldwork itself. In the same way that an apprentice will attach himself to an established potter in order to learn the trade (the keying results because what is work for the potter is an opportunity to practice for the apprentice, and to dabble for the fieldworker), so does the participant-observer attach herself to one or more informants to find out about various aspects of their lives which, for the informants themselves, have a very different everyday meaning than that experienced by the fieldworker.[35] As I wrote at the beginning of the actual description of the Akiyasama festival:

> At the time I was on a high. As I have learned in later research projects, fieldwork can intoxicate the newcomer who is charmed by the people he or she meets, by the ways they behave, and by the seemingly unstoppable flood of stories that they have to tell. It had been an exhilarating first few weeks in Sarayama.

It is very unlikely that this enthusiasm for the charms of the local inhabitants was shared by the latter themselves – they had, after all, known one another since before they went to school (and occasionally even harboured a grudge from those days of yore) – while the stories I had heard for the first time had for the most part been shorn of all novelty by the sheer repetition of their telling over the years (especially, perhaps, to wide-eyed visitors from the 'outside' world).

At the same time, though, we should keep in mind the fact that I am, perhaps, being unfair to my informants and that I am misperceiving the situation because in fact they *do* like one another unreservedly and enjoy telling stories. In which case, I am guilty of *miskeying* – wrongly oriented behaviour that results from ambiguities and thus misreading the meanings of a frame.[36]

Fabrications

A fabrication occurs when someone intentionally tries to manage an activity in such a way that one or more of the other participants in a frame will be induced into falsely believing that one thing rather than another is going on. For example, it might have been that Rikizō was only *pretending* to get drunk (and, in the end, it is only he who knows for sure) in order to be able to say a few of the things that were on his mind and that he hadn't had a chance to air. Since he was by temperament a man who often said what he felt or thought, it was possible – although rather unlikely – that, if I had happened to drop by his workshop earlier that afternoon, Rikizō would have said there and then what he later said during the Akiyasama celebration. Another example of fabrication used to occur regularly over a period of two to three months when Inoshige was ordered not to drink by his doctor, but still attended drinking sessions with cans of tomato juice in his pocket and proceeded to feign appropriate inebriation as the evening wore on, in order not to inconvenience other participants.[37] The various layers of activity that accrue as a result of fabrications and keyings (plus rekeyings) during the course of a frame are called *laminations*. Laminations can be said to give 'depth' to frame behaviour.

Fashion magazines are both cultural products and commodities. As cultural products, they include stories, interviews, information and news, and photographs of fashion, beauty, celebrities, ordinary women around the world, and so on, for the interest of their targeted *readers*. As commodities, however, they represent, primarily through direct and indirect advertising, the interests of various corporations which are persuaded that the magazines are the most suitable means of conveying information and images about themselves and their products to targeted *consumers*. Thus every fashion magazine's editor-in-chief has to keep in mind and appeal to two sets of customers: one of readers who are attracted by their magazine's contents; the other of advertisers who see those contents as an appropriate environment for their products and services.[38]

Provided that the 'cultural' and 'commercial' aspects of the magazine's contents are kept separate, all is well. For the most part, however, the dividing line between the two is far from clear. When a magazine informs readers in its cover photo credits, for example, that model Cindy Crawford is wearing a sequinned tank top by Dolce & Gabbana, using eyeliner, mascara, foundation, and other make-up by Revlon, and that her hair is styled with products from L'Oréal, are we as readers to accept this as 'information' or as 'advertising'? That it is surely the latter may be extrapolated from three unrelated facts. One is that make-up artists themselves use all kinds of different products, which may include one, or possibly two, of the advertised brand. The effect they create, however, is generally *not* by means of the products stated in the credits. Another is that, at the time of her appearance on the magazine cover, Crawford was under contract to Revlon to act as its main advertising endorser. The third is that a magazine will occasionally reveal its commercial hand when it adds in the credits that the model is wearing Lancôme's *Trésor* or some such perfume (which is usually linked to the brand of cosmetics said to be used). Given that the cover page is not impregnated with this fragrance, the nature of such gratuitous advertising becomes obvious and the fabrication is revealed for what it is.

Fashion-magazine publishing is a business that delivers readers to potential advertisers more than it does editorial content to readers. The fact that editors have to address two sets of customers tends to create conflicts of interest and further fabrications. Financially speaking, advertising is indispensable, since without it the cover price would need to be increased beyond the average reader's means (or so it is argued). To attract advertising, an editor needs to ensure that the contents of her magazine both support the idea of consuming fashion, cosmetics, health, interior and other related goods, and are aimed at the kind of reader who has money to spend. This may involve a magazine writer incorporating favourable comment (or laminations) about advertisers' products in her magazine. It almost invariably means providing what Gloria Steinem, former editor-in-chief of Ms magazine, has called 'supportive editorial atmosphere or complementary copy'. So, a fashion magazine will emphasize fitness and health, for example, to attract sportswear, health and special food advertising; and it will feature certain clothing brands in its fashion spreads to thank certain fashion houses for past patronage and to encourage them to continue to advertise in the magazine in the future. In short, editorial coverage is 'service journalism' designed to be 'sympathetic' and attract advertisers, while those who advertise get editorial coverage by means of 'special sections', advertorials, and revenue-related reading matter or 'fluff'.[39]

Theatrical frames

A theatrical frame is more than simple keying for a number of reasons. First, its boundaries sharply (and arbitrarily) cut off what takes place on 'stage' from what lies beyond it (in other words, the *zashiki* guest room from the rest of Yōjirō's house and the community of houses beyond). Secondly, an individual is transformed into a performer who is watched by, and consciously engages, an audience (as when Rikizō stopped being a participant drinker with his fellow villagers and launched into a series of very direct questions and comments which were listened to attentively by all present as they carefully watched the interaction between us). Thirdly, one person at a time is allowed to hold the stage and speak uninterrupted, ideally providing his or her audience covertly with the information necessary to sustain dramatic effect (as can be seen in the various tactics adopted by Rikizō to make fully public my present fieldwork activity, and to question my credentials by casting doubt on the mode of entry I had used to get permission to carry out fieldwork in Sarayama in the first place).[40] Fourthly, unlike in ordinary conversation, more or less everything that is spoken 'on stage' is significant and is treated as such by participants and audience. In all these respects, we might say that the interaction that occurred between Rikizō and myself was a theatrical frame, rather than simple keying, as first suggested above.

In the same way that the structure of a fashion magazine may be seen as either a primary framework in itself, or a primary framework surrounded by numerous brackets, the competitive presentation in advertising may be seen as not simply a primary framework, but as an excellent example of a theatrical frame in action. Presentations almost invariably take place in a special room that is not normally used for other purposes by an advertising agency and is thus marked out as a special performance stage. The person who makes the 'pitch' or presentation itself speaks, rather like an auctioneer,[41] in a special voice and with a special rhythm in order to engage his audience who, for its part, is continuously assessing his performance. Everything that is said in a presentation is deemed to be significant by both agency and client personnel, and is discussed at length in a question-answer session following an agency's presentation. As a result, a presentation – like an art auction or fashion show – is an integral part of the processes that serve to define and maintain the advertising community as a whole. This is the sociological importance of the theatrical frame.[42]

Out-of-Frame Behaviour

Although participants in a frame usually give the appearance of 'respectful involvement' in what is going on, it often happens that their attention is elsewhere and that they 'disattend' an ongoing activity.[43] On at least two counts, Rikizō showed a willingness to disattend during the course of his engagement with me: first, he systematically ignored his audience; secondly, he also systematically ignored any answer to his questions that I tried to give. In other words, he was more intent on saying what he wanted to say than in engaging in a dialogue of some kind. Similarly, by staring straight down at the table in front of him and not catching my eye when I turned to him for help, Takayoshi also gave the appearance of disattending the discussion between Rikizō and myself. This kind of disengagement from a frame of activity is known as out-of-frame behaviour.

In many ways, the distinction between 'front' and 'back' regions (*omote* and *ura* in Japanese) can be seen as illustrating out-of-frame behaviour. Opening speeches thanking us for attending a particular function when we are so busy, telling us how fortunate we are in having fine weather, reminding us why we are gathered, and so on are designed primarily to establish a particular frame. Participants are required to listen to these speeches, and to display an appropriate physical demeanour (usually kneeling formally on their heels with head bowed and the palms of their hands placed firmly on their thighs). But it is extremely unlikely that everyone is actually paying all that much attention to what is said (since most have heard it several dozen times before at the beginning of identical or similar occasions). So one person may be mulling over how to avoid a hangover, another wondering how best to cope with her son's complaint about being bullied by her neighbour's son at school, a third thinking of using the occasion to go drinking in town in order to meet up with his favourite bar hostess, and so on. Thus, while physically displaying an attentive front, each of these participants will in fact not be properly engaged in what is going on within the frame in which they are present.

The same might well be said of the ethnographer since one important aim of field-work is to observe who is saying or doing what, where, when, how and for what purpose while participating in a series of everyday events (or frames). Observation, however, necessarily obliges the fieldworker to reflect upon, and thus to distance himself from, what is going on, so that – while apparently joining in the fun of drinking or firing a kiln – he is in fact often 'out of frame'.[44]

Frame Breaking

Frame breaking is said to occur when the organization of activity, together with its expectations and norms of social behaviour therein, is disrupted in some way. In at least one respect, Rikizō's outburst during the Akiyasama drinking session can be seen as an example of frame breaking. Although it was to be expected that, in the course of exchanging *sake* cups, people would get rather drunk, there was also an expectation – or, at least, hope – that people would be able to remain in control of themselves and not lash out, with either their tongues or their fists, at other par-ticipants. The fact that everyone went immediately quiet when Rikizō launched his verbal assault on me suggests that, in fact, he was disrupting their own participa-tion in the festivities and that he was, as a result, breaking frame.

In this particular case, we might also note that my own surprise at what was going on (I had never before been verbally assaulted in this way by a Japanese) reflects a point made by Goffman himself: that participant observers, among whom he was himself supreme, often find it difficult to respond to situations in which they may have been thrown out by a person's behaviour, state of (un)dress, language and so on, but who need, nonetheless, to try to act as if what they are observing is more or less 'normal'.[45]

As an academic talking about an academic field – that of Japanese Studies – in the Introduction to this book, I was treading on dangerous ground. Although academics happily gossip in corridors and at conferences about who has done or said what to whom, they expect such conversations to remain firmly enclosed within the frames established by such corridors and conferences. They anticipate that colleagues will not make public what they have heard or come to know, and that they will not add in such a forum their own speculations, interpretations, information and analysis of the field in which they all operate. To do so, as I learned when I wrote and published a book in Japanese on my life as a Professor of Japanese Studies, is 'sacrilege' to those in the field and can lead to private demands for dismissal by those with sufficient political capital to make such demands, but insufficient respect for the 'freedom of thought' associated with educational capital to enable them to be met.[46]

All of the above terms – primary frameworks, brackets, keying, fabrications, the-atrical frames, out-of-frame behaviour and breaking frame – are useful tools for a participant observer carrying out fieldwork in an initially alien environment, and should be helpful in analysing what is going on among participants in any frame. I will try to use them here, therefore, as appropriate.

'Setting' and 'Frame'

And now let us turn from the work of Erving Goffman to that of Chie Nakane and her analysis of the structure of Japanese society. This is necessary because frames of activity are the means by which Japanese think about, explain and analyse social behaviour, and because there is probably no other society which is more sociologically aware of who does what to whom, where, when, how and why.[47] This is why Nakane was quite right to emphasize the concept of frame as a means toward analysing Japanese social behaviour.

In the mid- to late 1960s, Nakane published a best-selling book entitled, literally, *Human Relations in a Vertical Society* (*Tate Shakai no Ningen Kankei*). Translated into English as *Japanese Society*, this work soon became a Penguin Sociology classic, and, in its original Japanese version, was reprinted 98 times during the course of the following 30 years. Given the book's unprecedented popularity, human nature's propensity to undermine that which it sets up on pedestals to admire, and the historical context in which the work was written (during the peak of Japan's high-growth economy), it probably comes as no surprise to those unfamiliar with 'things Japanese' to learn that over the years Nakane's argument – in particular, her emphasis on the structure of 'the group' and the 'vertical' nature of Japanese social relations – has been roundly criticized.[48] Indeed, these days hardly an article or book in the field of the anthropology of Japan goes by without some denigrating reference to Nakane's work.

Surprisingly, perhaps, it is the *consequences* of Nakane's thesis, rather than the thesis itself, which has attracted critics' attention and produced enough written pages to destroy a few more square kilometres of precious forest. It is, however, the *thesis* that I wish to deal with here. In *Japanese Society*, Nakane started her discussion of the nature of Japanese society by making a structural distinction between 'attribute' (*shikaku*) and 'setting' (*ba*) or, as it was imprecisely translated into English, 'frame'. She used the term 'attribute' rather broadly to apply to the family line into which an individual was born, the education that he or she received, the occupation that he or she then took on, as well as gender and class affiliation. 'Setting' was used to refer to 'the structuring of individual persons into a collectivity, regardless of their different attributes, by means of a particular "frame" (*waku*)'.[49] By 'frame' she meant an institution like a rural village, company, government organization, school, and so on.

Nakane's thesis was that, in all societies, individuals belong to social groups or classes as a result of attributes and frames. Since these never exactly coincide, however, and since one always comes to be given precedence over the other, a distinction can be made between two types of society: one in which 'attribute', and the other in which 'frame', is given greater weight. In Japan, argued Nakane, the 'setting' or 'frame' was structurally more important than 'attribute' in the organization of social relations and people's understandings thereof. By way of illustration, she pointed out how, regardless of their specific attributes, a producer, cameraman and chauffeur in a Japanese television company, for instance, will all refer to themselves first and foremost as members of the Asahi or Mainichi Broadcasting Company, rather than by their job descriptions (which they are unlikely to have, anyway). In other words, the 'setting' or 'frame' plays a primary part in the structure and consciousness of a social group, and 'attribute' plays only a secondary role.[50] This is not to suggest that 'attribute' is irrelevant; after all, participants in the Akiyasama festival were seated according to both age and gender. Rather, it is the 'frame' that situates social structure – witness the fact that the frame for the gathering was established first by the demarcation (the two opening speeches [or brackets] exchanged between insider [the host, Yōjirō] and outsider [Tanuki, as senior male present]) and then by the blurring (through the toast joined in by all participants) of spatial boundaries.[51]

Although, in the English translation of her work, 'frame' is the single word used to describe 'a locality, an institution or a particular relationship which binds a set of individuals into one group,'[52] in Japanese Nakane shifts back and forth – not entirely clearly – between two words: *ba*, which I have translated here as 'setting', and *waku*, which I'm going to translate as 'frame'. *Ba* is rather close to my earlier outline of a 'spatial frame', while *waku* corresponds more with a 'temporal frame' (with a touch of instrumentalism thrown in). Although Nakane started out by stressing 'setting' as the special characteristic of a group's social interaction,[53] she gradually introduced more permanent groups, such as the household, rural community, company and bureaucratic organization, as examples of 'frame'. In this way, the concept of frame came to refer more to constant, stable and institutional environments than to provisional settings for social interaction. This enabled Nakane then to address issues such as ranking, leadership, fission, factions and one or two other aspects of Japanese social organization that have attracted such recent adverse criticism, and to ignore the shifting variables of people interacting in different social contexts.

There was thus a contradiction in her usage of terminology. 'Setting' (*ba*) was established originally in opposition to what she perceived as the constancy and stability of a person's attribute, but was then in 'frame' (*waku*) given precisely the stable, constant features found in attribute.[54]

The distinction between setting and frame in itself is no bad thing. After all, as participant in the Akiyasama festival, I was a full member of the temporary setting (*ba*), though not of the stable frame (*waku*) comprising membership of one of the fourteen households making up the community. It is, indeed, this tension between temporary and more permanent affiliations among people that influences their social behaviour and interaction. Precisely because I was not a long-term resident of Sarayama, but only a temporary – though active – participant in one of its formal gatherings, Rikizō was obliged to treat me with a certain amount of minimal respect. I was, after all, an 'outsider' rather than 'insider', even though granted provisional 'inside' status. As a result, Rikizō could not appropriately support his verbal attack with, for instance, physical assault – something that occasionally happened among Sarayama residents when they drank and argued on their own. But, precisely because I *was* given provisional inside status in the setting, Rikizō clearly thought it appropriate to launch his attack.

Comment

In this chapter, I have focused on the work of two scholars extremely well known in their respective academic fields, in order to show how and why I think frames provide an appropriate and useful method for analysing social interaction. In the settings in which such interaction takes place, in the purposes to which it is put and the way in which it then unfolds through time, frames provide participants with sets of ground rules about how to behave 'properly', and the fieldworker with a perfect opportunity to observe a social microcosm that can lead him or her to broader understandings of social organization in general.

This is not to suggest anything new. This kind of 'frame-based' fieldwork that I advocate here is not that different from either the interpretive case method espoused by Michael Burawoy or the extended case method developed by Max Gluckman and other members of the Manchester 'school' of social anthropology during the post-Second World War period. Each examines a particular social situation in the light of more general principles – as I have tried to do by relating drinking behaviour in a pottery community to a more general principle distinguishing between front stage and back stage behaviour in Japanese society. While the interpretive case method sees a setting as a micro-context in which a macro-level principle is enacted, the extended case method examines how that social situation is in fact shaped by external forces. Frames thus help participant observers 'examine the macro world through the way the latter shapes and in turn is shaped and conditioned by the micro world, the everyday world of face-to-face interaction'.[55] They help all of us who are not professional fieldworkers, too, to put together the pieces of each social jigsaw puzzle that we need to solve when we go to a concert, start work in a company, attend a wedding ceremony or hang out in a bar. If Celine Dion were an anthropologist, she'd have risen to fame by singing *The Power of Frames*.

Notes

1. Erving Goffman, *Frame Analysis* 1986 [1974], pp. 561, 564–66.
2. Goffman, *The Presentation of Self in Everyday Life*, 1959. Ulf Hannerz, *Exploring the City*, 1980, Chapter 6, provides a very useful summary of Goffman's work and shows how it may be used in urban anthropology.
3. Chie Nakane, *Tate Shakai no Ningen Kankei*, 1967b; *Japanese Society*, 1970.
4. E.g. Jane Bachnik and Charles Quinn (eds), *Situated Meaning: Inside and outside in Japanese self, society, and language*, 1984.
5. The growth of the Chinese economy will almost certainly radically alter the current intellectual, political, diplomatic and economic geography of the world within two decades of this book's eventual publication. The increasing centrality of China and Japan together should also lead to the anthropology of East Asia becoming more central to the discipline of anthropology as a whole.
6. Of course, they *are* different, but probably not much more different than are Americans from French, English from Greeks, and Danes from Rumanians.
7. Ruth Benedict, *The Chrysanthemum and the Sword*, 1946.
8. Takeo Doi, *The Anatomy of Dependence*, 1973.
9. E.g., among others, Jane Bachnik, '*Omote/ura*: indexes and the organization of self and society in Japan', 1989; Joy Hendry, *Wrapping Culture: Politeness, presentation, and power in Japan and other societies*, 1993.
10. I realize that there is an element of intellectual imperialism here, in that I am forcing Japanese concepts into an English frame, rather than vice versa. I have two not-very-justified justifications for this. First, I am working in an academic environment that is dominated by English-language and American outputs (something that may not be exactly acceptable, but that cannot be overturned overnight). Secondly, and more importantly, people reading this book are going to understand better what I mean by 'frames', 'front stage', 'back stage', and so on, than they would by *ba, waku, omote, ura, tatemae, honne* and so forth.
11. Goffman, *Frame Analysis*, pp. 16–20.
12. Bennet Berger, 'Foreword', to Goffman, *Frame Analysis*, 1986, pp. xi–xviii.
13. John Van Maanen, *Tales of the Field*, 1988, p. 131.
14. Goffman, *Frame Analysis*, p. 13.
15. Ibid.
16. Goffman, *Frame Analysis*, p. 11.
17. A comment which Goffman from his grave might make about my own particularistic use of frame analysis. See also Arthur Danto, *The Transfiguration of the Commonplace*, 1981, p. viii.
18. Goffman, *Frame Analysis*, p. 345.
19. Ibid., p. 11.

20. Ibid., p. 316. Goffman (*Frame Analysis*, p. 7) proposes 'frame' in roughly the sense in which it was employed by Gregory Bateson in a 1955 paper titled 'A theory of play and phantasy', reprinted in Bateson, *Steps to an Ecology of the Mind*, 1972.
21. Goffman, *Frame Analysis*, p. 10.
22. Ibid., p. 21.
23. Ibid.
24. Goffman does not mention 'secondary' or other frameworks that are not 'primary'.
25. Goffman, *Frame Analysis*, p. 22.
26. A very rare exception may be found in the February 2002 edition of the American version of *Harper's Bazaar*, on the back cover of which the new Editor-in-Chief, Glenda Bailey, placed a photo-from-behind in the same red dress of the front cover model, Gisele Bündschen, there photographed from in front. Given that the cover credits include the origin of the clothes and accessories worn by the cover model ('rayon plunge-front asymmetrical dress by Giorgio Armani, Lucite bangles by R.J. Graziano, and sandals by Manolo Blahnik'), however, this may be seen as a 'double advertisement' for the designers in question. In fact, this was one of two front covers run by the magazine that month (the other was a close-up of Gisele in the same red dress) and readers were asked in the Contents page to e-mail editors saying which one they preferred.
27. Brian Moeran, 'A tournament of value: strategies of presentation in Japanese advertising', 1993.
28. Goffman, *Frame Analysis*, p. 27.
29. Ibid., p. 499.
30. Ibid., pp. 251–2.
31. We should, perhaps, note that the distinction between spatial and temporal brackets is rarely as categorical as the words suggest and that spatial brackets tend to contain within them an element of time and temporal brackets one of space.
32. Brian Moeran, *A Far Valley: Four years in a Japanese community*, 1998.
33. Goffman, *Frame Analysis*, p. 45.
34. Ibid., p. 83.
35. Ibid., pp. 74–7, where Goffman refers to this kind of keying as 'regrounding'.
36. Ibid., p. 308.
37. Research fabrications also occur, of course, as when one scholar plagiarizes another's work but gives off the impression – or openly asserts – that it is his own, or a researcher – or, more often these days, 'undercover' journalist – carries out participant-observation fieldwork without the knowledge of those being studied (Goffman, *Frame Analysis*, p. 95).

38. Jenny McKay, *The Magazines Handbook*, 2000, pp. 196–7.
39. Eric Clark, *The Want Makers – Lifting the lid off the advertising industry: How they make you want to buy*, 1989, pp. 344–51.
40. Goffman, *Frame Analysis*, p. 143, also suggests that 'utterances tend to be much longer and more grandiloquent than in ordinary conversation'. Although this was not the case in the Akiyasama story, Rikizō did resort to a direct and in-your-face type of language that is not found in normal off-stage conversation in Japan.
41. Charles Smith, *Auctions*, 1989, pp. 116–25.
42. Victor Turner (in *Dramas, Fields and Metaphors*, 1974, p. 133) uses the term 'arena' to refer to 'a framework – whether institutionalized or not – which manifestly functions as a setting for antagonistic interaction aimed at arriving at a publicly recognized decision'. In this sense, his use of arena is close to Goffman's notion of theatrical framework.
43. Goffman, *Frame Analysis*, pp. 201–2.
44. Sometimes, while drinking, I found it necessary to remove myself physically from a frame in order to jot down notes of what was being said. I thus devised the ruse of staggering off to the nearest toilet from time to time to scrawl hurried keywords in my notebook, in the hope that they would help me recall conversations the following morning. My out-of-frame behaviour attracted the attention of one of my companions who, at one point, asked whether I would like him to introduce me to a doctor specializing in bladder infections!
45. Goffman, *Frame Analysis*, p. 352.
46. Brian Moeran, *London Daigaku Nihongo Gakka*, 1988.
47. I believe that this observation was initially made by Ronald Dore, although I cannot for the life of me find where he wrote it.
48. E.g. Harumi Befu, 'The group model of Japanese society and an alternative', 1980; Ross Mouer and Yoshio Sugimoto, *Images of Japanese Society*, 1986.
49. Nakane Chie, *Tate Shakai no Ningen Kankei*, 1967b, p. 27.
50. Nakane, *Tate Shakai no Ningen Kankei*, pp. 29–30; *Japanese Society*, p. 3.
51. Nakane, *Tate Shakai no Ningen Kankei*, p. 33.
52. Nakane, *Japanese Society*, p. 1.
53. It is clear that Nakane's interest is in 'small groups' (*shōshūdan*, a term that she prefers to 'primary group' [*Tate Shakai no Rikigaku*, p. 22]), which are defined quite simply as 'co-operation in work and sharing of space' (*shigoto no kyōryoku to ba no kyōyū*). She recognizes, moreover, the variable nature of such small groups that results from the different purposes for which they are formed and the different people who make up their membership (ideally between five and seven persons to maximize a full expression and free exchange of individual opinions and emotions). See Nakane, *Japanese Society*, p. 12; *Tate Shakai no Rikigaku*, 1978, pp. 22-4; and also *Tate Shakai*

no Ningen Kankei, p. 25.

54. It is the institutional rather than interpersonal, or individual, point of view that Nakane stresses throughout her argument.

55. Michael Burawoy, 'Introduction' to Burawoy et al., *Ethnography Unbound: Power and resistance in the modern metropolis*, 1991, p. 6.

−3−

Frames at Work

What I think the work of both Goffman and Nakane makes clear is, on the one hand, the extraordinarily wide-ranging power of 'frame' as an analytical concept and, on the other, the difficulty in tying the concept down and separating its components out sufficiently clearly for us to be able to use them effectively in our analysis of social organization in general. What I want to do in this chapter, therefore, is introduce some more fieldwork stories as a way of analysing different kinds of frame behaviour and relating it to more general social organizational issues of the kind that neither Goffman nor Nakane, for different reasons of their own, properly followed up.

There is a temptation here to try to create a classificatory framework of frame types, in the way that I began to do at the end of my account of the Akiyasama festival. After all, it is clear that spatial settings have some effect on participants' social interaction in frames of all kinds. For instance, one observation I made during the course of a couple of years' drinking in Sarayama was that the most senior men present very rarely strayed from their seating positions at the 'top' of the room by the *tokonoma* alcove during the course of each drinking session. Rather, as might be expected of men who held positions of authority in the community, the potters' cooperative or the valley in which Sarayama was located, they expected others to come 'up' to them to discuss matters. Similarly, the youngest – and thus most junior in the community and valley prestige hierarchy – tended to stay more or less in their positions at the 'bottom' of the room, although they might venture into groups of fellow drinkers located more centrally in a house's *zashiki*. Middle-aged men in their 40s and 50s, however, were extremely active during *sake* cup exchanges and would join groups of men in different parts of the room, depending on what they wanted to say to whom and when. It was these men who raised and discussed community, pottery cooperative, and valley affairs with both elder and younger men, and it was they who brought power to bear on those in positions of authority.[1]

This example of how a particular setting supported the social behaviour of old and young, senior and junior, in a community of Japanese potters is not particularly unusual. Settings for formal gatherings involving food and drink anywhere in the world almost invariably establish a hierarchy of space that places some people at the 'top' and others at the 'bottom' of a room. Thus, just as senior men in

Sarayama and other Japanese homes find themselves sitting with their backs to the *tokonoma* sacred alcove facing 'down' the room, the host at a Chinese banquet in a restaurant will be placed with his back to the wall so that he can survey both his guests and other customers in the restaurant, and quickly attract the attention of waiters (who, as in many other countries, are themselves dressed in different uniforms to signal their statuses and what kinds of dishes or drinks they are allowed to bring to the table). Moreover, the very layout of a 'horizontal' table across the upper part of the room with 'vertical' tables lined down the room is repeated time and time again in college dining halls, wedding receptions, royal banquets, and Nobel Prize-giving dinners. In other words, spatial layout tends to follow what appear to be almost universal distinctions between 'up' and 'down', on the one hand, and 'surface' (exterior) and 'depth' (interior), on the other.[2]

Senior managerial staff in large corporations invariably have their offices located towards the top of the building in which they work, while lesser personnel are assigned to lower floors where there is less light. The more senior the position, the higher the floor, so that, on the up/down axis, the hierarchy of corporate power is matched by the physical structure of the office building.[3] This power is generally seen to be economic. In magazine publishing houses, whenever editorial staff referred to publishers and advertising staff, they invariably pointed a finger to the ceiling above their heads – regardless of whether they were in New York, Paris, London, Tokyo or Hong Kong.

On any one floor, there is a horizontal axis of surface/depth in operation. The offices of more senior senior staff are located further away from the (elevator) 'entrance' than those of less senior staff. In open-plan office arrangements such as are often found in Japan, the desks of department or division managers are placed by windows, or, at least, as far away from the main door as possible. Those who sit nearest the entrance and deal with visitors (people from the exterior) are women and other 'non-permanent' members of the work force. 'Depth' is thus a symbolic classification which does not match the physical construction of the building itself.

As a result, we are almost always able to draw conclusions from such settings about who is sitting where in terms of the frame's status hierarchy (the distribution of important participants according to alternating left and right positions also helps) and can behave accordingly.

The distinction between exterior and interior is emphasized by the fact that the 'upper' part of a room is almost invariably located as far away from the main entrance as possible (a fact which, on certain occasions, allows the most high and mighty to parade through assembled silent guests from their entrance at the bottom to their being seated at the top of a particular framed setting). In many societies, this distribution of space is applied only to very formal frameworks. In Japan, however, it is applied rather more extensively in people's everyday environment.

Visitors shown into a company meeting room will be asked to sit at a table set by the window, and expected to line themselves in seniority from the window 'down' the room towards the entrance.[4] This standard arrangement means that the woman commandeered to bring tea knows at once whom to serve first. Members of the company receiving the visitor will place themselves in a similar order of seniority on the opposite side of the same table, with their backs to the door.

This setting places the symbolic interior in the physical exterior and reveals the basic structure of Japanese social organization which itself reveals the following order of oppositional principles: first, outsider vis-à-vis insider; second, senior vis-à-vis junior; third, male vis-à-vis female.[5] This classificatory axis, where low is to high as exterior is to interior, is even followed when members of different companies enter a taxi. Guest will enter first (to be seated behind the driver) and host last. In the event of four people riding in the same vehicle, the most junior member of the host company will sit in the front seat (turning round to talk is deemed difficult and uncomfortable and therefore not for guests or more senior members of one's own company), from where he or she will be expected to issue instructions to and pay the taxi driver as appropriate.

Art exhibitions, too, tend to reveal a general pattern in their framed setting. Lesser works are placed near the entrance to a show, and more important ones in the 'depth' of a gallery – that is, that part of the exhibition space furthest from the entrance. This mode of display is paralleled in jewellery retail stores, where less expensive items are placed near the entrance to attract customers who are then drawn further and further into the store by the display of more precious, rare and expensive pieces. In both cases, items that for one reason or another are seen to be particularly valuable are placed on pedestals or behind glass. In addition, monetary value is usually signified by the distance between one art object or piece of jewellery and another. Cheaper objects are placed close together; expensive ones quite far apart. This is how we know at once the difference between a bargain-basement sale and high-class goods.

The same standard principle of attraction is used in department stores, but on a vertical plane. Cosmetics, fragrances and perfumes, together with fashion accessories, are placed at street level to attract shoppers (who are mainly women). Fashion and clothing are located on the next floors, followed by interior items, like kitchenware, furniture, bedding, lighting and so on, until at or near the top are to be found art galleries and 'museums'. This vertical axis marks an overall progression of cheap/expensive items, on the one hand, and a move from exterior to interior (from make-up to clothing in the public, and from kitchen to bedroom in the private, sphere). To ensure that customers *do* move through this continuum of frames, department stores often locate restaurants and/or bargain sales at the very top of their buildings.

This is all common knowledge to those of us who keep our eyes open as we travel around the world. But social settings in themselves are not sufficient to explain the ways in which frames are initiated, develop and, finally, come to a (provisional) close. As the example about drinking behaviour and movement cited at the beginning of the chapter demonstrates, there is an obvious complementary time element built into every frame. Yet even this is not so straightforward a classificatory 'type' because, apart from the mere sequence of events, or strips of action (which, I have also suggested, may be regarded as 'mini frames' in themselves), that take place in a particular frame, participants bring with them from outside the frame certain social roles and individual characteristics or dispositions that themselves usually have a bearing on what kind of social and communicative exchanges do or do not take place. Thus, when drinking sessions involve people from all over the Ono valley (like the primary school's sports day, the valley's autumn marathon race, or the fire brigade's annual year-end bash), participants come as members of different households (which may be related by branching, marriage and/or adoption to the households of other participants), of different residential communities in the valley (Sarayama, Wada or Yashiki), of different occupational groups (like the pear growers' or carpenters' associations), and so on. Each of these institutional affiliations is ongoing, stable and constant and so stands in contrast to the provisional nature of the frame in which participants have gathered to celebrate.

The trouble with this sort of classificatory framework is that, in the end, the theoretical distinctions between space and time, between provisional occasions and constant affiliations, and doubtless many others (physical and abstract; interpersonal and institutional?) become so blurred that it becomes impossible to sustain them in practice. Rather than entangle myself in stale typologies, therefore, and mindful of the semantic overload that Goffman referred to, I want here to give several more examples of frames at work. It is in its *general* ability to help us analyse social behaviour, and not in its typological dissection, that the power of frame analysis lies.

All people in *all* societies throughout the world participate in frames of one sort or another. Almost – but not necessarily – all people are very aware of the existence of interactive frames and play the parts expected of them therein, although just what those parts are will differ for different people in different parts of the world. Many consciously and subconsciously exploit for their own ends opportunities arising during the course of framed activity. Some peoples (like the Japanese) are more conscious of the importance of primary frameworks in their everyday lives and are thus more adept at framing them with particular norms of verbal and non-verbal behaviour. (Think of the ubiquity of the suit for the salaryman employee, the short white socks and open-heel sandals of the young mother, the multi-pocketed flack jacket of the television cameraman or photographer, the floppy broad-brimmed hats and hiking boots of a couple out walking at a weekend.) Others (like the Danes) are less so. But even Danes, as we shall soon see, are conscious of appropriate frame behaviour on some occasions, if not others. Frames take on importance when what goes on in them *matters* to people.

This series of assertions in itself makes an assertion: that frame analysis can, and should, be used as a method of comparison. It is, therefore, the similarities and differences in frame behaviour among different people and peoples in certain situations that are, objectively, similar that should help us formulate the degrees to which they are and are not the same as, or different from, ourselves. In other words, if – as anthropologists or sociologists – our aim is to make comparisons and thereby arrive at the kind of generalizations expected of our social science, frame analysis is an excellent place to start. Not that I intend to make too many such generalizations here since the purpose of this book is to outline two other – what I regard as complementary – levels of sociological analysis to go with frames: networks and fields.

Let me start with a story that illustrates how business ideology can be upset by an unanticipated cross-cultural influence. In most countries in Europe and in the United States, people make a fairly strict distinction between work and play. For the most part, they do not discuss their private lives in the office (not, at least, unless they have a colleague there who is also a close friend); and they also tend not to give blow-by-blow accounts of humdrum office affairs unless something particularly noteworthy occurs (a colleague accuses her boss of sexual harassment; a customer throws a fit and threatens to hold up the bank; or students go on strike and lock teachers out of the school). There is no particular hard-and-fast 'rule' in this separation of work and leisure activities, but it is normally accepted that they *should* be separate. Thus, when invited to dinner at her home by an office associate, the guest (and his partner) will, during the course of an evening, engage in a wide-ranging conversation that covers the state of the weather, a recent rain-spoiled holiday abroad, the hostess's children and their schooling, the effect of media violence on children, recent displays of hooliganism by youngsters on the terraces of the local football team's stadium, and so on and so forth. Similarly, when playing a round of golf together, office colleagues will not mention their everyday life at work, since it is deemed impolite to 'talk shop'.[6]

In Japan, however, this separation of work and play is rather different. In one respect, the Japanese can be said to keep the two apart even more than do Americans or British, in that company employees hardly – if – ever invite office colleagues to their homes. If someone feels that some form of entertainment is appropriate, he will generally arrange for it to be done outside the home in a restaurant or bar, and his wife is thus spared the trial of being obliged to entertain someone she doesn't know at all, or with whom she has no more than a passing acquaintance. In other respects, however, the Japanese have few, if any, qualms about mixing work and leisure. Drinking and golfing are well-known examples of this conflation of activities that most of us would regard as occupying rather separate frames and, during my period of fieldwork in a Japanese advertising agency, I often used to hear stories about how an account executive had managed to clinch a deal with a client in a bar or on the golf course that he hadn't been able to do during office hours. For Japanese businessmen, drinking establishments and country clubs were very definitely 'primary frameworks'.

One such story, though, shows that the kind of leisure frame that permits the intermingling of work with play in Japanese society has begun to be affected by Western business norms separating the two. One Monday morning, I was sitting at my desk beside a Mr Yano (whom we will encounter again in the next chapter), managing director of the Account Services Division and a member of the agency's Board of Directors. He had returned late the evening before from a weekend in the foothills of Mt Fuji where he had been entertaining the newly-appointed advertising manager of a client company and, while looking a little tired (he had an enormous workload and was under considerable pressure in general because of his senior position in the agency), was obviously pleased with his weekend.

The telephone rang. Yano's secretary answered it and, holding her hand over the mouthpiece, told Yano who it was on the line. He immediately picked up the phone and embarked upon a series of polite phrases that Japanese frequently use to bracket a frame and link past and present activity shared by those concerned.[7] He then moved with his most unctuous voice to something that had clearly been discussed as part of his weekend activities. As he started to convey a series of thanks, he was rather abruptly cut short by the voice on the other end of the telephone line. This led to a complete change of expression on Yano's part as he grappled with what was clearly frame-breaking behaviour on the part of his conversant and, after one or two minutes of talk and counter-talk, initiated more 'bracket' phrases to close the telephone conversation's frame.

He put the phone down on its cradle, and sat thoughtfully for a few minutes. Then he turned to me.

'*Sensei*,' he began, using a form of address customarily applied to all teachers and 'people of knowledge' (from university professors and doctors to flower-arrangement instructors and masseurs), 'I really don't understand what's going on in Japan these days.'

I raised a quizzical eyebrow and asked him what he meant.

'In Japanese business,' he explained, 'it's quite normal for one company to invite another company out for a few drinks, or a meal, or even a weekend at a country club. We're all so busy during the daytime and weekdays that we think it appropriate to try to relax a bit over some good food, a few glasses of beer or whisky, or a round or two of golf. After all, business is driven by personal relations and these sorts of leisure activities allow us to get to know one another as *people* and not just as members of this or that company. Do you follow me?'

I did.

'Well, last Saturday, I invited the new advertising manager of a client of ours for a weekend at a country club of which our agency's a member. It was beautiful weather, as you know, and we played a lot of golf, but I'm so bad that he won all the time.' He smiled, and I knew that Yano had probably lost on purpose as part of his tactic to ingratiate himself with his new acquaintance. 'At one stage yesterday morning, when we were out on the course, I broached the idea of a new advertising campaign to my companion and he seemed very pleased with the idea and appeared to give me the go-ahead. But this morning,' Yano gave the kind of laugh that revealed his embarrassment and dabbed at his brow with a pocket handkerchief, 'when I mentioned our deal on the phone just now, the manager asked me: "What deal?" And when I reminded him of what we'd talked about on the golf course, he curtly replied: "That was on the golf course. Business deals are made in the office, not on the golf course." Can you believe it?'

I couldn't, and asked Yano how this could have happened.

'Well, that's just it, *sensei*. I've been thinking things over and now I think I understand. As I learned during our first evening together at dinner, this particular advertising manager has spent a long time working in the New York branch of his company. As a result, he's learned *American* ideas about how work and leisure shouldn't be mixed. And now that he's been transferred back to Japan, he's decided to carry on an American style of business. What's worse,' Yano continued with a wry smile, 'he's not the only one to do so. These days a lot of Japanese businessmen have either been trained abroad or have worked in Europe or the United States. And they seem to prefer the "dry" interpersonal relations they find there to what we call the "wet" endless give-and-take that characterizes the Japanese business environment. The problem for me is I never know which of my clients is going to stick to which method of doing business. It's made life really tricky.'

There is, of course, an interesting question underlying this story: to what extent is the globalization of American business affecting not just consumer cultural communities, but different cultural ideologies about how business should be conducted in the first place? This particular frame, therefore, shows a dimension not normally emphasized by proponents and critics of globalization theory and reveals the subtleties of intercultural 'flows' of exchange.[8] But what this particular story also tells us is that frames are always subject to participants' varied interpretations. Different people tend to produce different understandings of what goes on in a particular frame, construing and misconstruing verbal and non-verbal behaviour, and then acting accordingly. It is usually when things go 'wrong' that we learn to step back and examine more closely the assumptions that we bring to the frames in which we take part.

Another example of cultural misunderstandings and intercultural frame-breaking is provided by Dominique Bouchet in his discussion of the behaviour of a panel of French and Danish journalists who had been brought together to discuss the European Union in front of an invited audience. Before the meeting began, the French journalists talked, bantered and joked together, using body language in a way that a Dane would have found rather 'childish', although the French themselves would have seen it as simply 'collegial'. After all, they knew one another quite well and the meeting had not yet begun. But once they were bidden on stage, all three Frenchmen adjusted their ties, checked their hair and walked on stage with upright bearing and heads held high, before sitting down in a slightly stiff and formal manner that was a far cry from their earlier playful posture. This, however, merely raised several eyebrows among members of the Danish audience who regarded them as rather arrogant and typical 'little Napoleons'. As one was heard to remark: 'Hark at the way they look down at us with their noses in the air.'

Then it was the turn of the Danish journalists to appear before the audience. Before the meeting their body language had been only a little more serious than that of their French colleagues, who had not remarked anything especially strange about them. But the French journalists were immediately upset by the casual and nonchalant way in which the Danes appeared in front of the audience, 'almost as if they were pals at a teenage party' – making no attempt to adjust their back-stage behaviour in any way. This, felt the French, was an insult to the audience and showed that the Danish journalists' popularity with the general public had obviously gone to their heads.[9]

In fact, of course, both groups of journalists were adjusting their behaviour to meet their own perceived expectations of their audience in the context of a public meeting and discussion. But, whereas the French clearly distinguished between front- and back-stage behaviour, the Danes did not. The misconceptions on both sides, therefore, resulted from different cultural attitudes toward appropriate frame behaviour. If the meeting had taken place in the presence of a French audience, of course, the Danes would have been berated for their casualness and apparent lack of respect.

As an English-born foreign professor holding an Irish passport and employed in a Danish institute of tertiary education, I find myself continually coming up against this kind of confusing, and often irritating, frame behaviour (or apparent lack of it) – in the classroom, as well as in various kinds of meetings involving colleagues, administrative staff and students.[10] Part of the difficulty lies in the differing ideological principles according to which every society is organized. For example, precisely because of the egalitarian ethos that prevails in Danish society – an ethos that refuses to recognize any essential difference between professor and student, or CEO and rubbish collector – there is, in general, little distinction between front-stage and back-stage behaviour. This is unimaginable in Japan, where what Chie Nakane calls the 'vertical principle' of hierarchical organization encourages particular kinds of verbal and non-verbal behaviour among particular sets of people in particular frames.[11]

Moreover, because of the acceptance of egalitarianism, an awful lot of time has to be spent ensuring that everyone who is a participant in a particular frame (let us say a Study Board meeting) has his or her say in discussions of changes to a curriculum, problems surrounding a particular course, comments made by an external examiner, and so on. There is absolutely no publicly recognized conception that someone who has had experience in organizing course curricula, for example, might know better than others how to make such changes; or that someone else who is a 'specialist' in a particular subject (let us say, Japanese management) might be able to judge for him- or herself what should or should not be included in a new course he or she plans to teach on that subject, and in which year of their studies it might most usefully be taken by students. Rather, everybody is treated as an equal; students have as much right as professors to say what should or should not be taught; and decisions are ratified by consensus.[12]

It has been frequently – indeed almost too frequently – remarked about the Japanese, too, that they live by consensus. Indeed, both Danish and Japanese societies pride themselves on ensuring that individual people do not get their own way all the time and that 'the nail that sticks out is hammered down' – a proverb they both share.[13] But, and here lies the difference in frame behaviour, while Danes are generally quick to pounce on an upstart member of their group, usually by means of sarcastic put-downs, for their part Japanese very often encourage differences of opinion among their colleagues. There is an understandable logic at work here. Both Danes and Japanese, as I have said, practise consensus decision-making, but while the Danes do it by virtually eliminating alternative visions right from the start, Japanese encourage novelty of thought as a means toward moving in new directions. As a result, Japanese tend to encourage minor social and cultural changes through frame behaviour, while the Danes prefer to retain the status quo.

All this is not to suggest that Danes *never* adjust their behaviour and forms of non-verbal communication between formal and informal levels of frame behaviour. They do so when it really matters. And what matters in Danish society is the family. For example, when gathering for a baptism, birthday party or golden wedding anniversary, all guests will stand around outside the chosen venue (church, restaurant or hotel) until *all* the other guests have arrived and they are bidden to move inside. During this time, every new arrival will move from one invited guest to the next, shake hands and, where necessary, say his or her first name. This is unthinkable in Japanese society and indeed in many other neighbouring societies in Europe.

What is going on here? What is the point of introducing yourself to fifty-odd people and trying rather desperately to remember their names (a near total impossibility) as you endlessly repeat your own? Are you trying to break the social ice formed by the sheer variety of people drawn into such frames? So far as I can judge, the function of this introductory circuit – and guests will indeed be standing in a large oval or circle as they await the call to file inside – is to establish through name exchanges a basic egalitarian structure among all participants in the event in question. Names (and it is first and not family names that are exchanged) permit individual people to engage with other frame participants as individuals and not as persons with social roles of one sort or another. Introductions thus clear the ground for any frame interaction that is to follow.

So far, so good. But this process of establishing what kind of social interaction is to be expected during the course of the event concerned does not mean that all is now plain sailing for the outsider. Nor does it mean that, in fact, invited guests *are* allowed to behave in an entirely egalitarian way. During the actual course of the reception that they are attending, these normally oh-so-casual Danes who caused the three French journalists such discomfort in the earlier story proceed to exhibit *the* most formal displays of behaviour. For a start, guests are strategically distributed around a number of tables in the room (a seating plan and hand-written name cards help them locate their proper places), so that each table brings together some who do and others who do not know one another from before the occasion. Having ensured that those on either side of them know their names, everyone then sits down to a three-course meal, generally orchestrated by a 'toastmaster' who proceeds to stage various interruptions (frame-breaking strips of activity) during the course of the afternoon or evening. These consist for the most part of speeches, toasts and songs, but may include entertainment of some sort.

As we have seen, speeches, toasts and songs are also part of gatherings participated in by my potter friends in Sarayama, but their overall style is a bit different – reflecting certain anomalies in people's understandings of how ideally they should interact. For example, in Denmark, speeches are almost invariably followed by toasts when all present are bidden rise and raise their glasses to the happy couple, baby or birthday celebrant, or whoever. Unlike the initial single communal chorus of '*kanpai!*' in Japan, these formal toasts of '*Skol!*'[14] continuously punctuate such Danish events and thus frequently bracket the flow of the overall frame – so that each person making a speech or proposing a toast in fact exerts his or her power to disrupt the egalitarian pattern of behaviour so painstakingly established by guests upon their arrival. The same is true of the singing which invariably accompanies such gatherings. Whereas in Japan singing is an opportunity for individuals to give vent to their voices and so silence the gathering – whatever happened to the 'group' ethos here? – in Denmark, all present are bidden rise and sing well-known songs together.[15] These frame-breaking interruptions are thus accompanied by physical interruptions of one sort or another – from standing up and sitting down, to co-ordinated singing and drinking, by way of the would-be speechmaker's tinkling of a knife blade on a wine glass to attract people's attention.[16]

The examples of frame behaviour provided here are designed to emphasize how participants bring with them a number of preconceptions about what should and should not take place in any context. As I said earlier, it is when frames are broken, and things go wrong as a result, that we tend to reflect upon the cultural baggage that we bring to bear on frames. For example, from time to time, during my – alas! increasingly infrequent – visits to Tokyo, I am invited by a Japanese couple for a meal in their apartment near Roppongi. When Mariko places a pleasingly arranged dish before me, she invariably laughs and tells me what 'a worthless thing' (*tsumaranai mono*) her carefully prepared food is. In fact, this is a standard polite gesture – close to fabrication – on the part of a hostess obliged to serve food to guests in Japan (and reveals a double set of oppositions between insider and outsider and women and men), but its humorous intonation in this instance arises because I once jokingly retorted (she is a good enough friend for me to have got away with it): 'Well, if it's that worthless, don't you think it's pretty rude of you to serve it to a guest in the first place?'

After the initial thunderbolt had struck, Mariko quickly explained away my frame-breaking behaviour by saying, with an obvious measure of relief, 'Oh! You foreigners! How you love to joke!' In this way, she re-keyed the incident and glossed over the fact that at this particular stage in frame behaviour I had been expected to display a serious demeanour and thank her for all the inconvenience to which she had been put by my visit. Afterwards, however, she clearly reflected on the fabricated nature of certain forms of etiquette that housewives in general are obliged to perform in front of guests, and now gives as good as she gets in our reframed rituals of politeness.

Such good-humoured acceptance of a breach of form is not usual and most examples of frame-breaking behaviour do not end so harmoniously. Not long ago, somewhere on the reclaimed land beyond Tokyo's International Airport Bus Station, I witnessed the shooting of a hair product poster campaign. The job was simple enough: one close-up photo of a model's face and hair, to be used in a European company's annual New Year poster distributed to its franchised hairdressing salons all over Japan. The day's activities, too, went according to plan and I was able once more to witness the tripartite division of responsibilities in the studio environment between art director, photographer and hair stylist (rather than make-up artist). Even though all were Japanese, the studio team's behaviour and activities followed fairly closely what I had already witnessed in another context in Hong Kong, as well as what I had read elsewhere.

The most interesting part of the day's activities, so far as I myself was concerned, was the fact that the photographer used a digital camera hooked up to his computer. When the time came, therefore, to gather around to discuss his first shots, everyone stood as near to the portable computer as possible. In the meantime, photographer, art director and hair stylist conferred over what they saw. Was the gel used on the plate of glass in front of the camera lens sufficiently thickly applied to give the multi-spotlight effect they sought around the model's head? Should the model's expression be a little less serious? What about those stray wisps of hair falling across one cheek? Was her eye make-up a little dark, perhaps? And, every so often, the photographer would select a particular image and blow it up for a closer look, advising his colleagues that there was really little need to worry about such minutiae of the picture's composition, since the computer program that he was running could iron out all blemishes and make everything perfect. To prove his point, he isolated one of the model's eyes, clicked here and there on the screen, made the highlighted area disappear and then reappear comparatively lighter than the other. Then, to make absolutely sure that the others realized the power of his new technology, he also quickly removed the offending stray wisps of hair.

Not surprisingly, perhaps, the art director quickly retired to a couple of tables set up in one corner of the studio and there went into out-of-frame mode as he sipped a cup of green tea and flipped through the first of several magazines. He clearly signalled that, so far as he himself was concerned, the photographer knew what he was doing and had decided to leave him to his devices. The hairstylist, however, needed convincing. As the shooting continued and the photographer lined more and more shots up on his screen, she started suggesting that the model's hair should be this way, not that; brushed looser; tinted more auburn; given greater length, and so on. The photographer made it clear that she was the expert in how the model should look, and let her have her way.

And so the afternoon wore on. The hair stylist prepared the Eurasian model who, when ready, sat on a swivel stool in front of the camera and gazed into the depth of its lens. The photographer pressed the shutter, issued the occasional instruction to the model, and carried on with his work until there were a dozen photos filling the screen. These he and the hair stylist examined and discussed before isolating one or two that they particularly liked and from there moving onto a new photography session with the model. Finally, after taking six dozen pictures, photographer and hair stylist started to narrow down their earlier selections. Without too much difficulty, they were able to discard most of the shots and before long had agreed that there were three that were particularly good and appropriate for the client's poster.

At this stage, the photographer turned to the client company's advertising manager and asked him which of the three he preferred. The latter hesitated a little, but the photographer quickly led him through the reasoning behind his and the hairstylist's selection, pointedly adding that he himself preferred one particular shot.[17] The advertising manager agreed with his choice. The photographer then turned back to the hair stylist who, until that moment, had shown very slight signs of discomfort with the photographer's final choice. She gazed at the enlarged photo of the model on the screen, nodding to herself indecisively for a few seconds before agreeing that it was the best. The photographer asked if she was sure and, when she nodded again, he looked around and said the accustomed phrase that signals the end of a working frame in Japan: '*O-tsukaresama deshita*' ('Thank you for your trouble').

These words were repeated loudly by all on the set, and people immediately moved and started talking again as they went about their separate tasks to finish up the day's work. One photographer's assistant unscrewed the camera from the tripod on which it was standing, and then dismantled the tripod itself; another started rubbing the strategically squirted gel from the plate glass, while two studio assistants began unscrewing the clamps that held the sheet of glass in place; another took away the stool on which the model had sat while posing and then reached up to take down the roll of grey-white paper that had acted as backdrop to the poster photo. The photographer himself, at my request, was printing me out a copy of the finally selected photo, although he warned me that he was secretly going to make one or two computer-programmed changes to the image on which we had all agreed. 'But don't tell the hair stylist,' he said quietly in my ear, 'or she'll get upset.'

Just at that very moment, the hair stylist herself appeared from the back room where she had been working with the model's hair all day, and where she and her assistant were now getting it back to 'normal'.

'I'm not happy with the final picture,' she said, taking the print that was then in my hands. 'I want to do one more set of photos.'

There was a sudden and deathly hush in the studio. In spite of the noise and bustle, everyone seemed to have heard the hair stylist's words. Faces turned toward the hair stylist; hands remained as if glued to the furnishings and equipment. The frame froze.

'Why's that?' Asked the photographer politely, although it was obvious that he was surprised at what seemed to him to be frame-breaking behaviour.

'Because I don't like the way the model's hair is arranged. I think I should give it more volume and brush it in a slightly different way.'

'But you said you were satisfied with what we've already selected', the photographer pointed out.

'I was,' she answered a little stubbornly, 'but I'm not any more. I think we can make the photo even better.'

The photographer – a man slightly younger and less experienced work-wise than the hair stylist – was sympathetic.

'You're right in a way,' he said, 'and I'd be very happy, normally, to shoot a few more pictures, if you felt that that's what's necessary. But as it is, things are a little tricky. I mean, my assistant's packed away the camera and tripod and the studio assistants have already begun to dismantle the set. Even if we put everything back together again, it's going to be virtually impossible to get *exactly* the same camera placement and gel effect that we had before. You've seen how long it took me to get everything arranged this morning while you were working hard on the model's hair.'

The hair stylist nodded, while the photographer continued.

'If you don't mind waiting another four hours, something can probably be done. But, of course,' he turned now to the advertising manager who was standing impassively behind him, seemingly out-of-frame, but clearly not, 'that means we'll be obliged to hire the studio for the night as well, and pay the crew and model overtime.' He turned back to the hair stylist. 'I guess what you have to consider is, is all the extra trouble and expense worth the marginally better results we might get from a new batch of photos?'

The photographer had produced some sound technical and financial reasons for leaving matters as they were, and the hair stylist knew it. But still she persisted.

'Well, I think so,' she began, tapping my precious print. 'This picture here isn't quite what we set out to achieve.'

It was then that the art director spoke – for the first and only time that afternoon – from his place at the table in the corner of the studio, keying in the commercial forces underpinning creative work.

'Look!' he said, addressing the hair stylist in a louder voice that carried across the space between them and turned several heads in his direction. 'The photographer has brought you in and consulted you throughout the photo session this afternoon. He's accepted the changes you've wanted to make because he's recognized that, when it comes to hair, you're the expert. This much you've shown in the work you've produced for us today, and that's why, of course, we employed you in the first place. But he's an expert, too, you know, in his own field. He knows what makes a good photograph and if that photograph doesn't quite show a model's hair to the very utmost perfection that you as a hair stylist are seeking, then something has to give. You've already said that the photo you've chosen together is OK. And the advertising manager here has agreed with your choice. You can't now put the client to extra cost and everyone else to extra work, just because you think you can make things a little more perfect.'

There was an icy silence. The hair stylist stood in the very midst of the assembled crew and was totally silent for half a minute. Then she bowed her head quickly, apologized: '*Dōmo sumimasen deshita*', and went back to the make-up room.

The photographer looked inquiringly at the advertising manager who nodded his head imperceptibly. Once more he called out clearly for all to hear: '*O-tsukare-sama deshita*.' The broken frame 'unfroze' as everyone went back to their work dismantling the set.

The question that arises from this example of conflict is: does the fact that the disagreement between photographer and hair stylist take place in Japan have any bearing on its resolution? It is rather harder to make a stab at an appropriate answer, if only because I never witnessed a similar set-to between personnel on a studio shoot in New York or Paris. But what is almost certain is that there *are* disagreements between different specialists on a set from time to time. After all, photographer, make-up artist, hair stylist, (fashion) stylist and art director all want to make their individual mark in any ad campaign or fashion story. Indeed, one of the interesting things about such events is the way in which an original idea may come to change rather subtly as a result of the different input that each specialist gives.[18] Just *how* those disagreements are dealt with, however, is difficult to gauge.

There are a number of points about this example that I myself find interesting. First, there is the fact that, although frequently accused of irrational behaviour and an inability to present logical arguments, these particular Japanese backed up their positions with sound and pragmatic reasoning. Indeed, it was almost certainly because of the logic of the arguments presented by the photographer, as compared with the somewhat vaguer explanations of the hair stylist, that the former won the day. This goes against much of what is written about the ideal behaviour of the Japanese[19] and, in my own opinion, makes them seem much more like the normal people they are.

Secondly, both photographer and art director emphasized the cooperative nature of the work that everyone had been involved in that day. They thereby implied that this was not the time, perhaps, for individual egotism to make an appearance. At the same time, though, they made sure that the hair stylist knew how much they appreciated her work, and that their criticisms were not directed at her own expertise, but more at her failure to appreciate another's expertise, as well as to consider the financial implications of her request for another set of photos. Her professional craft credentials were thus upheld, rather than undermined. The disagreement was framed as an issue regarding overall group dynamics, rather than as a clash between individuals. Although it is possible that the latter might have been the case in an American or European studio situation, this Japanese example parallels another come across in Hong Kong, so that we can at least avoid the often adopted stance that the Japanese are somehow 'unique' in their social behaviour.

Thirdly, the dynamics of the provisional frame of a studio photo shoot were soon reinforced by longer-term institutional power. Both photographer and hair stylist were freelance specialists employed by an advertising agency for this particular job. The art director employed by the agency was content to let the two conduct the opening exchanges of their disagreement, but very soon stepped in.[20] During his speech, he reminded the hair stylist that she was employed by his agency for a job (and thus that he was her boss for the day). He then strategically involved the advertising manager as representative of the agency's client, on the one hand, to back up the validity of the choice of photo already made, and on the other to intimate that all of them there owed their living to the money provided by the client for this poster campaign. In short, there was an institutional and positional hierarchy paralleling the flow of money down from client through advertising agency to freelance specialists and studio crew. My suspicion is that this realization would have characterized the working-out of any similar situation anywhere else in the world, but that the Japanese are, perhaps, a little more conscious of its social processes and ramifications.

Fourthly, what difference did it make – if any – that the hair stylist was a woman arguing her point with three men?

As I say, I do not know how this kind of conflict might have been resolved, or exacerbated, in another cultural context and can only make a few informed guesses. Would everyone have stood so still and silently watching in a Paris studio? Would the client have permitted himself to be more involved in the discussion in New York? In other words, would those present have accepted that the photographer, art director and hair stylist represented the division of responsibilities that a studio shoot incurs? Or would they have felt that they were 'individualistic' enough to have their own say? And would a gay hair stylist have fared any better with his arguments in London?

These are the sorts of questions frame analysis raises. They are also the ones it must seek to answer in the long term.

Notes

1. Moeran, 'One over the seven', 1986.
2. George Lakoff and Mark Johnson, *Metaphors We Live By*, 1980.
3. Cf. Rosabeth Moss Kanter, *Men and Women of the Corporation*, 1993 (1977), pp. 34–6.
4. When there are three, as opposed to two, visitors, the most senior should sit flanked on either side by his colleagues – the more senior of whom should be by the window.
5. This set of social oppositions is neatly paralleled by a similar set of linguistic oppositions in the structure of the Japanese language. See Samuel Martin, 'Speech levels in Japan and Korea', in D. Hymes (ed.), *Language in Culture and Society*, 1964, pp. 407–15.
6. One general exception to this norm is among members of the academic world, who often find it extremely difficult to disengage from their scholarly activities and, in particular, the gossip surrounding such activities and the institutions in which they take place.
7. Yano at this point exhibited out-of-frame behaviour, since he was still scrawling a few final words on a document that he had been reading when the telephone rang.
8. At the same time, though, we cannot ignore the way in which *Japanese* business methods have had their effect on American business organization – in particular, perhaps, the idea of 'corporate culture'. See Graeme Salaman, 'Culturing production', in P. du Gay (ed.) *Production of Culture/Cultures of Production*, 1997, pp. 235–84.
9. Dominique Bouchet, 'Kulturforskelle – en styrke', in P. Milner, T. Morsing and K. Overø (eds), *Mit Europa*, 2003, pp. 36–7.

10. This confusion and irritation are undoubtedly mutual, since all three groups of personnel involved often see my own interventions as breaking frame.

11. Nakane, *Tate Shakai no Ningen Kankei*, 1967b, and *Tate Shakai no Rikigaku*, 1978. The workings of the parliamentary Diet are a good example of this working-out of front- and back-stage behaviour. See Chalmers Johnson, '*Omote* (explicit) and *ura* (implicit): translating Japanese political terms', 1980.

12. For someone used to the Hong Kong academic tradition, where the title of full professor conferred on an individual unquestioned intellectual and social superiority, and where the interests of students were largely ignored, all this came as a salutary reminder of my negligible significance in the world at large.

13. Danish journalists, in particular, like to cite this proverb when writing on Japan. Unfortunately, in translating it, they use 'nail' in the sense of the 'hard terminal covering of finger and toe' (*negl*) rather than of a 'small spike of metal' (*søm*), thereby invoking a macabre Orientalist image of Japanese as sadistic torturers.

14. By coincidence, the Danish word for 'Cheers!' actually means 'pot'.

15. Songs written especially for the occasion have their lyrics passed round in Xeroxed form for each guest who remains seated while singing.

16. An excellent example of such formal frame, and frame-breaking, behaviour is to be found in Thomas Vinterberg's film *Festen* (*The Banquet*).

17. In general, people in the advertising world tend to lead their clients in the direction they themselves want to go. See Timothy Malefyt, 'Models, metaphors and client relations: the negotiated meanings of advertising', in T. de Waal Malefyt and B. Moeran (eds), *Advertising Cultures*, 2003, pp. 140, 149-51.

18. Brian Moeran, *A Japanese Advertising Agency*, 1996, Chapter 4.

19. Peter Dale, *The Myth of Japanese Uniqueness*, 1986.

20. This was partly reinforced by his having positioned himself in a corner of the studio, roughly half way between the photographer and his computer, on the one side, and the hair stylist's room, on the other.

Part II
Networks

–4–

Managing Impressions

In his discussion of Goffman's work on impression management and the history of the study of networks, Ulf Hannerz suggests that there are 'advantages in integrating the dramaturgical perspective with network analysis',[1] since there are ways – other than those discussed by Goffman – in which variations in self presentation may be affected by and/or themselves affect how networks are put together and function.

The example of a particular fieldwork situation that I describe in the first chapter of each part of this book, in which the concept of frame, network or field is introduced, is, of course, itself an exercise in self presentation and impression management on at least two counts. First, I wish to convey to my readers the 'fact' that the situation described has been chosen primarily for its heuristic value. The contents of the story are there to illustrate the argued potential for a particular method of studying social interaction, rather than to entertain (although entertainment value is not insignificant since the book's commercial potential will need to be evaluated by an eventual publisher). Secondly, each story is designed to impress by its 'honesty' – revealing that the fieldworker is prone to the most naive suppositions and idiotic mistakes, as well as self-interested tactics, and that fieldwork itself is as much a messy business – what Danny Miller has called 'the muddle in the middle'[2] – as a social scientific method of study.

In this chapter, I will move from a focus on frames to one on networks. This does not mean that frame analysis will be put entirely to one side, but rather that it will be used as appropriate to complement and inform my discussion of networks since the two frequently work in tandem. The story told here reinforces the link between impression management and network analysis and starts with how I managed to get permission to study what was at the time a medium-sized Japanese advertising agency (then known as Asahi Tsūshinsha or Asatsu) and which is now the third-largest agency in Japan (now known as ADK), and what happened as a result of a connection made soon after my acceptance into the company. It was one set of connections or network that got me into Asatsu and enabled me to carry out fieldwork research in the first place,[3] it was another, linked personal connection that then helped that research and even allowed me to enter the back stage of Japanese advertising practices. Once again, though, as in my story in Chapter 1, I need to start by 'bracketing' this tale from the field with two or three explanatory background paragraphs.

Entering the Field

When I was in the middle of a second two-year period of fieldwork on the art world of Japanese ceramics (more of that in Part Three of this book), my elder son, Alyosha, dived into the local Ono Valley primary school swimming pool as instructed, hit his head on the bottom of the pool (it was only 82 centimetres deep) and suffered a compressed fracture of three bones in his neck that, together with other injuries, kept him in and out of hospital for the best part of nine months. Since Japanese hospitals generally require that a patient always be accompanied by a family member who administers to all the patient's non-medical needs, I found myself spending a lot of time with Alyosha, reading stories, preparing him extra meals ('Dog food', he called it!), talking about life, and watching television (I had rigged up a mirror to enable him to see the screen from his supine position on the bed).

Most television stations in Japan – at least, the ones putting out the kind of programmes that a twelve-year-old-boy enjoyed at the time – are commercial. This meant that programmes were punctuated by television commercials, many of which we both found, if not incomprehensible, at least curious. As we sought to understand the logic behind fifteen – at most, thirty – seconds of quickly framed images, music and words, it occurred to me that my next research project ought to be the study of the social processes underpinning the production of advertising.

Some years later, when finally the promise of a sabbatical beckoned, I decided that I did indeed want to do fieldwork in an advertising agency and so set about trying to find one that would accept an academic in its midst. This is where my networking began. At the time, I was in charge of the undergraduate programme in Japanese Studies at the University of London's School of Oriental and African Studies (SOAS). One of the innovations that my colleagues and I had decided to introduce as part of our overall upgrading of the programme was a compulsory term abroad for all students after the first six months of their studies. The difficulty, of course, was finding an appropriate Japanese educational institution that would not only want to enter into an exchange agreement with SOAS, but would teach our students more or less according to the regulations binding London University degree programmes *and* do so at an extremely reasonable cost.

The institution with which we eventually established what turned out to be an excellent and, I think mutually rewarding, working partnership was the Hokkaido University of Education, located in Sapporo, the largest city in Japan's northernmost main island of Hokkaido. Coincidentally, just before negotiations began, I was contacted by a Mr. Suzuki, the *Hokkaido Shinbun* newspaper's foreign correspondent in London, who asked me to write a regular feature article for his newspaper every three or four months as part of its process of 'internationalization' (at the time much in vogue in Japan). This I did over the next few years, even after Suzuki himself was transferred back to Tokyo, and, since the *Hokkaido Shinbun* publicly supported the exchange programme we had set up between students in London and Sapporo (the fact that I had been independently recruited as a feature writer helped, of course), I made sure that I paid a courtesy visit to its offices whenever I visited Japan.

It was to Suzuki, therefore, that I first mentioned my plan to study an advertising agency, since I realized – from the effect of an advertisement on the front page of the *Asahi Shinbun* newspaper for a book that I had written in Japanese – that newspapers, and not just television, were an important advertising medium. He promptly pointed out that he was a mere correspondent and knew nothing about the advertising side of his newspaper (a typical division between editorial and publishing activities that I was to encounter again in my study of women's international fashion magazines), but suggested instead that we talk to a Mr. Honda, the advertising manager of his newspaper's Tokyo office. After telephoning to ensure that Honda was there, we then went downstairs two floors and I found myself once more explaining who I was and what I wanted to do by way of research.

Honda listened intently and, after a moment's reflection, suggested that Asahi Tsūshinsha might be a good choice of fieldwork site. 'We do a lot of business with them,' he said by way of explanation, before adding for my obvious benefit, 'and it's a very *Japanese* company.'

Never having heard of Asatsu, and slightly nervous – as a social anthropologist who believed in comparison as a methodology – about doing fieldwork in a very 'Japanese' company, I asked a few questions. Honda told me that the company had only started business some 40 years previously, but – thanks to the dynamism of its CEO, Masao Inagaki – had since risen to become Japan's sixth largest advertising agency. It was a full-service agency that handled virtually any business requested of it (except, I soon found out, anything to do with political parties and politicians), but was particularly famous for having pioneered the development of *anime* televised cartoons and associated merchandising products.

This seemed good enough for me – especially the bit about animation programmes – so I asked Honda if he could possibly introduce me to someone at Asatsu. He said that that was no problem and promised to get back to me the next day.

True to his word, he called me the following morning and said that he had set up a meeting for me at 9 o'clock two days hence, a Saturday. I was to meet Inagaki himself, and Honda would be there to effect the introductions.

And so, having spent an abstemious evening in the company of friends the night before, I arrived at Asatsu's head office and met Honda in the lobby of the somewhat less-than-imposing building near Shinbashi Station. We took the elevator up to the eighth floor and presented ourselves to a receptionist who, obviously primed about our arrival, at once took us along a screened-off corridor to a large sunlit room with a long table suitable for Board meetings. Honda and I sat on the far side of the table by the window, with myself to his left and furthest from the door. A minute or so later, an energetic, smiling man wearing gold-rimmed glasses came bustling apologetically into the room, followed by a grey-haired, stern-faced man who introduced himself as Takano and a woman called Fujii. We exchanged name cards and I learned that Takano was in charge of the CEO's Office, while Fujii was Inagaki's PA. Inagaki himself motioned to us to be seated, and himself sat down flanked by Takano to his right and Fujii to his left nearest the door. We then passed one or two pleasantries – including polite praise for my knowledge of both spoken and written Japanese (a form of bracketing that marked me out as a foreigner, but potentially included me in among all Japanese present in the room) and questions about how long I had lived in Japan, where I had studied, and so on.

After these opening brackets, Honda turned to the business at hand. 'As you can see,' he started, referring to my name card on the table in front of himself and Inagaki and his colleagues, 'Moeran *sensei* is Chair Professor of Japanese Studies at the University of London where he has initiated a student exchange programme with the Hokkaido University of Education in Sapporo. This, of course, has been of great interest to our newspaper and we've also asked *sensei* to write some feature articles for us on a regular basis. Because he's now interested in doing research on the Japanese advertising industry, he not unnaturally turned to us for advice and assistance. And because we at the *Hokkaido Newspaper* are very indebted to Asatsu for the advertising revenues that you have procured for us, and because of the good relations that exist between our two companies, I suggested to Professor Moeran that he talk to you.'

This masterful introduction performed a number of crucial tasks in framing the meeting between Inagaki and myself.[4]

First, it established my personal credentials as a senior academic at a highly respected British university. I did not rank as high as a corporate executive officer in the respective hierarchies of our academic and advertising worlds, of course, but Honda was intimating that I *was* sufficiently senior to enable Inagaki and myself to engage in conversation on a fairly level playing field.

Secondly, it established a link between my institution and the *Hokkaido Newspaper* through the student-exchange programme that I myself had been instrumental in initiating. In this way, Honda traced the *genealogy* of our relationship at an organizational level – an important part in network relationships where participants must be given the opportunity to know how to (re)act with regard to a request for assistance.

Thirdly, by then mentioning that his newspaper had contracted me to write feature articles for it on a regular basis, Honda conveyed something crucial to the smooth working of network connections at a personal level: that there already existed a relation of *trust* between us. By implication, Inagaki could trust Honda's trust in me.[5]

Fourthly, Honda's introduction showed the obvious logical connection between my chosen subject of research and the *Hokkaido Newspaper*, as well as that between the *Hokkaido Newspaper* and Asatsu. In other words, it showed that Honda was *not abusing his connection* with Inagaki in any way and that it was entirely justifiable for him to turn to the CEO for assistance in this instance.

Fifthly, Honda gently reminded Inagaki of an ongoing (financial) relationship between the latter's agency and his own newspaper in which he himself was involved on a day-to-day, hands-on basis as advertising manager. In this way, he intimated that his request was not just personal, but backed by institutional authority and appealed to that ongoing relationship as a means of obliging Inagaki to take seriously my request to conduct research in his agency.

Like almost all Japanese in such situations, Inagaki nodded as each of the points was made and, once Honda had finished his introduction, looked inquiringly at me. It was then that I realized that – not unlike an advertising executive – I had to make a succinct presentation of my research interest and its underlying reasons and practical aims, as well as what, specifically, I wanted Inagaki to do for me. This presentation is what in the advertising industry itself is called a 'pitch' and, to be successful, it has to be persuasive. The difficulty for any academic, when talking to people who are not themselves in academia, lies in putting across complex ideas in as straightforward a manner as possible and in persuading others of the practical relevance of one's research.

And so I began (with a bracket or two, to frame my research in Japan). I explained that I was a social anthropologist who had studied under Professor Nakane of Tokyo University and written a doctoral dissertation on a community of potters and its involvement in the Japanese folk-art movement. I then said that, as part of my ongoing interest in how people related to things and in how things themselves tended to organize people, I wished to study an advertising agency. Hitherto, virtually all academic studies of advertising had been concerned with advertisements as *products*. I was interested, however, in the social *processes* underlying these products. How was an advertisement made? What kinds of people were involved in which stages of its production? And what kind of problems and challenges did they face, and why? This could only be found out by carrying out fieldwork in an advertising agency and I would be extremely grateful if Mr. Inagaki (I referred to him by the role title of *shachō*, or CEO) would allow me to study in *his* agency.[6]

There was a short pause after I had finished my two-minute pitch, and I waited nervously, conscious of Inagaki's piercing gaze behind his amiable smile. He was sizing me up, although he had been noticeably impressed by my link to Professor Nakane and thus to Japan's most prestigious university. His first comment, however, was a little unexpected.

'I see. Well, it's certainly true that we need people these days to explain Japan to the outside world,' he began, with a flicker of a glance towards Takano on his right. 'Just look at the way the Americans are treating us these days with their so-called "Japan bashing" tactics.'

I nodded respectfully and made one or two noises of agreement, although a little at a loss as to what to say, but Inagaki continued by asking me some rather direct questions about how I was going to finance myself throughout my research, where I would find an apartment, whether I was sure I could afford to live in Tokyo, and so on. I assured him that I would not be asking him or his agency for a 'salary' of any sort and that I hoped to get a research fellowship of some kind. As for finding somewhere to live and Tokyo's high cost of living, that was something for me – and not him – to worry about. Would it be possible, though, to do fieldwork in his agency?

What did this 'fieldwork' entail exactly? I explained as best I could about how I hoped to get an all-round picture of how an advertising agency functioned and how it prepared its advertising campaigns, and that this could best be done by talking to all sorts of people in the agency, getting them to tell me their experiences, and – hopefully – being able to sit in on a campaign's preparations. I compared a fieldworker to a new employee who had to learn the ropes of advertising if he or she was to be of any use to the agency.

Inagaki nodded at that. And when would this fieldwork begin and how long would it last? He looked surprised when, after mentioning a start date over a year ahead, I replied 'one year' to the second half of his question. Clearly, I needed to justify the length of time that I felt to be appropriate. This meant that I told him how I would be a mere apprentice who knew less than his annual intake of recruits every April (since I wasn't Japanese in the first place) and so would need to study, and study as hard and as long as I could.

Mention of the word study seemed to please him. And what did I intend to do once my fieldwork was finished? Would I write a report of some kind? I told him that I wanted to write a book – not a piece of popular journalism, but an academic book. And would I use Asatsu's name? Not unless he thought it appropriate. 'I don't see why not,' he mused. 'It could be advertising for us, after all.'

There was a brief pause. Once again I felt uncomfortably aware of his piercing gaze, but it seemed that he had made up his mind.

'One year's rather a long time,' he said. 'Why don't we say three months to begin with? You will liaise with Mr Takano here. He's the one who'll organize your time in Asatsu.'

I thanked him profusely, while also daring to add that I hoped that the three months would be extended to a year. Inagaki smiled again and said we would have to see how things went. And with that he stood up, signalling that the meeting was at an end. Honda and I rose, too, made our farewells, took the elevator down to the lobby and walked out into a beautiful sunny autumn day. I had got permission to study an advertising agency. My networking had worked. I had successfully managed an impression.

Developing Contacts

By the time of my next visit to Tokyo, in the late spring of the following year, I had just received news that I had been awarded a one-year senior fellowship by the Japan Foundation for my proposed study of an advertising agency. I therefore made sure to get in touch with Takano and inform him of developments. He seemed pleased at the news – possibly because he realized that now it was extremely unlikely that I would make any financial demand on his agency; but also because the prestige of a Japan Foundation fellowship rubbed off from the researcher onto the object of his research. I had given Asatsu a little cultural capital that it was to use from time to time as appropriate during the course of my field-work research. It also meant that, without anything being said on either side, my initial three-month trial period was extended to a year.

Before I left, Takano asked me to wait in our meeting room for a moment or two while he went to call one of the agency's managing directors who wished to talk to me. A few minutes later, I met Mr. Yano, the senior executive who later had such trouble working out appropriate frame behaviour with an American-influenced client on the golf course.

'Ah! *Sensei*!' He said with a welcoming smile, the moment his head was round the door – a little bit like Sir Humphrey Appleby in *Yes, Prime Minister*. 'My name's Yano and I'd like to thank you so much for choosing our poor company to study. I've heard so much about you from Takano and the CEO, and I look forward to working with you once you come here in January next year.'

And having set this particular frame with his (fabricating?) allusion to Asatsu, my fieldwork study, and his link to mutually known colleagues in the company, we exchanged name cards and sat down. Yano then commented on my position as chair professor, asked about Japanese Studies at London University and elsewhere in England, mentioned a trip he had taken to London with his wife some years previously, and finally got to the point.

'As a matter of fact, *sensei*, my son is about to go to London University for a year to do an intensive English-language course. Yes, *isn't* that a coincidence? Of course, he doesn't tell me very much these days – you know how sons are when they grow up – but I understand that he's going to be at your very own School of Oriental and African Studies. It *is* a small world, isn't it!'

While noting the clever links he had made in our opening conversation between myself, my academic institution, England, and his family as part of a tactic to make the reason for his being in the room with me less out-of-the-ordinary, I made the appropriate noises of surprise and delight at such a coincidence.

'I realize you're an extremely busy man, *sensei*,' Yano continued, blithely ignoring both his own seniority and the frantic pace at which he lived his own life at the time, 'but I wonder if you'd be so kind as to keep a distant eye on that young rascal of mine and be there to help *if* he gets into any trouble. I realize this is making a great imposition on you, but . . .' His voice trailed away in a manner commonly practised by Japanese who like to allow their conversationalists to fill in the unspoken part of requests, denials, partial admittances of truth, and so on.

I promised Yano that I would do as requested and, after a few more pleasantries, took my leave.

A couple of months later, a young man knocked on my office door at SOAS and introduced himself as Yano's son. After making sure that everything was more or less satisfactory regarding his settling-in arrangements, I then invited him out for a drink a few days later and we spent a pleasant summer evening downing a bottle of Chablis in a courtyard outside a bar somewhere near the British Museum. On my next trip to Tokyo in the late summer, Yano insisted on meeting me and making effusive apologies for my having wasted my precious time on his insignificant son. It seemed that he was especially impressed by the Chablis (which had been spectacularly effective in breaking down the young man's reserve).

By the time I began my fieldwork in Asatsu, therefore, I already had in Yano an influential supporter in the company. This was to stand me in good stead when – as part of a plan that saw me placed each month in a different divisional 'office' of the agency so that I could learn what kind of work people did in media buying, marketing, promotions and so on – I found myself in Account Services or Sales (*eigyō*). This was the name used for agency-client relations and was in many ways the most difficult part of an agency to study – partly because account executives often moved in extremely mysterious ways in an attempt to bring in new business to the agency, and partly because agency-client relations were by nature sensitive and thus not open for external observation.

Fortunately, however, Yano prevailed upon one junior executive to take me under his wing and, having cleared my presence with a couple of clients, to let me sit in on some of the negotiations surrounding the agency's preparations for an ad campaign.[7] But there were still a lot of things that I sort of knew were going on in the Account Services office, but never had a chance to observe. These included the so-called 'competitive presentation' – an opportunity for an agency to compete with rival agencies for an account (that is, the sum of money handed to an agency by a client) by preparing an advertising campaign based on marketing and other information provided by its potential client at an orientation meeting. I realized that such presentations were absolutely crucial to the success or failure of an advertising agency (although I could only vaguely guess why), but I had no idea what they involved in terms of the agency's internal organizational dynamics. Nor, given the issue of 'client confidentiality', could I see how I was going to get around this impasse in my research.

During my stay in Account Services, it was Yano who took me under his wing, insisted that I sit at a desk beside him in the open plan-office, and generally made sure that my research proceeded as I hoped. When I mentioned one day the difficulty of being able to sit in on and observe a presentation, he nodded his head in agreement and simply said: 'You're right, *sensei*. It *is* very difficult, isn't it?' and left things at that.

Late one evening a couple of weeks later, Yano called me at home. '*Sensei*,' he began in his customary unctuous voice, 'I *do* hope I didn't get you out of bed. No? Oh, that's a relief. You see, I'm phoning to ask for your help.'

Me? Help? I did my best to tone down the excitement building up inside me as I asked how I might be of assistance.

'Well, you see, *sensei*, we've been asked by a potential client to prepare an advertising campaign in English to be run in Germany and the United States. Because you come from Europe and know English, we thought it might be a good idea if you could comment on the work the creative team's been doing.'

I said I would, of course, be delighted to help and promised to be at Yano's desk by 8.30 the next morning.

Once I had arrived, Yano whisked me downstairs to one of the windowless rooms that agency people used to use for internal meetings of one sort or another.[8] There we found half a dozen men, all sitting round a table smoking, with dozens of ad mock-ups lined around the walls behind them. I was briefly introduced by Yano who then left and immediately found myself being given a quick run-down of the situation. The agency had been asked by a major Japanese corporation, Frontier, to come up with a print advertising campaign that was to be run in Germany and the United States as part of its preparations for a competitive preparation. I was needed on two counts. First, could I ensure that all the English used in the ad headlines was correct? Secondly, could I give my opinion as someone from Europe, who had also spent some time in the United States, about the content of the campaign's visuals?

I set to work and made such comments as I could. The English was easy enough, and I was able to correct one or two howlers – like *The Kane Mutiny* in conjunction with a photograph of the film director, Orson Welles (*Citizen Kane* was intended) – together with various misprints. I also gave my (at times, I suspect, somewhat injudicious) opinion about the six different ad series that were placed around the room. What caught my attention most, however, was the tag line that the creative team was using for Frontier: *the Pulse of Entertainment*. I asked why this had been chosen, heard that the team had been offered two others at its orientation meeting with Frontier,[9] and offered to try to come up with something more appropriate.

I do not intend here to detail all the ins and outs of what followed during the next few days.[10] The important point is that I managed to make what turned out to be a significant contribution to Asatsu's presentation to Frontier, by coming up with a rather different but acceptable tagline of my own: *It's in the Name*. My connection with Yano not only gave me back-stage access to the nitty-gritty grind of daily work in an advertising agency. He also arranged for me to be present at Asatsu's presentation to Frontier. ('Wear that white linen jacket of yours, *sensei*,' he advised. 'Very Manhattan Avenue!') This in itself opened doors that allowed me to attend, even help pitch, several other competitive presentations made by the agency to potential or existing clients.

All this helped me in at least two important ways. I was able, on the one hand, to gain an in-depth understanding of agency-client relations and, on the other, by coming up with a tag line that won Frontier's acclaim, to show people in Asatsu itself that I could be more than a mere 'professor' doing research and that I had ideas which might prove useful to them in their own work. This led to my being consulted from time to time by people I hardly knew, but who had heard through the grapevine about my contribution to the Frontier presentation (which Asatsu had won), and who asked my 'advice' about all sorts of issues that came their way, from naming All Nippon Airways new business class service (*Club ANA*), to marketing a clothes softener (*Happiness is a Soft Blanket*). These requests in turn led to my learning more about the different and varied kinds of accounts that the agency handled and thus increased my overall knowledge of the Japanese advertising industry.

Comment

Writing a tale from the field that succinctly encompasses the analytical potential of network analysis is rather more difficult than composing a story that illustrates one of frames. This is partly because, by their very nature, frames are situated, compact and limited (in terms of place, time and participants) and so allow for 'thick' description and analysis. Networks, on the other hand, tend to be much more dislocated and open-ended, which means that stories about them, too, are 'thinner' and less satisfactory as neat exemplifications of a methodology. It is precisely this sociological difference that encourages me to talk of 'network-based fieldwork' as a methodologically different kind of participant observation from 'frame-based fieldwork'.

What, then, can we learn from the tale told in this chapter? First and foremost, as we also saw in Chapter One, entry into the chosen fieldwork site is a critical event that, in Japan at least, requires some kind of personal introduction to those who are being asked to provide the kind of information that the fieldworker seeks. In the case of my research in Sarayama, it will be remembered, I had two lines of access. One of these was academic, and involved the head of my department who was an anthropologist of India and who introduced me to Chie Nakane who was herself a specialist in the north Indian sub-continent. The network connection here, therefore, was really quite strong – being based on personal interaction between the two scholars concerned, and a shared regional and disciplinary interest backed by institutional authority. However, although extremely strong within the academic field, this connection did not cut much ice with the potters of Sarayama who, having had to deal with a number of academics involved in the Japanese folk-art movement over the years, were less than impressed by so-called 'scholarly' credentials. So far as they were concerned, and in the context of what they themselves knew from lengthy experience in making pottery that had been labelled 'folk art' (*mingei*), the academic critics they had come across could only talk in ideological, and for them irrelevant, terms.

The second line of access, then, that brought me to one particular potter, Inoshige, in Sarayama was via Kim Shuefftan and Toshio Sekiji in Tokyo, to whom I had been introduced by Bernard Leach. This set of connections was far more effective, although my own link to Bernard had been limited to three meetings, one of which consisted of little more than a brief 'hello-goodbye' exchange following a public appearance by the great man. Bernard had himself spent a month in Sarayama a couple of decades previously and had been much loved and respected by the potters who remembered well his courtesy, his practical pottery knowledge, his willingness to learn, and the way he was prepared to 'mix it' with them (even though, as his wife Janet once remarked, Bernard spoke a brand of Meiji-period Japanese that was fast becoming incomprehensible to modern Japanese). Toshio, too, had spent a month or so in Sarayama during the shooting of a short documentary film on Onta (and neighbouring Koishiwara) pottery and had come to know and be known by most of the potters there. Despite my own negligible knowledge of the craft of pottery at the time, it was my contacts in the world of folk-art pottery that gave me access to one particular potter in Sarayama. Although Inoshige had an extremely wide network of friends and acquaintances, he was not in any position of authority within Sarayama at the time. This meant that all he could do was pass me on to his colleagues, whom I then had to persuade of the reasonableness of their allowing me to carry out a year's fieldwork in the community.

It was the 'working world' connection that helped me gain access, too, to a Japanese advertising agency. What started as an educational arrangement was picked up for comment and praise by a local newspaper, one of whose remits was to report anything of 'significance' occurring in the region in which it was published and distributed. At the same time, a personal relationship developed between the foreign correspondent of that newspaper based in London and myself because of the request that I write for the newspaper every so often. This relationship was not purely confined to visits to my office on his part, but extended to 'off-duty' socializing both in public places and, with his family, in the privacy of my home. I kept up this relationship with Suzuki even after he had been transferred back to Tokyo because he was the one who still handled and translated my articles and because I still headed a university department that sent its students regularly to the region in which his newspaper was based.

What followed was a fairly simple connection through the newspaper's advertising manager to advertising agency CEO. Of course, Honda recommended Asatsu, rather than a larger agency like Dentsu or Hakuhodo, because he had already met Inagaki and knew that it would be much more sensible to introduce me to someone who had decision-making power than to someone who did not. In this respect, Honda himself exhibited an advertising man's experience, in that much of the time and energy of those working in an agency is spent trying to work out precisely who in any client company is invested with the power to make decisions (and it is *not* necessarily the person highest up the corporate hierarchy).

The decision, once made, was made rapidly and quickly delegated. There was always the danger, of course, that Inagaki's stern-faced assistant, Takano, might not understand why his CEO had chosen to act as he did when faced with my request to conduct fieldwork in Asatsu. This was, I think, one strategy behind the way in which Inagaki himself questioned me after my initial 'pitch'. The comment about needing foreigners who understood the Japanese, for example, was probably made (to judge from Inagaki's sidelong glance) for Takano's, rather than my own, benefit. He wanted his aide to know one line of reasoning behind the decision that he was to make ten minutes later.[11] Similarly, his questions about my financial situation, and the reassurances that I gave in my answers that I did not intend to be a burden on the agency in any way, were probably designed to allay suspicions about my intentions and potential subsequent gossip among employees once I started my fieldwork, as much as to satisfy Inagaki's curiosity. At the same time, though, the CEO made sure that he was accompanied to this meeting by two of his subordinates. There were two reasons for this. First, Takano and Fujii could act as observers of my overall appearance and bearing. Was my tie knotted correctly, or was it askew and loose? Were my fingernails bitten to the quick, or overly long and not properly cleaned? Did I fidget with my watch strap or signet ring as I spoke? They were there to provide supplementary assessments of my character besides that made by Inagaki while he was directly involved in questioning me. Secondly, they could be called upon to act as witnesses should anything go wrong.[12]

Once admitted to Asatsu, I found myself almost immediately involved in a new set of networks involving employees of the agency and their contacts in the advertising and media industries. My being approached by Yano with a request to keep an eye on his son during the period of his studies at my university was an opportunity to be seized upon by an incoming fieldworker. Previous experience of life in Japan had taught me that. I knew that treating Yano's son (and myself) to a bottle of Chablis would stand me in good stead once I started fieldwork, although I did not think far enough ahead at the time to realize how the business of getting accounts was bound to be surrounded in a mist of secrecy and how much Yano would be able to help me see through these mists.[13] After all, just *how* money is earned – as I should have remembered from my salutary experiences in Sarayama – almost invariably affords certain kinds of people (family businesses, entrepreneurs, free-lance photographers, fashion models) some discomfort when directly questioned about it. Anyway, my taking Yano's son out for an evening was a calculated act on my part – calculated in the sense that I knew that a favour given created the kind of sense of obligation that would in the end result in a favour being returned. In short, I relied on the mutual expectation of what Marshall Sahlins has called 'balanced reciprocity' which characterizes most network relations in Japan.[14]

If the way in which I took advantage of the opportunity offered by this new network connection was calculated, so, too, it might be said, was Yano's own request made to someone he had never met, but had just heard about from Inagaki and Takano. In which case the initial exchange between these two points in a network was, like many initial exchanges between people introduced to each other through networks, instrumental. It was only later that the relationship developed into an affective one.

It is just possible, however, that Yano was used to test me. After all, I was an outsider (and a foreigner, as well) who had just been given permission to study, without apparent restraints of any kind, everything that went on in Asatsu. But, even though Honda of the *Hokkaido Newspaper* had vouched for me, there was no hard evidence that I really could be trusted. Yano's request to keep an eye on his son, therefore, may have been designed to see whether I would behave as a Japanese personal connection would and, therefore, whether future exchanges between us could be framed appropriately according to Japanese norms and expectations.[15]

The personal connection established between Yano and myself was primarily to my advantage. This is to be expected. After all, I was the foreign scholar trying to find out about the social organization of an advertising industry. Being neither Japanese nor an advertising man myself, I was an outsider twice over and needed all the help I could reasonably get. Yano provided me with that assistance, suggesting that I talk to one account executive about the back-stage negotiations leading up to this event, or ask another creative director about the reasoning behind the visuals in that campaign, and so on. He also provided me with contacts, or suggested whom I should go through, when, for one reason or another, I wanted to talk to somebody outside the agency about something.

There were occasions, however, when I was able to 'repay' the 'debts' that had built up through his providing me with one favour after another. At his request, therefore, I gave a lecture to the new recruits during their three-week training period in April that year. I was also invited to attend one or two expensive dinners in the company of (would-be) clients, when Yano felt that the presence of an educated foreigner, who also held a chair professorship at a prestigious university, would be to his overall advantage. Here, to be true, the gains were mutual, since I had a chance to witness an ad man's suave wooing of a client first hand.

When it came to involving me in the preparations for the Frontier presentation, Yano almost certainly expected little more than a cultural and linguistic input from me ensuring that the account team had made no embarrassing – and so potentially disastrous – mistakes. The fact that, by chance, I was able to come up with a suitable tagline for the client company, as well as with one or two other ideas incorporated in Asatsu's presentation, was the icing on the network cake, so far as Yano (and, indeed, I myself) was concerned. It certainly contributed to a change in attitude on his part because thereafter he began to treat me less as a 'professor' and more as an 'ad man' (although he never failed to call me '*sensei*'), and thus moved into back-stage discussions of gossip and personalities, tactics and strategies, rather than keeping to front-stage information, institutions and ideal practices as previously. In other words, the nature of our own relationship established through networks led to my realising that Japanese business – and, by implication, business elsewhere in the world – operates according to two principles. One is the rather obvious institutional structure of more or less stable organizations operating in a particular field (which, in this fieldwork account, has been advertising). The other is that permanently shifting web of interpersonal networks linking different people in different constellations for different intents and purposes. Just how these formal and informal relations complement and affect one another is the subject of the remaining chapters in this book.

Notes

1. Ulf Hannerz, *Exploring the City*, 1980, p. 234.
2. Daniel Miller, 'Advertising, production and consumption as cultural economy', in T. Malefyt and B. Moeran (eds), *Advertising Cultures*, 2003, p. 76.
3. As Malcolm Chapman points out (in 'Social anthropology and business studies: some considerations of method', 2001, p. 32), 'many business researchers rely upon the exploitation of previous contacts, friendships, and the like, for first access to a company'.
4. Erving Goffman (in *The Presentation of Self in Everyday Life*, p. 22) points out that the information that each participant *initially* possesses about fellow participants is crucially important, 'for it is on the basis of this initial information

that the individual starts to define the situation and starts to build up lines of responsive action'.

5. As Francis Fukuyama writes (in *Trust: The social virtues and the creation of prosperity*, 1995, p. 26): 'Trust is the expectation that arises within a community of regular, honest and cooperative behavior, based on commonly shared norms, on the part of other members of that community.'

6. As Goffman (in *The Presentation of Self*, p. 18) notes, an individual sometimes expresses him- or herself in a particular way because his or her status or social group requires that it be so. As a 'scholar', I was more or less obliged to play the part of a 'university professor' in my initial pitch to Inagaki, even though – as fieldworker – I was going to have to throw this academic role aside and try to make myself seen and be accepted as an 'ad man' (and, in other fieldwork situations, country potter, writer, sympathetic environmentalist in favour of sustainable development, and so on).

7. Brian Moeran, *A Japanese Advertising Agency*, 1996, Chapters 3 and 4.

8. These meeting rooms were reserved for internal use because, without a window, they did not provide a clear indicator of how best to frame the inside-outside and hierarchical relations characterizing interaction with visitors.

9. The two others were: *The Art of Entertainment* and – wait for it – *The Joy of Light and Creativity*.

10. That has already been done in Brian Moeran, 'Imagining and imaging the other: Japanese advertising international', in Malefyt and Moeran, *Advertising Cultures*, pp. 91–112.

11. Asatsu had, at the time, entered into partnership with the New York-based agency, BBDO – a partnership which involved difficult, protracted and often seemingly fruitless negotiations over everything from mutual share-holding to global advertising clients. As I was to be told time and time again, the agency's American partner seemed not to understand the long-term reciprocal nature of Japanese business methods – something that caused Inagaki and fellow members of the Board of Directors much soul-searching.

12. It did. Much later, after I had finished fieldwork and was writing up my data, I showed an early draft of one article to Takano who, as well as correcting one or two mistakes and censoring some of my interpretations of fieldwork information, upbraided me for using the agency's name. I had to remind him of my initial conversation with Inagaki in his presence when the CEO had said that he saw no reason why I should not use Asatsu's name. In fact, however, Takano's view prevailed during the time leading up to publication of my monograph, *A Japanese Advertising Agency*. The fact that I am now allowed to use the agency's name is partly to do with at least four different facts: first, Takano's retirement; second, a change in top-management style; third, written material about advertising goes out of date very quickly and is soon perceived

as unthreatening; and fourth, my monograph was seen to be sufficiently faithful to reality at one stage for it to be recommended for reading by all new recruits to the agency.

13. As Goffman (*The Presentation of Self in Everyday Life*, p. 17) has observed: sometimes an individual knows exactly what he or she is up to and calculates very precisely how to give off an impression; at other times, he or she is less aware of how calculating he or she is, even though the activity is still going on in that way.

14. Marshall Sahlins, 'On the sociology of primitive exchange', in M. Banton (ed.) *The Relevance of Models for Social Anthropology*, 1965, pp. 139–236.

15. As Ronald Burt says (in 'The network entrepreneur', 2000, p. 288): 'With this kind of uncertainty, players are cautious about extending themselves for people whose reputation for honouring interpersonal debt is unknown.'

–5–

Making Connections

What the previous chapter makes clear is that in the advertising and media industries, and in business more generally, connections and networks of one kind or another frame social interaction. People are brought together through connections, and bring others in their wake. Because these connections themselves form networks which extend seemingly ad infinitum into all kinds of different organizations and institutions that make up society, they help us study and analyse the concept of field addressed in the third part of this book. Networks thus link the two research methods of frame and field in the same way that they link individual people and organizations.

But the expansive reach of networks and the sheer variety of connections in operation at any one time makes them extremely difficult to talk about coherently. Thus the study of networks has itself become extremely broad and varied, ranging from informal interpersonal relations of the kind studied by anthropologists[1] to various kinds of institutional networks and inter-organizational alliance structures studied by organizational and economic sociologists.[2] The recent revolution in information technology has encouraged, too, the idea that society itself is a highly dynamic and innovative 'network'. While primarily concerned with institutional networking and with how business projects are themselves enacted by networks, Manuel Castells goes so far as to suggest that 'the network society represents a qualitative change in the human experience'[3] – not that I intend to contribute here in any way to such intellectual euphoria, if only because I have my doubts about this aspect of Castells' thesis. Instead, in this and the following chapters, I wish to look at the relation between networks and connections, on the one hand and, on the other, at how best we might analyse and properly integrate relations between individuals and relations between business organizations. In the process, we will see how economic action is, in part at least, embedded in social relations which themselves generate and are sustained by moral dimensions.[4]

Given the more grounded and extensive work with network analysis that has been going on in organizational and economic sociology over several decades, we might wonder why anthropologists these days tend to disregard it almost totally. Such neglect may have something to do with the tendency of a few sociologists to go in for such quantifying devices as adjacency matrices, polynomial transformations, Guttman scales, the Bonacich eigenvector measure of network centrality, and so on, as a result of which their analyses make little – if any – sense to those untrained in the finer arts of calculus (that is, to the great majority of anthropologists). Indeed, to the occasional cynic, they might appear designed solely to make their authors eligible for the Nobel Prize in Economics.[5]

But anthropologists' neglect of network analysis during the past two decades and more is also partly connected, I think, with the domination of the discipline by a particularly American take on anthropology, which is more concerned with 'culture' than with detailed and in-depth analysis of social organization after the manner of British, Scandinavian and some other forms of European anthropology.[6] I suspect, too, that the fact that these days the discipline of anthropology as a whole (but especially, perhaps, the American branch thereof) tends to be driven by academic celebrities and intellectual fashions, contributes to the neglect of network analysis. As Ulf Hannerz wryly pointed out more than a decade ago,[7] social-network theorizing was unfashionable even then because of its link to action and exchange theories – both of which had been found wanting by those propelling the discipline in new directions. In an academic field in which participants are judged primarily by their ability to contribute to (meta-)theoretical discussions of postmodernism when postmodernism is all the rage, or of globalization, de-territorialization and diasporas when they happen to emerge as the sine qua non of anthropological theorizing, research that fails to incorporate such intellectual fashions is quietly but promptly consigned to the dustbin of irrelevance.[8] As Richard Wilk points out in a slightly different context, 'when theory becomes a domain where small elite groups can strut the latest hot French fashion down the runway . . . we have problems'.[9]

And yet a number of scholars have quietly endorsed the idea of network analysis – partly because it focuses and builds on sets of relations linking persons, objects and/or events;[10] partly because of its openness[9] (unlike the essentially closed nature of frame analysis, for example); partly because, in taking account of the different kinds of relations (practical assistance, advice, information, friendship, and so on) that both exist and do not exist among people, it shows how they are connected to social positions within a system and how these positions themselves bring to light various levels of social structure, or field of forces.[12] As Srinivas and Béteille put it four decades ago, 'the concept of social network paves the way to an understanding of the linkage existing between different institutional spheres and between different systems of groups and categories'.[13]

This, indeed, was why anthropologists started to study networks in the first place. Dissatisfied with structural-functional approaches that favoured apparently enduring relationships in a social institutional framework, some anthropologists examined, instead, how networks cut across such enduring groups and institutions while also revealing other areas of the social landscape. In the process they showed how, rather than allowing themselves merely to accept and be restrained by institutional boundaries, individual actors actively crossed and manipulated them by means of networks.[14]

There is, though, another reason for studying networks, one primarily taken up by sociologists who, as part of a long ongoing discussion in their discipline, have argued that the kind of social relations found in networks affect economic behaviour and institutions. Networks are part of what Mark Granovetter calls the 'embedded' dimensions of economic activity.[15] This argument runs counter to the claims made by economists that social relations only minimally affect behaviour which is primarily rational and self-interested. Networks, therefore, become the focus for those interested in trying to separate or bring together the social and the economic in our everyday lives.

Network Analysis

The word 'network' is used in two senses in the anthropological and sociological literature.[16] First, as we have just seen, it refers most commonly to informal social systems that operate alongside the more formal institutional structures in which people generally find themselves. Much of the early anthropological study of networks, for example, was concerned with personal networks formed and maintained through face-to-face interaction – the kind of material that I presented in the last chapter.[17] Secondly, it is made to apply to a formalized methodology, as in 'network analysis'. In either case, however, the idea of 'network' implies an emphasis on agency vis-à-vis structure, informal vis-à-vis formal patterns of behaviour, and, when concerned with the economy, the 'embeddedness' of cultural ideals like trust,[18] goodwill[19] and *guanxi*[20] in economic action.

> Yano was known and respected as a man with 'a broad face' (*kao ga hiroi*). If anyone in the agency knew how to get from point A to an apparently distant and unconnected point B, then he was the one. His networks (*jinmyaku*) spread in all directions, communicating reliable information of all kinds back and forth, and he knew how to behave with the appropriate balance of spontaneous generosity (*ninjō*) and obligation (*giri*) expected in interpersonal relations in Japan. Many others in the agency tried to emulate him in these respects. After all, his senior position was clearly due, in large part, to the social capital that he had acquired through connections.[21]
>
> The informal connections followed through by Yano and his colleagues were in constant play with the agency's formal organizational structure. The Account Services Office was divided into seven major divisions, which were themselves organized into departments, sections, groups and teams, each of which was headed by an employee who had made some important contribution to the agency's financial welfare by bringing in a new client or expanding an existing account. However, every account executive made use of informal connections to carry out the business at hand and it was the successful manipulation of these informal ties that led to the acquisition of a new,

or expansion of an existing, account. Such successes needed to be rewarded by promotion of some kind. As a result, Asatsu's Board of Directors was constantly reorganizing the agency's formal structure to take account of informal successes. In so doing, it created new teams and groups and, occasionally, a whole new department.

This juggling with the formal structure did not stop at the formation of new components. The Board also believed that each of the seven divisions in Account Services should be more or less equally balanced in terms of overall income generated. Thus, if one division suddenly expanded its business dramatically, adjustments would have to be made to its component parts and a department, with relevant sections, groups and teams, transferred to a new division, which itself might have to shed one or two of its component parts to another division, and so on, until all were back in financial equilibrium. The circulation of client accounts predicated on informal connections between account executives and advertising or product managers thus induced a parallel circulation of different components in the formal organization of the agency.

Relations act as the building blocks of network analysis, but just what *kind* of relations and just *how* they should be studied is problematic. Here we are faced with difficulties surrounding both the content and level of analysis. All sorts of different kinds of relations come into play among people involved in networks or interpersonal connections of one sort or another.[22]

My relationship with Yano (and his with me) brought different elements into play at different times: help, advice, information, collegiality, eventually a form of friendship. It involved a communication of messages, ideas and information, together with transactions and other exchanges of various kinds (both directly and indirectly connected to the advertising business in which we were both participants). Into these were woven notions of instrumentality (to secure information and services deemed valuable by at least one of us); sentiment (a mutual respect, for instance, for the different ways in which we went about our tasks and the contributions each could make to the other's work); and authority and power, based primarily on Yano's elevated position in the agency hierarchy, but also, initially, on my own academic position vis-à-vis Yano's son's forthcoming study at London University. We were also both men of a similar age who could share musical and literary interests, as well as 'events' that had impinged on our lives – such as the long-running battle in the very late 1960s and early 1970s between students, farmers and police over the building of Narita International Airport. We could talk together of what we were doing then, of how we felt, and what we thought we should have been doing. All these things together gave rise to a sense of mutual trust between us.

Other networks involve other kinds of relational content. In Sarayama and the Ono Valley, for example, kinship (both descent and exchange) was important, but so was membership of a residential community, occupational group, and the local school PTA. So someone like my potter friend Inoshige would find himself linking up with several younger potters who quietly admired his work and who wanted to produce pots that took some account of the aesthetic ideals of the folk-art movement for which Onta pottery was famous. But he would also discuss with fellow fathers of children at the North Ono Primary School who were carpenters, rice farmers, wood cutters and pear growers the ongoing issues affecting *their* work groups and cooperatives, as well as the quality of education their children received, the personality of individual teachers employed in the school, and the relative merits of one hamlet chief's determination to widen the valley road in such a way that it would cut into the school's playground (and, in so doing, destroy a few old and beautiful cherry trees). In each of these situations, different sentiments, aims and strategies would be brought to bear by Inoshige, depending on whether he was more or less directly involved and on whether he was called upon to intervene on others' behalves. These overlapping network memberships were – as is usually the case – reinforced by extensive gift-giving and other material exchanges that made each network extremely 'dense'.

Given the way in which all kinds of different communicative content come into play in varying rations throughout people's participation in interpersonal relations, the question that arises is: *which* part or parts of this content is more important at any one time? One problem affecting any answer to this question is that what participants bring to bear during the course of a single frame – let alone in different frames – will vary during its enactment as each seeks a mutually satisfactory resolution to what is at issue.

The road-widening discussion may have started as a point of general concern to all parents of primary school children living in the upper half of the Ono Valley, and in this respect Inoshige had as much interest as the others present at the gathering since his youngest daughter was in her final year at the school. But it soon shifted to a more strictly residential issue focusing on the hamlet in which the school was located, and thence to the person nominally in charge of that hamlet's affairs, which affected Inoshige only to the extent that he did not like the man concerned, but was a close friend of his main protagonist. But from there the matter broadened in scope again because the hamlet chief was said to be in cahoots with the person elected to administer matters affecting the Ono Valley as a whole, and this administrator was no less than Tanuki, senior member of Sarayama, former leader of the potters' cooperative, and related by descent to Inoshige. It was this combination of shared residence, work and household kinship connection that then encouraged a number of those present to urge Inoshige to have a word with Tanuki to see if something couldn't be done to stop the proposal to widen the valley road.

Now how all this is to be *measured*, in order to make a single isolated case into something of comparative significance is yet another problem faced by network analysts. Are they to measure the time spent on different aspects of communicative content (locality, residence, occupation, mutual interest, kinship, and so on) and assign them to some kind of quantitative scale of importance? Should they then count the number of voices and people making use of each aspect at any one time, and convert this into a percentage that they can then recalculate vis-à-vis the already measured minutes? In which case, why not also measure the decibels of noise generated for each aspect during the heat of the discussion and bring this into the overall calculation? Are the aspects in themselves to be ordered according to a scale of hierarchical values that gives occupation, say, a greater 'weighting' than kinship? If so, on what grounds is this scale to be arrived at? Prior knowledge? Whose prior knowledge? Prior knowledge of what and whom exactly? And when, where, how and by whom was such knowledge acquired? And so on and so forth. If not, on what grounds are all aspects to be treated as equal?

As if this were not enough to induce the sort of headache that we would normally attribute to an excess of locally brewed *sake*, network analysts then have to remember to take into account participants' and speakers' relative ages, positions, household wealth, and overall kinship relations (fortunately, in this instance, all the participants were at least men, so that gender is not an issue), since all of these would have had some effect on who said what to whom, when, why, for whose benefit, with what effect, and so on. And even if, by some mathematical miracle, they were able to reduce all this to a few succinct tables of descriptive statistics making use of positive coefficients, correlation matrices, time-constant and time-varying vectors of covariates, and so on and so forth, some might reasonably ask whether these tell us any more than the kind of 'thick description' provided in the first place. This is what Michael Burawoy calls sociology's 'uncertainty principle': the closer we get to measuring some dimensions – connectedness and values – the further we recede on others – objectivity and validity.[23]

If the sheer variety of relational *content* makes thorough network analysis extremely difficult, the *levels* of analysis to be accounted for are no less complex. Precisely because of their informality and the difficulty in co-ordinating on a grand scale their seemingly innumerable participants, networks prove extremely difficult to study. This is exemplified in the various classificatory terms that are brought to bear at this point. Some scholars recommend that we cut the analytical cake into four slices: egocentric networks, dyads, triads and complete networks.[24] Others prefer categories which seem less precise at first glance but which are then usefully qualified. Ulf Hannerz, for example, in his exemplary discussion of networks and their value to the study of urban society, suggests that we start with ego-centred networks (a phrase, surely, to be preferred to ego*centric*), before moving on to partial networks which emerge around the primary content of actors' relationships (like political, business or academic networks). We may then, thirdly, combine the two by looking at partial networks from the point of view of individual actors (such as was done by Adrian Mayer in his study of Indian electoral politics).[25]

The field of magazine publishing, like many other businesses, is a curious mix of institutions and interpersonal relations which effectively bar entry to those outside such networks, while simultaneously smoothening connections within and enabling the immediate cooptation of new personnel as and when required. The problem for the fieldworker is how to gain access to those networks, in order to be able to move effortlessly within and between institutions.

My research on international fashion magazines has been an exercise in such networking practices. All have their origins in coincidence. In Hong Kong, Pamela Lam was so enthused by a course in Japanese advertising and media that I once gave with Lise Skov that, on graduation, she found herself employment in the magazine industry and, after two or three years, ended up as assistant editor of the Hong Kong edition of *Harper's Bazaar*, before moving on to other things in her life. It was Pamela who opened doors for me in Hong Kong, by introducing me to the editors of both *Harper's Bazaar* and *Marie Claire*. Thank you, Pamela.

During one of three interviews with the latter, the editor-in-chief, Olivia Wong, suggested I get in touch with Katie Breen, who was in charge of all *Marie Claire*'s international editions round the world. This I did by e-mail, mentioning Olivia's name, and received a reply in due course from Katie who asked for more details of my research. I explained briefly, but appended for her information the five-page research outline sent in my successful application to the Danish Research Agency to 'prove' that I was a '*bona fide* researcher' and not some 'muckraking journalist'. I did not expect her to read it. Within a day, Katie replied to say that she had read my research outline, found it fascinating and my research 'important', and suggested that I visit her in Paris as soon as mutually convenient. It transpired, when we met some months later, that she had a PhD in history from the University of Geneva and that she had, as a result, been interested in my academic approach.[26] Katie introduced me to members of *Marie Claire International* as well as to others in the French edition of the magazine, and advised me about whom to contact in the London office. She also exerted pressure on the editor of the Japanese edition to accede to my hitherto unanswered requests to interview him on my next trip to Tokyo. Thank you, Katie.

In both Japan and the United States, 'cold' letters and subsequent e-mails requesting interviews with editorial and publishing staff met with silence. Repeated telephone calls were answered with the customary 'I'm afraid so-and-so is not in the office right now.' In a desperate search for alternative but related research directions ten days before a scheduled trip to New York, I decided to try a model agency and, after checking on the Internet, opted for DNA – mainly because it handled two famous models: one whom I rather liked, the other whom I thought extremely ugly. An e-mail message in reply asked me to telephone a Jérôme Bonnouvrier. This I did and found myself explaining to a very French-sounding gentleman what I was doing and asking whether he might be able to give me an interview. This he politely evaded by saying that what he did wasn't really of importance to my research,[27] and that I should get in touch with Guillaume Bruneau, art director of Elle in New York. Did I know him? Well, by name, yes, but no more. 'Just call him up,' advised Bonnouvrier, 'He's a nice guy. French, like myself. Just say you know me. He'll give you an interview.' The French Connection worked. Bruneau gracefully acquiesced. Thank you, Jérôme.

In Tokyo – where, for once, nothing worked – I had more or less given up on getting access to any magazine editor or publisher and had resigned myself to the fact that, on this trip, I was going to get no more than the single, OK-so-far-as-it-went interview with the editor of *Marie Claire Japon*, plus quite a lot of useful talks with readers. But then, during a courtesy call to Asatsu (now transformed into ADK and located in a magnificent new building in Tsukiji), I was chatting with an old friend, Nakamura Kintarō (or 'Kinchan'), who had been running the agency's magazine media-buying department for more than a dozen years (and who had taken me off to Kodansha for the practice of a media-buying session after one-and-a-half days of theory at the beginning of my fieldwork in Asatsu). Kinchan asked about my research, and I told him about the difficulties I was having in getting access to magazine staff. He looked surprised and upset on my behalf. 'But that's ridiculous,' he exclaimed. 'Leave it with me for a day or two. I'll sort things out for you.' By the end of the week, I had interviews with the editor-in-chief of *Harper's Bazaar*, the assistant editor and advertising manager of *Elle Japon* (the editor-in-chief was out of town), and the fashion editor and advertising manager of *Vogue Nippon*. Thank you, Kinchan.

Given that networks can extend almost indefinitely, transforming themselves in the process from – say – a cluster of intellectuals whose primary purpose is to maintain the 'purity' of a folk-art form to one that includes one or two of these intellectuals at its core but also a number of folk-art dealers and retailers, whose main aim is to sell whatever kind of folk art will sell regardless of perceived aesthetic purity, where are we to draw the limits of our analyses? Hannerz himself distinguishes between what he calls first-order stars, first-order zones (which include one or more indirect contacts among those liaising with ego), second-order stars (where other actors in ego's star/zone have their own separate star relationships), and so on.[28] But he rightly recognizes that this kind of analysis quickly becomes unmanageable since most people cannot see beyond their primary and secondary contacts, even though most chains are usually quite short, varying between three and ten links.[29] This means that other criteria need to be brought in to measure networks, and here the shifting ground of analysis itself begins to imitate the social relations it is analysing. Hannerz, for example, mentions range, reachability, network density (the ratio of actual to potential ties among actors in a network), and clusters of ties that develop around particular individuals. Herminia Ibarra, on the other hand, prefers density, connectivity (the degree to which actors are linked through direct and indirect ties), and hierarchy which, in her opinion, together provide network organizations with flexibility and ease of communication.[30]

But range, reachability, density, and so on, are not in themselves sufficient criteria for successful network analysis. Indeed, even size can be a mixed blessing. In an important contribution to network analysis, Ronald Burt points out that more contacts do not necessarily mean greater diversity.[31] He thus distinguishes between 'sparse' networks, which provide more information benefits, and 'dense' networks which provide more or less information for more work and are thus relatively inefficient. This kind of redundance may come from the fact that a lot of ego's contacts are themselves directly connected with one another at the level of first-order star, or because three or four direct personal contacts have exactly the same extended cluster (or, in Hannerz's terms, second-order zone) of contacts who provide ego with the same information. The way to overcome this kind of cohesion and structural equivalence, and thus to balance network size and efficiency in order to make it efficient, is to create and optimize what Burt calls 'structural holes' around as many contacts as possible.[32] In other words, ego should cultivate people who do *not* have the same contacts (since one is enough for his own particular purposes) and who have *different* kinds of knowledge and information to impart. In this way he or she will get a much higher rate of return from networking activities.[33]

In my study of ceramic art in Japan, it was critically important for me to find contacts with structural holes, because the sheer density of interlocking networks among potters, dealers, and department-store representatives very quickly produced the same pieces of gossip and information and reproduced the same ideological positions with regard to the aesthetic appreciation and commercial exploitation of ceramics. In order to overcome this 'structural wall', I developed one set of contacts around Jimbei Hagiwara, a potter working locally in Koishiwara; and another around a local city-based dealer, Eisuke Minamoto, who was in touch with potters and department-store representatives all over northern Kyushu. A third network tapped into was that of a museum curator in Kurashiki – between Osaka and Hiroshima, and near the pottery centre of Bizen – who provided me with entry into the world of ceramics outside northern Kyushu. A fourth was that of a Kyoto-based critic. Although the last two networks overlapped to some degree, the critic in particular provided a structural hole in the *type* of potter I could gain access to, since he specialized in sculptural ceramics and abstract art.

Networks and Connections

'Connections' are, in differing degrees, crucial to the conduct of business of all kinds. Anyone who doubts this need merely recall the ubiquity of phrases like 'old-boy network', 'in the family', 'members of the club', '*who* you know, not what you know', 'got in by the back door', 'contacts' and 'well connected' to realize that, behind the formal faces of market and welfare capitalism, all sorts of informal goings-on – from exchanges of information to job appointments, by way of blatant bribery – are taking place. As Carol Heimer aptly says, it is only by 'helping friends' that anyone can ever do business.[34]

What are the mechanisms by which connections can be, and often are, made? Because their networking is so arbitrary, people feel somehow that it should be anchored to social norms or rules. Different societies, and different social worlds within a society, have different practices and expectations in this regard. In Japan, for example, people are always looking for suitable excuses or justifications for being together. Age is one. Two people will happily call each other 'class mates' (*dōkyūsei*) and use this link to cement a relationship between them, although they were never in the same class together, or even at the same school, but merely entered the national education system in the same year. Geographical origin is another. The fact that two people living and working in Tokyo happen to come from Kyushu is sufficient to encourage bonding, even though they may come from very different parts of the island. Indeed, when in Kyushu, they would stress their differences (like Minamoto Eisuke, the Fukuoka-based pottery dealer, who was very proud of the fact that he was *not* born in Fukuoka, but came from Nagasaki). University is a third. Again, regardless of when either party might have attended university or what each might have studied, the fact that both graduated from Keio, Kobe or Kita Kyushu University is enough to enable a relationship to develop. Finally, there is kinship, although these days this tends to be limited to rural communities like those I lived in and studied in the Ono Valley – unless you happen to be one of those elite people who make sure that they intermarry with other elite people.

> When all else fails, there is always the fallback position of 'fate' (*go-en*). A man may pore over a visitor's name card, examining the fine print, asking questions about the other's past and present life, searching for a connection. How long has he been in his company? So he must have graduated from university in such-and-such a year (indicating a possible age connection)? And where did he go to university? Does that mean he is from the such-and-such region of Japan? Perhaps he knows so-and-so in such-and-such a company who also went to the same university and is from that part of the country? And so on, and so forth.
>
> This kind of enquiry borders on the hopeless when conducted of a foreigner in Japan. Once age has been found wanting as a method of bonding, there is little likelihood of the foreigner being able to satisfy other criteria like kinship, geographical origin or university. A potential line of help exists if the foreigner is married to a Japanese, because questions can then circle around the spouse. But generally the only way in which the informal relationship can be formally sanctioned is when, having socialized with the foreigner sufficiently to be able to judge whether he or she wishes to continue the connection or not, the Japanese can exclaim with unconcealed pleasure, 'It's fate that's brought us together, isn't it?'
>
> The Japanese word for fate (*en*), a little like the Greek *moira* (thread), literally means 'connection'.

With the possible exception of the socialized concept of fate, none of the mechanisms described above is particularly unusual. Kinship, age, origin and education are all standard means of justifying interpersonal relations all over the world. In Japan, though, because people tend to introduce people to others who share the same backgrounds, they quickly form dense networks which themselves often take on the form of factions.

Factionalism is something frequently mentioned in discussions of government and political networks. One feature sustaining political factionalism is the idea of 'locality', which enables all those from a particular prefecture or region to band together and help one another in times of need. This is sustained by the regional electoral system. University background is a particularly common device for creating a sense of unity among some (and, as a consequence, division among other) government ministry bureaucrats. Indeed, a ministry may recruit only from a certain faculty within a university. Marriage, and resulting kinship relations, unite political, business, finance, industrial and court families, in such a way that selective genealogies make it seem as if they have entered into a conspiracy of power in order to rule Japan.[35] Although commonly criticized by those writing about Japanese society,[36] these kinds of alliances are found all over the world in one form or another and are neither particularly different nor necessarily conspiratorial.[37]

In Asatsu, factions were not an issue, even though at one point something like 10 per cent of the employees were graduates of the same university (Waseda). When I asked Yano why they didn't all get together from time to time, his short answer was: 'We haven't got the time.' When I asked him whether the Waseda graduates could form a power block within the agency, he retorted: 'What's the point, *sensei*?' He then continued by explaining that a business was not a bureaucracy. It had to be open to growth and take advantage of all money-making possibilities that arose. A faction would be counter-productive in this regard.[38]

In other words, if networks are used to link people, things and events, and if they are characterized by their openness, they also have the parallel and simultaneous potential to *close* certain avenues of interaction. By choosing one connection rather than another, by operating through one network and not others, we automatically cut off access to the rest. As Inoshige once said, in reply to my comment about people not being close friends in Sarayama: 'Two friends are the beginning of a faction and that would upset the harmony of the community.'

Yano broadened the discussion to the field in which the agency operated. 'Remember, *sensei*', he smiled, 'we're an independent agency. We haven't joined any of those large industrial, bank or intermarket *keiretsu* alliances. We're not like the Tōkyū Agency, for example, which is basically in-house for the Tōkyū Group. It's true that we'd get a lot of new business if we were to act that way. Our biggest client, Mitsubishi Motors, for example, could introduce us to Mitsubishi Bank who'd give us an account for the asking and put us in touch with Mitsubishi Heavy Industries, who'd do the same. And they'd hand us on to the cement, construction and other related companies that form part of the Mitsubishi Group, and Asatsu would end up becoming Mitsubishi's in-house agency. But if that happened, we wouldn't be able to touch anything that was *not* part of the Mitsubishi Group – Mitsui, Sumitomo, Fuji, Sanwa and all the rest of those Japanese *keiretsu* that spend a lot of money on advertising. So, you see, alliances cut off business opportunities, as well as making them. You have to steer a fine line between independence and involvement.'

That fine line taken by the agency was a result of thousands and thousands of personal contacts made daily by its 900 or so employees. I remember, very early on in my fieldwork, being irritated around about five o'clock in the afternoon by the seemingly endless ringing of telephones and voices of people talking to one another, having impromptu mini-meetings at spare desks set up for that purpose, and shouting the occasional command across the open-floor office. Resisting a culturally induced impulse to tidy up my desk and leave the office after yet another long day, I tried to work out what was going on and soon realized that a large number of the agency's account executives, marketers and creative people had been away from their desks during most of the day, visiting clients and media organizations, following up on research data, checking on locations for a television commercial, and so on. Once they returned to the agency's headquarters, however, instead of calling it a day and going off home, all these employees began to talk to those around them in their section, as well as to relevant others in different departments and organizations on the phone, about the various things that they had seen and heard during the day.[39]

In other words, their networks and contacts were used to acquire and relay information that would be of assistance to the agency's work in general – from the fact that rival Dentsu had just lost an important account to news of a TV station's need for a sponsor for one of its programmes, by way of all sorts of gossip and information about local celebrities, client personnel, and possible 'events' in Japan (visits by the Rolling Stones, Manchester United football team, an opera company, and so on and so forth). The information relayed was then incorporated as appropriate into different people's business strategies and formed the basis for the start of their next day's work. One reason for the agency's success was this direct line through connections to strategies and thence action and results.

But how do these contacts and networks actually work in business? At the heart of connections is the need to get access to, and the opportunity to pass on, information of one sort or another. Everyone is processing information. Everyone is calculating who might find a particular piece of information useful. And everyone wants to get access to information that he or she hasn't had the time or opportunity to process him- or herself. Networking and networks, then, are concerned with access to information, the timing of its dissemination (the early bird catches the worm), and the naming of people therein who might be able to help with another's problem. In this respect, networks are 'an important screening device'. They filter information about others to you, as well as about you to others.[40]

Still, one more problem with network analysis is that network becomes a kind of 'catch-all' word, used sometimes to comment on and analyse individual, at other times organizational and inter-organizational, connections without being of very much *practical* help. Ibarra, for example, distinguishes between 'prescribed' and 'emergent' networks. The latter are regarded very much in the way I have been discussing networks here, as 'informal, discretionary patterns of interaction where the content of the relationship may be work-related, social, or a combination of both'.[41] But, in reality, it is the *connections* made – the processes of networking – rather than the overall networks per se,[42] which form the basis of everyday business behaviour. In this respect, like the Japanese who distinguish between *tsukiai* (personal relations)[43] and *jinmyaku* (literally, 'human arteries'), we need to keep the two categories analytically separate. Connections are a part of a person's network and, although other connections within the network will often be referred to in the initial stages of a meeting between two people brought together by a third party (as in Honda's introductory speech when we visited Inagaki at Asatsu) to put those concerned 'in the picture', so to speak, it is the one-to-one relations thereafter that count. In this respect, a person's network is little more than a framing device for ongoing social interaction.

Put differently, we may say that connections are what people *practise*; networks are how they analyse them *theoretically*.

Notes

1. E.g. Adrian Mayer, 'The significance of quasi-groups in the study of complex societies', in M. Banton (ed.) *The Social Organisation of Complex Societies*, 1966, pp. 97–122; J. Clyde Mitchell, 'The concept and use of social networks', in his edited *Social Networks in Urban Situations*, 1969.
2. E.g. Michael Gerlach, *Alliance Capitalism*, 1992; Ranjay Gulati and Martin Gargiulo, 'Where do interorganizational networks come from?' 1999.
3. Manuel Castells, *Network Society*, 2000 (1996), p. 508.
4. Mark Granovetter, 'Economic actions and social structure: the problem of embcddedness', 1985.
5. Let me quickly make it clear that I have absolutely no objection to quantitative research methods which I believe *should* be used in tandem with qualitative fieldwork and in-depth interviews. The issue here is one of presentation and understanding, and relates to a conundrum that has faced intellectuals from time immemorial: whether to write in precise terms that constitute a jargon for the benefit of the few; or whether to write in equally precise but more widely understood language for the benefit of the many.

6. This domination results, among other things, from the sheer number of departments of anthropology located in hundreds of universities right across the United States. Viewed from the outside, American-based anthropologists appear at times to be rather self-centred in their general lack of interest in and disregard for anthropological traditions and writings elsewhere in the world (like, for example, Brazil, Scandinavia and Japan). This problem was bravely addressed by June Nash and Judith Freidenberg, who ran a panel (whose ensuing discussion was attended by fewer than half a dozen North Americans) entitled 'Institutionalizing the discipline of anthropology in international arenas' at the meeting of the American Anthropological Association in Washington, DC in November 2001.

7. Ulf Hannerz, 'The global ecumene as a network of networks', 1992, p. 39.

8. We can be fairly sure, therefore, that this particular book is destined for a lengthy lying-in-state in the publisher's warehouse – that mausoleum for thoughts, bad writing and the world's rain forests.

9. Richard Wilk, 'When good theories go bad: theory in economic anthropology and consumer research', 2002, p. 240.

10. Mitchell, *Social Networks*.

11. Hannerz, 'The global ecumene', p. 40.

12. David Knoke and James Kublinski, 'Network analysis: basic concepts', in G. Thompson et al. (eds), *Markets, Hierarchies and Networks: The coordination of social life*, 1991, p. 174.

13. M.N. Srinivas and André Beteille, 'Networks in Indian social structure', 1964, pp. 165–6.

14. Ulf Hannerz, *Exploring the City*, 1980, pp. 173–5.

15. Granovetter, 'Economic actions and social structure'.

16. Gerlach, *Alliance Capitalism*, p. 67.

17. John Barnes, 'Networks and political processes', in J. Clyde Mitchell (ed.) *Social Networks in Urban Situations*, 1969; Elizabeth Bott, *Family and Social Network*, 1957.

18. Edward Lorenz, 'Neither friends nor strangers: informal networks of subcontracting in French industry', in G. Thompson et al. (eds) *Markets, Hierarchies and Networks: The coordination of social life*, 1991.

19. Ronald Dore, 'Goodwill and the spirit of market capitalism', 1983.

20. Mayfair Mei-hui Yang, *Gifts, Favors and Banquets: The art of social relationships in China*, 1994; Andrew Kipnis, *Producing Guanxi: Sentiment, self, and subculture in a north China village*, 1997.

21. Cf. Ronald Burt, 'The network entrepreneur', in R. Swedberg (ed.) *Entrepreneurship*, 2000, p. 286.

22. Knoke and Kublinski, 'Network analysis', p. 177.

23. Michael Burawoy, 'Introduction', to Burawoy et al., *Ethnography Unbound:*

Power and Resistance in the Modern metropolis, 1991, p. 2.

24. Knoke and Kublinski, 'Network analysis', pp. 178–9.
25. Hannerz, *Exploring the City*, pp. 177–8; Mayer, 'The significance of quasi-groups'.
26. 'You were lucky,' she smiled across the table of a small restaurant in Mairie d'Issy, Paris, 'I'm probably the only person in the world of women's magazine publishing with a doctorate. Not that it is of any use in my job, but . . .' A very Gallic shrug of her shoulders finished the sentence for me.
27. The 20-minute telephone call, however, provided me with enough snippets of gossip and information to reassure me that he certainly would have been a good informant!
28. Hannerz, *Exploring the City*, p. 179.
29. This corresponds with Stanley Milgram's 'Six Degrees of Separation' theory, whereby, given a completely unknown person's address somewhere in the United States of America, respondents surveyed were generally able to reach that person via no more than six network contacts (in Karsten Bengtsson, 'Netværksteorier blomstrer i USA', 2003).
30. Herminia Ibarra, 'Structural alignments, individual strategies, and managerial action: elements toward a network theory of getting things done', in N. Nohria and R. Eccles (eds), *Networks and Organizations: Structure, form and action*, 1992, p. 170.
31. Ronald Burt, *Structural Holes: The social structure of competition*, 1992a; 'The social structure of competition', in N. Nohria and R. Eccles (eds) *Networks and Organizations: Structure, form and action*, 1992b.
32. Burt, 'The network entrepreneur', p. 293.
33. In her discussion of Chinese *guanxi* networks, Mayfair Yang (*Gifts, Favors and Banquets*, p. 123) arrives at more or less the same – though not so precisely formulated – conclusion: 'It is a rule that the larger one's guanxi network, and the more diverse one's guanxi connections with people of different occupations and positions, the better becomes one's manoeuvrability in society and with officialdom to obtain resources and opportunities.' And see also Burt, 'The social structure of competition', pp. 61–7.
34. Carol Heimer, 'Doing your job *and* helping your friends: universalistic norms about obligations to particular others in networks', in N. Nohria and R. Eccles (eds) *Networks and Organizations: Structure, form and action*, 1992, p. 143.
35. Satō Tomoyasu, *Keibatsu: Nihon no new establishment*, 1981.
36. Karel van Wolferen, *The Enigma of Japanese Power*, 1989.
37. See, for example, the discussion of education cliques in the British government by Anthony Sampson, *Anatomy of Britain Today*, 1965; kinship and affinal relationships among elite families in Britain by T. Lupton and S. Wilson, 'Background and connections of top decision-makers', 1959;

Michael Useem on 'The social organization of the American business elite and participation of corporation directors in the governance of American institutions', 1979; and Adam Kuper, 'Fraternity and endogamy: the house of Rothschild', 2001.

38. What Yano did not add was that the fact that a large number of employees had been to the same university facilitated socialization, problem-solving and decision-making processes within the agency. (cf. Paul DiMaggio and Walter Powell, 'The iron cage revisited: institutional isomorphism and collective rationality in organizational fields', 1983.)

39. Advertising executives, like most managers around the world, prefer oral to written communication. (cf. Henry Mintzberg, *The Nature of Managerial Work*, 1973.)

40. Burt, 'The network entrepreneur', p. 287.

41. Ibarra, 'Structural alignments, individual strategies, and managerial action', p. 166.

42. Rosabeth Moss Kanter and Robert Eccles, 'Making network research relevant to practice', 1992, pp. 521–2.

43. Reiko Atsumi, 'Tsukiai – obligatory personal relationships of Japanese white-collar company employees', 1979.

–6–

Doing Business

Connections work along two sets of double axes in the world of business. At the *individual* level, they operate within and between organizations. At the *organizational* level, formal relations between firms are established as a result of informal individual contacts. We have already seen how connections work, and on occasion don't work, at the individual level. So in this chapter, I will focus a little more on the organizational level and the links between individual connections and corporate alliances of one sort or another. I will also look at the moral and ethical issues underpinning people's reliance on and use of networks and connections.

What do we mean when we say that an 'advertiser', 'client' or 'corporation' is doing business with an 'agency' or other kind of organization? All organizations are constituted by dozens and dozens of different frames of activity involving individual members thereof (from meetings to task forces, by way of product launches, canteen lunches and organizational maps), so that an organization can usefully be described as *a framework of frames*. At the same time, though, organizations are also in important respects themselves social networks which constrain people's actions and are in turn shaped by them. Given that organizations have business relations with other organizations which are also social networks, an organizational field may be seen as being formed out of *a network of networks*.[1] Any comparative analysis of organizations has to take into account both the characteristics of each organization's networks and the overall structure of the field in which it operates.[2]

The fact that an organization is a network of people interacting within and across organizational boundaries means that it is sometimes hard, both for observers and for participants, to distinguish the difference between actions carried out by individuals *qua* individuals, and those performed by individuals as representatives of the organizations to which they belong.

When my son, Alyosha, broke his neck diving as instructed into a shallow (82 cm) diving pool at the North Ono Primary School, the accident was first handled by the headmaster and his assistant at a personal level. Before any inquiry had been made, they offered to fire the teacher in charge. They unofficially informed the Local Education Authority, the school's administrative office located in the Hita City Hall, of what had happened but made no formal report of the accident.

The Local Education Authority consisted of half a dozen personnel, and the man designated to deal with Alyosha's accident, as and when I had the time to make enquiries, quickly distinguished between the 'official' LEA position and his own 'personal' interest as someone who 'lived in the same valley' (regional connection) and who was the uncle of my landlord (kinship connection). It was at the personal level that negotiations between the LEA and myself continued for some time.

When it came to the issue of Alyosha's future welfare and possible compensation, my personal contact explained that 'compensation' was not a word that the LEA could possibly accept since it implied responsibility for the accident, and responsibility had by no means been proven. However, because of the personal connection between us, he added that the LEA would be prepared to pay what it referred to as 'going away money' (*senbetsukin*), customarily given to people going on holidays to help them buy souvenirs to bring back home (and return to the donor). Unlike 'illness money' (*mimaikin*) given to patients in hospital, 'going away money' would not set a precedent (since we were foreigners intending to leave the Ono Valley as soon as Alyosha recovered and local people, by definition, could not do likewise). In other words, it would not make the LEA liable for similar payments in the future to other children injured in school accidents.

During these negotiations, I sought the advice of the managing director of the Kyushu branch of the *Asahi Newspaper*, with whom I was acquainted. Because of his long association through the journalists' club in Tokyo with Japan's politicians, he was quick to suggest that he get in touch with the Diet member for the neighbouring prefecture of Kumamoto (rather than Oita, where we lived). There were two reasons for this tactical move. First, the Diet member concerned was a senior politician to whom the Mayor of Hita owed factional allegiance. Secondly, he had served as Minister of Education in a previous government.

I was thus introduced to the private secretary of the politician concerned. I met him late on a Friday afternoon in his Diet office in Tokyo. He heard me out, asked several questions and told me to leave matters with him. By the time I had returned to the Ono Valley on Sunday afternoon, the Ministry of Education had telephoned the Hita LEA, demanding to know what was going on (they mistakenly thought that Alyosha had been killed), and the LEA had in turn demanded that the North Ono Primary School submit a formal report of the accident which was written and submitted on the Saturday – at least two months after the accident itself. The report was then sent from the LEA to the Ministry of Education, and institutional links were thereby sealed. From that point on, it was Brian versus the full opaqueness of a bureaucratic system – an unequal struggle between individual and organizations which could only be concluded in court.

At other times, the connecting lines between individuals and the organizations they represent are clear to themselves, but not necessarily to others.

When I was persuaded to hold my own one-man pottery exhibition in a Fukuoka department store, a question that quickly arose was who would act as my official 'sponsor'. It was customary for art exhibitions at the time to be backed by national newspapers, like the *Asahi* and *Mainichi*, since they gained cultural capital from being seen to support activities that brought 'art to the people'. Eisuke Minamoto, the dealer organizing the exhibition, therefore approached an acquaintance in the *Mainichi Newspaper* to ask for his support. For reasons that will become clear in the following chapter, the latter felt that I might be better served by being sponsored by a cultural organization of some kind, rather than his newspaper. He therefore suggested the Anglo-Japanese Cultural Association, whose chairman he knew and introduced me to. I told the chairman (an academic) and two colleagues about the 'philosophy' underpinning my pottery and they quickly agreed that their association should act as official sponsor of my one-man show. Another contact, this time my own, was the director of the British Council in Tokyo who also agreed that the exhibition could be officially backed by the British Council. Neither of these institutional forms of support would have been possible without these personal connections which themselves, of course, were not made public to those visiting my show. It was the institutional, not personal, support that counted.

Connections thus involve a continuous movement back and forth between individuals and organizations. It is their very opaqueness that defies analysis.

An account executive may be able to massage his connection with an advertising or product manager, so that the latter agrees to invite his agency to participate in a competitive presentation. The account team may then strive to produce impressive market analysis and eye-catching creative work in the presentation itself – advertising's quintessential theatrical frame – to win the account. But, however impressed the client's senior management decision-makers may be by the presentation, they will almost always tell the newly hired agency to go back to the drawing board and create a new campaign, based on additional marketing information and corporate strategy that, as a matter of principle, they have hitherto withheld. That is how power relations between advertiser and agency are enacted in the field of advertising as a whole.

So account executive and advertising manager find themselves back together in almost daily contact, but this time their discussions and negotiations have been formally ratified by the advertiser's decision to hire the agency. The personal connection is now backed up by institutional authority.

Connecting Organizations

So personal connections intermesh with, reinforce and are reinforced by the institutional frame or field in which each participant operates. But how are they transformed into organizational alliances? What do we mean when we say that firms form intercorporate relationships and are members of 'alliance structures' of one sort or another? One answer is provided for us. Intercorporate alliances are 'institutionalized relationships among firms based on localized networks of dense transactions, a stable framework for exchange, and patterns of periodic collective action.'[3] The tendencies that define these *keiretsu* or corporate business networks are affiliational ties, long-term relationships, multiplexity, extended networks and symbolic signification.[4] But why were these particular affiliations chosen? Whose extended networks are operating in a business alliance? What role does individual agency play in organizational structure?

One obvious link between individuals and organizations here is that of inter-locking directorships. Since important people tend to be thought of as representa-tives of an organization, ties with directors and people in power tend to be seen as ties to the organizations that they work for.[5] Certainly, there is a link between indi-vidual authority and organizational activity. The activities of the various presi-dents' councils (*shachō-kai*) that regularly bring together the CEOs of corporate business networks in Japan support such a view, since they facilitate intra-network trade and initiatives. In Japan, too, large corporations often place senior managers who have reached or are nearing retirement age as directors in affiliated and sub-contracting companies, to facilitate the maintenance of a vertical linkage between main and satellite firms.[6] But still we do not know how or why particular individ-uals are appointed, nor what the long-term effects of their appointments may be. Nor do we know in detail how these vertical firm linkages came into being in the first place. Rather, as with network analysis in general, analysis takes place at an external 'objective' level. What we need, therefore – and only qualitative fieldwork can provide this – is a study of the processes of strategic exchanges that enable organizational alliances.

Some scholars have argued that organizational networks are formed because of particular external needs that a firm cannot meet from within: the acquisition of resources, for instance, or the development of technology.[7] Thus ties are created with another organization that has the resources or technology required to satisfy that need. But there is uncertainty here in the managerial domain. How is a firm to choose its partner in the first place? What makes its Board of Directors opt for one rather than another organization? How does it get the necessary information about the potential partner's competences and capabilities to allay the uncertainty that necessarily surrounds such an alliance decision? After all, it is a partnership that is being entered into – one in which each party (like individual participants in a network) gives something in exchange for something else. Both needs and bene-fits must be accurately assessed and weighed.

And then a second set of questions arises. Is the proposed partner reliable? And how does one know? On what basis can one judge an *organization* to be trust-worthy? Here there is uncertainty in the moral domain. Ranjay Gulati and Martin Gargiulo suggest that decision-makers in companies 'rely on past partnerships to guide their future alliance decisions'.[8] Every new tie created contributes to the history of a network as a whole and enhances its overall potential. But *how* is that tie formalized, and *who* decides that it should be so, and on what *grounds*? Gra-novetter remarks on 'the widespread preference for transacting with individuals of known reputation', and adds that having 'trusted informants' is what matters.[9] In

Japan, as we have by now come to realize, personal relationships among individuals are what count in everyday interaction, and those between key participants play a crucial role in generating trust between organizations as a whole.[10] In general, it seems that, beneath the formal arrangements linking two or more corporations, there are all kinds of interpersonal relations at work and that it is via these that information is actively exchanged and the necessary trust built up to encourage more cooperation. In this respect, there is a 'relational embeddedness' in an organization's economic behaviour.[11]

But how do the frames and networks involving individual employees in organizations get transformed into alliances between *organizations*? What is the relation between networks built on particularistic ties and organizations aiming to achieve universalistic ends?[12]

In the field of advertising, accounts are the sums of money distributed, primarily by corporations, to advertising agencies which are usually asked to create appropriate campaigns (appropriate in terms of both product and corporate branding), for which they must then find suitable media outlets with appropriate target audiences. But how and why is an advertising agency awarded an account? On the surface, at least, an advertiser chooses an agency because of the work that it is currently doing and because it feels that it, rather than any other agency, appears best suited to its advertising needs. This is economic rationality as it ought to be. In actual fact, however, rather different criteria are usually brought to bear.

Probably the most important factor contributing to an advertising agency's winning or losing an account is the personal relationship developed between an account executive (AE) and his opposite number (advertising, sales, product or brand manager – let us call him Tanaka) in the client company. Indeed, it is this relationship which first *allows* an agency to participate in the kind of competitive presentation that I described in the previous chapter. Now, if no business connection exists between an agency and a potential advertising client, we may wonder how an account executive goes about creating a personal relationship with someone whose existence he may be aware of, but whom personally he does not know at all. One way, of course, is to get out and knock on doors.[13] Another is to tap into already existing networks and try to find a route through contacts to the person he wants to meet. This can be particularly effective if the targeted company is in some way allied – through relations of production, supply, distribution or finance – to one with which the agency is already doing business (something that is fairly common in a country which places great value on 'alliance' or 'welfare'[14] capitalism). A phone call to the account executive in charge of the account can lead to an introduction to the related company's representative who can then be persuaded to effect the necessary introduction to someone in the targeted company, who with luck will then arrange a meeting with the appropriate colleague and leave matters to develop from there.

Our AE's contacts may, however, come up short, especially if – like Asatsu – an agency is doing its best to remain independent, and/or when he needs to approach a totally unknown company. In the latter instance he may well ask the help of senior colleagues in the agency and see if they cannot use their connections to help him. Alternatively, and probably more likely, he will get in touch with people in newspaper, publishing or broadcasting companies, with whom he has come into contact during the course of his work in previous campaigns, and these contacts can probably help him get in touch with Tanaka.

And then the courtship begins. However eloquent, however persuasive, however smart and impressive the AE may be, Tanaka is never going to hand over his company's business to a virtual unknown. So the account executive begins the long, hard grind of showing the seriousness and diligence of his agency, on the one hand and, on the other, of impressing Tanaka with his personal integrity and so earning the latter's trust. In the Japanese advertising industry, the best way to do this – it is generally agreed – is to be assiduous in one's attentions. So the AE concerned will find all sorts of excuses to visit his would-be client, by casually dropping into his office with some privately prepared marketing data one week, a new product idea another, or tickets for an event sponsored by the agency.[15] Sometimes Tanaka will not be there; at other times he will be busy; but occasionally he will talk to the AE, exchanging, perhaps, a bit of gossip here, rumours about competitors' activities there, and inevitably – however buoyant things may appear to be – pessimistic ruminations on the future state of the Japanese economy.

These visits to Tanaka's office will be supplemented from time to time by the AE's invitations to 'have a drink' and, as we can already guess from previous examples in this book, the first drink will lead to a second, which will itself encourage a third. Tongues will be loosened on both sides and more information exchanged (and stored well in their respective memories until the next day, however intoxicating the effect of the liquor at the time). Who knows, then, how quickly or how slowly the relationship will develop.[16] Almost certainly, Tanaka will test the account executive in some way or other – calling him on one of his claims to be able to do something if required, perhaps, or letting loose a nugget of apparently confidential information to see what happens – and if the AE passes this test, then mutual trust will probably be established and the road opened, if but gradually, to Tanaka asking the account executive to do a small job – often unrelated to advertising per se – for his company. And if the outcome of this proves satisfactory, and if it so happens that Tanaka is not happy with the currently retained advertising agency (which information probably formed the very basis for the AE's decision to cultivate him in the first place), then, finally, our tenacious adman may get asked if his agency might be willing to participate in a competitive presentation (with no promises of its being awarded the account, he is firmly led to understand).

It is at this point that the development of informal contacts between two persons employed in different organizations reaches a new level.[17] Until now, we have been discussing two people, one *representing* a major corporation, the other an advertising agency. The invitation to take part in a competitive presentation, however, brings the two organizations *as organizations* into contact with each other. Given the strong possibility of the agency's being asked to take on a new client's account, the AE at this point – if not before – calls in his senior manager for back-up support. And so Yano, as executive director in charge of the Account Services Office, will be introduced to the – let us call him advertising – manager and will in the process do his utmost to persuade Tanaka of *his* reliability and the reliability of his agency. This initial contact may well be reciprocated by the advertising manager introducing to Yano the senior manager to whom *he* reports, and, if it clearly looks as if the agency is going to win the account (or at least the moment after it has done so), these two men will arrange for the CEOs of each company to get together over a meal so that they, too, can get to know each other and get a feel for the other's organization by asking various pertinent questions relating to current business activities, future plans and so on. Thus, links between the two organizations – one awarding, the other receiving an advertising account – are primarily formed by two individuals who then reinforce their personal contact by creating further connections between structurally equivalent personnel located in higher positions in their respective corporate hierarchies. As Granovetter remarks, 'it is not only at top levels that firms are connected by networks of personal relations, but at all levels where transactions must take place.'[18]

> Through its involvement in what are known as 'below-the-line' activities – that is to say promotion and sales outside space and time buying in the four main media of television, newspapers, magazines and radio – an advertising agency is from time to time able to establish perfect frames in which its senior management may interact with the senior management of a client company. For example, the co-ordination by Asatsu of an American football competition sponsored by Asahi Beer provided it with an annual opportunity for 'CEO play' (*shachō play*) between the two organizations. Over a period of two to three hours, while paying more or less attention to the game going on below them, senior staff could relax in the luxurious surroundings of a private box furnished with appropriate refreshments, and discuss the latest gossip, business, politics, the economy, and the meaning of life. Is this, perhaps, the back-stage reason why corporations generally are so eager to sponsor sporting events?

This descriptive detail shows how organizations form alliances, even inter-organizational networks, on the basis of interpersonal contacts and networks. In the Japanese advertising industry, at least, a relation between two companies usually starts out as a relation between individual members thereof and *not* between the institutions concerned. If we ignore these one-on-one contacts between differently located personnel in the organizations concerned and talk only in terms of 'Apple has invested $2.5 million in Adobe Systems', or 'Daimler Benz has entered into a technology development agreement with Mitsubishi', then we are misrecognizing what is actually driving organizational alliances.[19] In the example above, the first line is thrown between the AE and Tanaka, but to secure the agency ship to the client dock other lines must be secured – between Yano and Tanaka, between Yano and Tanaka's superior, between Inagaki and Tanaka's CEO. Each of these lines creates communication and exchanges of information at different levels of the organizational hierarchies, and each is then extended through those managerial links to involve others within each organization. But these personal lines of communication are fragile; they can only take so much tension before they snap. Which is why those concerned do their utmost to reinforce them by first creating, then maintaining other personal contacts. Thus, if one line should for some reason be broken, the others, it is hoped, will be strong enough to keep the ship moored to dock and the relationship afloat.

There are two ready ways in which those lines may suddenly snap. The first is a failure of some sort in the personal relationship between the two people most closely involved in the business at hand (in the case above, the AE and Tanaka). This may result from something said in the heat of a moment, or from some other kind of *faux pas*.

One senior account executive in Asatsu, who was in charge of an extremely prestigious 'blue chip' account, seduced by formal authority rather than by informal decision-making power, made the tactical error of switching his attention to the Japanese vice-president of his client – a major European car manufacturer – from the non-Japanese sales manager who was, strictly speaking, the AE's opposite number. The ad man clearly thought he was cultivating the real decision-maker in the local office of the car manufacturer, but failed to take into consideration the fact that the German sales manager had a direct line back to his headquarters in central Europe and was thus quickly able to persuade his superiors that Asatsu was not performing well enough. As a result, headquarters demanded a competitive presentation and, although a lot of energy was devoted to repairing the broken line of communication, the agency lost the account.[20]

The second, and more common, way a line between two organizations snaps happens when the contact in the client company is suddenly promoted or transferred[21] and is replaced by a new advertising manager who proves far less amenable to the AE's advances, since he has his own prior-existing network of contacts that lead him to favour the account executive of a rival agency. It is this potential rupture of one-to-one relations that threatens *every* account. In Japan, where companies employ generalists who may well be transferred to a new job in the spring of every year, the possibility of such ruptures is particularly acute. For this and other reasons (connected with seasonal media advertising and sponsorship), a lot of senior executives in the agency tend to go around with ash-grey faces (*aoi kao*) in the month or two leading up to the transfer season.

There is, however, an interesting sociological side-effect of all this social networking. The very existence of these formalizing personal contacts and related networks to some extent actually *drives* the circulation of accounts and thus the different and shifting alliances which advertising agencies and their clients enter.[22] Keeping up connections, making sure they are properly 'lubricated', demands a lot of time, energy and goodwill on both sides. It brings with it, though, certain expectations – about acceptable behaviour, about what a partner can or will or should do. And if someone fails to meet these expectations, lines of communication can be, and often are, irretrievably broken. There is always someone else, the injured party feels, who can better fill the gap between expectation and practice. Thus an agency might, through little obvious fault of its own, lose clients in the automobile and soft drinks industries, but gain, through little objective merit of its own, new clients in textiles and computers. In other words, the unpredictability of personal contacts gives rise to unpredicted organizational alliances which themselves are in the long run unpredictable.

But this in itself is no bad thing. With every new alliance with a client, an agency gains new market information, learns new strategies, and generally increases its overall knowledge of how the economy works and thus of how its client might take advantage of a situation. In all of this, personal contacts create, sustain and occasionally destroy organizational alliances.

Moral Dimensions

Because business relations are a form of economic behaviour which is inevitably intertwined with and embedded in more general ongoing systems of social relations, certain 'moral' issues come to the fore. In particular, businessmen and women worry about the self-interest of their connections being transformed into 'opportunism', on the one hand, and about how themselves to avoid being so accused as they create, recognize and sustain 'trust', on the other.

Connections have the ever-present potential to cause network members unforeseen difficulties in their ethical choices. One afternoon, when Inoshige and I were quietly making pots, two men stepped into his workshop, introduced themselves and – after a few bright comments on the weather, when Inoshige expected next to fire his kiln and so on – embarked on explaining the reason for their being there on a cold, late-autumn day. Would Inoshige perhaps be good enough to produce for them a couple of hundred ash-glazed badgers? There was an important 'do' somewhere over in Oita and the gentlemen wished to present all guests with a gift of Onta pottery.

Inoshige demurred. Politely reminding his visitors that Onta wares were primarily functional and that they had been designated one of Oita Prefecture's Traditional Cultural Properties, he said that making badgers was not part of that tradition. One of the visitors – himself somewhat badger-like in appearance – persisted. Inoshige felt himself obliged to change tack. He had never made any badgers and didn't really know how to do so. Easy, came the reply. A sample would be brought for him to copy. Inoshige changed tack again, pointing out that technically it would be impossible to make any badger with the kind of clay potters used in Sarayama. The clay would crack, either during drying and certainly when fired. In that case, perhaps if the badgers were made elsewhere, Inoshige could glaze and fire them in his kiln and call them Onta ware? But they wouldn't be Onta ware, because they weren't made in Sarayama. Yes, but he could stamp them to make it look as if they were, indeed, badgers from Onta. Inoshige agreed that he *could*, but added that he never stamped any of his pots and that, anyway, he had mislaid his seal.

And so it went on. Inoshige would not be moved and eventually the two men left. When I asked who the visitors had been, he replied that one (with the badger-like face) was a dealer. The other – how the two men were connected he didn't know – was a member of the Oita Prefecture's Committee for the Protection of Traditional Cultural Properties.

In Japan, as elsewhere,[23] trust is an extremely component in interpersonal networking. It will be recalled that this was one important, if implicit, thread woven into Honda's introductory speech when we met with Inagaki to ask for permission to carry out fieldwork in Asatsu. Honda's trust in me was reciprocated by Inagaki who never asked me to sign any confidentiality agreement in relation to what I was to learn or had learned about his agency during the course of my participant observation there. Even now, I am from time to time supplied with marketing information that is clearly 'marked '*Confidential*' and those concerned have never questioned the uses to which it might be put.

On the negative side, it will also be remembered that one of the things Rikizō said when he got at me during the Akiyasama gathering was:

How can we *trust* you? You're a foreigner. You *say* you're doing research. You *say* you know Bernard Leach. You *say* you've got a Japanese wife and children living near Nagoya. But how do we know if that's all true or not. *You* can see us here in Sarayama. You can see our houses, our families, the way we work. You can ask your questions, get your answers, and form opinions about us. But *we*'ve got nothing at all on you. Your life's an empty space, so far as *we*'re concerned.

Trust matters. For the most part, it is built up along a line of connections – which is why Inoshige could come to my rescue at that point and say, as someone who had introduced me to the other potters, that *he* had no evidence that I wasn't telling the truth. He indirectly asserted that his connections were reliable and therefore that I myself was also be trusted.

I was sitting with an editor of an international fashion magazine in Hong Kong, and found myself asking her about the difficult relationship between editorial and advertising matter. Noticing a slight hesitation on her part to open up on the subject, I tried to allay her fears by promising that whatever she said would be reported anonymously. I was a serious scholar trying to gain a clear and unbiased understanding of the field of women's fashion magazines.

'Don't worry,' she smiled, patting me on the forearm, 'Pamela introduced you to me. I trust you.'

But what *is* trust? It is more, surely, than believing that someone is not going to take advantage of you. In Japan, at least, it means knowing when and how best to help another, and knowing, too, when and how best to return assistance or favours rendered by the other. In other words, people know that life is exchange, and that norms of reciprocity and obligation will more or less ensure that what I give now I will be able to take back later on, albeit in different form, as the opportunity arises.

In the agency, much talk was devoted to the concept of the 'Asatsu man'. It was the Asatsu man, after all, who had – in the eyes of an older generation of employees, at least – contributed markedly to the agency's success over the years. But what *was* an Asatsu man? For a start, he was 'honest' (*shōjiki*). That was the first prerequisite. He wouldn't cheat a client, whatever happened. And then he was 'meek' (*sunao*) – meaning that he wasn't the kind of businessman who would manipulate you into doing something you didn't want to do. He should be 'broad minded' (*kokoro ga ōkii*), too, always open to new ideas and suggestions that would help clients (and thus the agency) expand their business. And, of course, he had to know when to pay back dues (*giri-gatai*). That was an Asatsu man, and that was what differentiated him from people employed in other advertising agencies both in Japan and around the world.

Such ideals – and they *were* only ideals, even though, in fact, much practised – are not sufficient in themselves to guarantee trustworthy behaviour, of course. Certain paradoxes can arise. The very existence of trust between two people, for example, actually encourages the opportunity for wrongdoing of some kind – as virtually every major business and political scandal, from Lockheed to Recruit in Japan and from Watergate to Enron in the USA, reminds us. Most forms of force and fraud, too, can only be carried out by teams of people who maintain some level of internal trust which, if broken, can have painful consequences (witness gangland 'disappearances').[24]

Still, what was – and still is – good for Asatsu is not necessarily good for other companies, although in Japan it would seem that there is in fact quite a close parallel between generalized morality and particular practices. Why else would it be possible to distinguish the Japanese (and, let us quickly add, German) from the Anglo-American form of doing business and call it 'welfare' capitalism? But is there not a danger here in relapsing, as the Japanese themselves tend to do, into cultural explanations of behaviour that is primarily economic?

Just how much social relations affect behaviour and institutions has been the subject of much debate in anthropology, sociology and economics.[25] At one extreme it is assumed that economic behaviour is rational, self-interested and only minimally affected by social relations (the economists' view). At the other it is argued that social relations can in no way be construed as independent from economic behaviour and associated institutions which are, on the contrary, substantially 'embedded' in them (the so-called 'substantivist' school of economic anthropology).[26]

An additional issue raised in this debate has been concerned with historical development. A majority of anthropologists and sociologists (as well as historians and political scientists) have taken the line that social relations strongly affected economic behaviour and institutions in pre-market economies, but that with modernization they have ceased to do so. As a result, economic transactions in modern markets are no longer influenced by kinship, residence and other social obligations, and the economies themselves can be classified as 'autonomous'. For their part, economists have mostly rejected this interpretation of economic development and assert that there has been little, if any, change in the way in which economic behaviour and associated institutions are, or are not, embedded in social relations of the kind that we have been discussing in this book.

The second half of this disagreement need not concern us here, since we are dealing, in Japan, with an extremely modern economy. The issue of 'embeddedness', however, lies at the heart of the last two chapters, where I have been at pains to show how social networks and personal connections affect economic behaviour and results in various ways. This is not in doubt. What is in doubt, though, is how *much* they do so (and the spectre of measuring the seemingly immeasurable and reducing them to obscure tables once more emerges), and Granovetter reminds us that we should be careful not to exaggerate the extent of people's socialization in economic transactions.[27]

This can be difficult, especially for scholars writing about societies whose historical and cultural development appears so different from our own. As a result, and it is a problem that continues to haunt discussions of social relations in East and Southeast Asia, cultural differences are often used as a mode of 'explanation' for what may well be no more than run-of-the-mill forms of economic behaviour.

Mayfair Yang, for example, argues that the practice of Chinese *guanxi* relations is 'different from the rationalized and impersonal exchange relations of capitalism',[28] while Reiko Atsumi says that personal relationships (*tsukiai*) in Japan represent 'a uniquely Japanese cultural pattern'.[29] Neither of these statements is based on right assumptions. Not only do Chinese *guanxi* relations operate in a socialist-capitalist system; exchange relations in 'purer' forms of free-market capitalism are *not* necessarily rationalized or impersonal. Moreover, the Japanese are *not* the only people in the world to develop 'obligatory' personal relations (as Yang's discussion of *guanxi* clearly illustrates, and as we have ourselves noted earlier when mentioning 'old-boy networks').

As Michael Gerlach points out in his study of the *keiretsu* system, Japanese corporations' alliance structures are *not* 'the inevitable consequence of distinctive, unchanging, and widely accepted cultural values'.[30] Similar organizational networks exist elsewhere in the world, not because of cultural norms, but because they have specific business functions that make them a viable social form.[31]

In illustration of this, let me briefly discuss one example of similar relations between business functions and economic behaviour in France and Japan. In an article discussing the introduction of new technology in small and medium-sized engineering firms in France, Edward Lorenz shows how large firms created 'partnerships' based on 'loyalty', 'mutual trust' and a 'moral contract' with smaller firms to whom they started to subcontract both basic (turning, milling and drilling) and more specialized (gear grinding and heat treatment) operations that they had hitherto carried out in-house. Pertinent issues raised by Lorenz include opportunism, partnership and trust.[32]

First, firms operate on the principle of mutual trust. As a result, they do not write contracts between contracting and sub-contracting firms, so that if a dispute arises it is settled by means of ongoing discussions rather than in court. Precisely because trust is not contractually binding, however, the problem of opportunism arises. In order to avoid being taken advantage of, a large firm solicits tenders from at least three subcontractors to ensure that production costs are not distorted in any way. It also splits its orders between two – and preferably more than two – subcontractors, so that if it has difficulties with one, it can switch to the other(s). Moreover, if its own business suffers a recession, the fact that it has only given orders equivalent to 10 to 15 per cent of the subcontractor's total sales prevents the latter from being financially crippled by the contracting firm's problems.

To know whether a subcontractor is or is not trustworthy, a firm relies initially on reputation, but only assigns short-term contracts for a year or two until the subcontractor has proven itself. Thereafter, as part of its promotion of the idea of partnership, a large firm will make every effort to guarantee a particular level of work, providing that the subcontractor keeps improving its performance. It will also not dump a subcontractor just because one of its competitors comes up with a better price or quality, but will give its current partner time to improve to the new standard. In short:

> Partnership entails a long-term commitment and reflects a condition of mutual dependency where both client and subcontractor are in a position to influence the other by their behaviour. Partnership is a set of normative rules, determining what behaviour is permissible and what constitutes a violation of trust. The rules are designed to facilitate exchange in a situation otherwise open to exploitation.[33]

Those who have spent the best part of their careers studying things Japanese might be excused for imagining that the above paragraph was written about Japanese, not French, business behaviour. Other comments – about contracts and dispute resolution, for example – will also have rung true. But what I find particularly interesting about Lorenz's discussion is the direct parallels in behaviour between clients and subcontractors in the French engineering industry and clients and agencies in the Japanese advertising industry. For example, first, Japanese advertisers also try to avoid opportunism on the part of an advertising agency by obliging a number of agencies (between two and as many as six, but generally three) to participate in a competitive presentation. This is partially to see what kind of work each agency is capable of, but also partially to ensure that the media plan that it presents (and it is the media plan that reveals how the client's money is to be spent) is realistic and within the client's advertising budget. The client will not dump its current agency, even though it may be performing below par (the reason for calling for the presentation in the first place), but allow it to participate. If it manages to satisfy its client that it really *can* do the job properly, this agency may well retain the account.

Secondly, depending on their size, Japanese advertisers, like large French engineering firms, split their accounts between at least two, and generally half a dozen, agencies as a way of 'hedging their bets'. If one agency fails to produce the goods, then the client has others to fall back on. At the same time, though, precisely because it is only allocating a relatively small proportion of its total advertising budget to any single agency, a client knows that that agency will not suffer too much in overall terms if it has suddenly to reduce its advertising appropriation because of a recession or some other reason. The fact that large Japanese advertising agencies take on hundreds and hundreds of comparatively small accounts (as compared with the few dozen lodged with an American or European agency) means that they are not at financial risk when, for one reason or another, they lose an account.

A third point, not mentioned by Lorenz, is that, by dividing the work that they ask French subcontractors and Japanese agencies to carry out on their behalves, clients in both countries maintain firm control by means of a 'divide-and-rule' mechanism. In the Japanese advertising industry, this encourages agencies to liaise with media organizations since the latter have overall knowledge of a client's total advertising strategy through all the separate accounts handled by different agencies, but often placed finally in the same media.

Finally, every new advertiser – and, indeed, every newly established advertising agency – has to satisfy the media organization with which it is placing its advertising that it can pay the rates demanded and is, as a result, (financially) trustworthy. This means that media organizations will, initially, demand payment up front when an advertising order is placed. Only when this is properly managed a few times will they relax conditions and ask for payment when the advertising in question appears in print or broadcast form. And only after an advertiser has proven itself time and time again and trust has been firmly established, will media organizations accept payment in arrears (although whether it is three or six months will, again, depend on the corporate social status of the advertiser *and* of the agency representing its interests, plus how often the client advertises and how much it spends with a particular media organization).

In all of this, it is social connections and relational networks that generate mutual trust and discourage cheating in any way (what sociologists and economists like to call 'malfeasance') – whether you are trying to strike a million dollar deal or merely looking for a plumber to mend your drains. As Mark Granovetter nicely summarizes it:

> Better than the statement that someone is known to be reliable is information from a trusted informant that he has dealt with that individual and found him so. Even better is information from one's own past dealings with that person.[34]

Trust, then, is efficient. You save yourself a lot of time and trouble by being able to rely on someone's word.[35] Through exchanges of information and the gradual development of mutual understanding, personal connections allow each party in a business deal to adapt to economic contingencies.[36] Along with organizational alliances, they rely on the notion of reciprocity, on what the Japanese like to call in English 'give-and-take', since giving, receiving and reciprocating are the essence of social interaction.[37] Underpinning the kind of social relations that we have been looking at in this chapter, therefore, are sets of moral values that may include virtually everything from generosity to calculated self-interest, trust to opportunism, and obligation to egoism. Personal connections involve 'ethics, tactics and etiquette'.[38] The exact content of these ethics, the tactics adopted, and the etiquette adhered to, may differ from one situation to the next, as well as from one society to another, but it is the specific practices of this 'generalized morality' that should make us take extremely seriously the social relations embedded in our economic transactions.

Notes

1. Ulf Hannerz (in *Exploring the City*, 1980, p. 201) uses the phrase 'network of networks' to describe the constitution of 'the city as a social order'.
2. Nitin Nohria, 'Is a network perspective a useful way of studying organizations?' in N. Nitin and R. Eccles (eds) *Networks and Organizations*, 1992, pp. 4–8.
3. Michael Gerlach, *Alliance Capitalism*, 1992, p. 3.
4. Gerlach, *Alliance Capitalism*, p. 4.
5. Carol Heimer, 'Doing your job *and* helping your friends', in N. Nitin and R. Eccles (eds) *Networks and Organizations*, 1992, p. 156.
6. Michael Gerlach and James Lincoln, 'The organization of business networks in the United States and Japan', 1992, p. 498.

7. Ronald Burt, *Corporate Profits and Cooptation: Networks of market constraints and directorate ties in the American economy*, 1983.
8. Ranjay Gulati and Martin Gargiulo, 'Where do interorganizational networks come from?' 1999, pp. 1444–5.
9. Mark Granovetter, 'Economic action and social structure', 1985, p. 490.
10. James Lincoln, Michael Gerlach and C. Ahmadjian, 'Keiretsu networks and corporate performance in Japan', 1996.
11. Gulati and Gargiulo, 'Where do interorganizational networks come from?' pp. 1445–6.
12. Heimer, 'Doing your job *and* helping your friends', pp. 143–4.
13. Walter Powell, *Getting Into Print*, 1986, p. 75.
14. Ronald Dore, *Stock Market Capitalism: Welfare Capitalism – Japan and Germany versus the Anglo-Saxons*, 2000.
15. He may even, on the pretext of 'being in the neighbourhood', deliver some women's magazines to Mrs Tanaka at their home.
16. Eight years was one of the longest periods of courtship mentioned in Asatsu's corporate story-telling.
17. As Powell observes (*Getting Into Print*, p. 76), 'Every social relationship is constrained and shaped by its own history.'
18. Granovetter, 'Economic action and social structure', p. 496.
19. As Howard Becker (*Writing for Social Scientists*, 1986) puts it, 'If you leave those actors out, you mistake the theory, both in letter and in spirit.' See also Tony Watson, *In Search of Management*, 2001, p. 28.
20. Brian Moeran, 'A tournament of value', 1993.
21. In Europe and the United States, this kind of instability arises more from people changing jobs and moving from one corporation to another. However, job mobility also enables new alliances along the lines described below for the advertising industry.
22. As we shall later see, the other force behind the circulation of accounts is what is known as the split-account system. See also Brian Moeran, 'The split account system and Japan's advertising industry', 2000.
23. Powell, *Getting Into Print*, pp. 50–1.
24. Granovetter, 'Economic action and social structure', p. 492.
25. The discussion and argument presented in the next few paragraphs are in large part based on Granovetter, 'Economic actions and social structure', pp. 481–3.
26. See Richard Wilk, *Economies and Cultures: Foundations of economic anthropology*, 1996, pp. 3–13, for a discussion of the differences between 'substantive' and 'formalist' schools in anthropology.
27. Granovetter, 'Economic actions and social structure', p. 483, in which he cites Dennis Wrong, 'The oversocialized conception of man in modern sociology', 1961, pp. 188–9.

28. Mayfair Yang, *Gifts, Favors and Banquets*, 1994, p. 145.
29. Reiko Atsumi, 'Tsukiai', 1979, p. 69.
30. Gerlach, *Alliance Capitalism*, p. 25.
31. Ibid., pp. 32–6.
32. Lorenz, 'Neither friends nor strangers', 1991.
33. Ibid., pp. 189–90.
34. Granovetter, 'Economic actions and social structure', p. 490.
35. Kenneth Arrow, *The Limits of Organization*, 1974, p. 23.
36. Lorenz, 'Neither friends nor strangers', p. 191.
37. Jacques Godbout, *The World of the Gift*, 1988.
38. Yang, *Gifts, Favors and Banquets*, p. 109.

Part III
Fields

Exhibition of Virtue

It was another hot and humid afternoon. The monsoon rainy season had begun. People had changed to their summer clothes – lightweight suits, pastel-coloured sleeveless dresses, short-sleeved shirts and blouses, cotton underwear. A late-June afternoon in Fukuoka and it wouldn't be comfortably cool again until the first typhoons in early September.

I had spent another frustrating day pursuing the cause of fieldwork. An early start from our house in the Ono Valley had made no appreciable difference to the level of traffic on the long main road into the city, controlled by a 40-kilometre an-hour-speed limit, a double yellow line to prevent overtaking, and an endless array of traffic lights. Two hours to drive 50-something kilometres was not my idea of fun. Once in Fukuoka, I had gone through the usual difficulty of finding some-where to park and then presented myself at 10 o'clock sharp for my first interview of the day.

My interviewee was pleasant enough – a man in charge of a local department store's Arts and Culture Department and smelling faintly of *Brut* or some such after-shave that I had come to expect from previous such interviews. The answers he gave to my questions, too, were what I had come to expect after almost three months of research on the world of Japanese ceramic art. Why did department stores hold art exhibitions? To give aspiring artists the opportunity to present their work. What was in it for the stores? Well, there was very little *commercial* benefit, of course. It might seem strange to a foreigner who came from the cradle of culture (the reference was to Europe), but the Japanese people yearned after culture and the store helped satisfy this yearning. Why not use the space to sell bargain under-wear or furniture or fans? A slightly embarrassed smile as my interviewee admitted that in some stores – not *his*, of course – art 'museums' were overnight transformed into bargain sales areas. But, honestly, the reason *his* department store exhibited art was that it wished to return 'culture' to the customers who patronized it and spent their money there. This was his store's way of saying 'thank you' to its customers. It was giving back in cultural form what it had received in material – that is, financial – form. This was part of the 'give-and-take' that characterized Japanese society. End of story. End of another unsatisfactory interview.

It was a nice idea, this culture-for-commerce exchange. It had a good old Con-fucian ring to it, and revealed nicely the importance of reciprocity in the everyday lives of institutions as well as of ordinary people. But since I had already heard this same answer given to the same question posed to various Art and Culture Department representatives working in other department stores in Fukuoka, as well as in Kita Kyushu, Kumamoto, Osaka and Tokyo, I was frustrated with my seeming lack of progress. Was this all there was to the art exhibition world? Department stores 'nurtured' artists and craftsmen by providing them with space to show their work to a general public which was being given culture in exchange for the money it spent there (sometimes on this very artwork)? The sheer parrot-like repetition of this explanation was beginning to get to me. Either I was asking the wrong questions, or my interviewees were lying or, at least, flannelling over the truth. Because truth, surely, it was not.

I had tried changing tack in my questions, but sooner or later we would end up back at the point at which I'd begun my fieldwork and I found myself obliged to ask about Japanese department stores' role in promoting art and culture.[1] My research question was very simple. How did a potter like Shōji Hamada, close friend of Bernard Leach and doyen of the Japanese folk-art movement, manage to be designated by the Ministry of Cultural Affairs as a holder of an important intangible cultural property (*jūyō mukei bunkazai*)? More popularly known as a 'national treasure', this appointment was one of the two highest honours of artistic achievement in the land. The answer turned out – like most things once you start enquiring into them in some depth – to be somewhat complex. But one obvious route, and this was something I had realized from Bernard's own reminiscences about Japan, was by exhibiting one's work. Just *where* Japanese potters (and, indeed, other artists and craftsmen) chose to exhibit, however, came as a slight surprise, since their favoured venue was a department store. It was only when they had become *very* famous or dead (ideally both) that potters' work would or could be exhibited in museums.

So there I was, seemingly endlessly doing the rounds of department stores, looking at the works that they displayed every week in their art galleries and, in Tokyo, even the occasional art museum. These visits had helped give me an overall view of what was going on in the world of Japanese ceramics, and I had begun to get a very general picture of the Who's Who of potters in Japan. (There were books to help, though entries were for the most part paid for by individuals wishing to market their names.) Still, apart from one or two slightly inconclusive initial talks with pottery critics in Tokyo and Osaka, that was as far as I had got. In my interviews with department store representatives, I'd come up against a bland brick wall of what I was sure were platitudes and prevarications. In a way, I felt rather like Alice who, having followed the White Rabbit down a hole, opens a little door in an empty hall and glimpses at the end of a small passage not much larger than a rat-hole 'the loveliest garden you ever saw'. The beds of bright flowers and cool fountains that she saw, but couldn't reach, were for me the nuggets of information that as a fieldworker I knew existed, if ever I managed to work out how to move from front stage to back in the world of Japan's department stores.

And now it was late afternoon, and I was driving across town to meet a pottery dealer called Eisuke Minamoto whom I had met briefly at the opening of a Kyushu Traditional Pottery Exhibition and who, one or two of my potter acquaintances said, often acted as an intermediary between potters and department stores. The appointment had been fixed for six o'clock because that was when Minamoto closed his gallery for the day. As a result, I'd had to spend the best part of the afternoon wandering round one or two more gallery shows and kicking my heels in a couple of the city's many coffee shops.

The traffic was, as usual, bad. This made me irritable, to add to the fact that I was already tired and dispirited. I faced the prospect of another fruitless interview, followed by a two-hour drive home to the Ono Valley. So, why bother? Why not drive straight home? Tomorrow I could take a day off, make some pots and enjoy myself for a change.

And so, as I turned into the street leading to Minamoto's gallery on the edge of the centre of town, I decided to give the appointment a miss and drive straight home. I passed the gallery with no more than a quick sidelong glance. No dealer was going to tell me anything I didn't already know. Dealers had their hands on the money and nobody likes to talk about money to those they don't know. Rikizō's outburst more than two years previously still rang in my ears.

Just beyond the gallery, the road had to cross a railway line and, as luck would have it, the level-crossing gates decided to lower themselves just as I was approaching. Warning lights flashed. The car two in front paid no attention and speeded across the tracks. So did the van ahead of me. I nearly followed suit, but thought better of it, brought my trusty Mazda to a halt, and waited for the train to pass, serenaded by the monotonous ting-ting-ting of the level-crossing bell.

And as I sat there, I thought about my family waiting for me back home. I thought about my fieldwork frustrations. I thought about the fact that my university and a research council in England together had funded my research for a year. And, as the train rattled towards me, I put the car into gear, did a three-point turn and drove back to the gallery for my interview. An exhibition of virtue.

In one respect, at least, embarking on my research on 'ceramic art' (*bijutsu tōgei* in Japanese) was easy. This time, there was nobody I needed to ask for permission to carry out my research, because I wasn't going to be located in any one place. This was a very different kind of fieldwork from what I had become used to during my stay in Sarayama (Onta). I no longer had the security of a set frame: 14 households and 82 inhabitants in a residential-cum-occupational hamlet, cosily nestling in a valley of other similarly isolated hamlets with which it interacted like a Russian doll in valley, town and city events. This time, I intended to range far and wide across Japan's southernmost island of Kyushu, where a large number of famous, not so famous, and infamous potters lived and worked, and to follow their work as best I could around the country through exhibitions. This was network ethnography, for which the more connections I had the better.

Once again, I was lucky in what happened to me before I got to 'the field'. During a long period of limbo between handing in my doctoral thesis and having it examined six months later by Professor Ronald Dore, I was asked to act as interpreter for a Hiroshi Hirose, the curator of a well-known folk-art museum in Kurashiki during his visit to Bernard Leach's widow Janet in St Ives. He and another famous critic, Akio Akita, were involved in arranging an exhibition of Bernard's work at the museum and had come to pick out some of his more famous pots which Janet had agreed to loan for the occasion. As it turned out, their English was mostly good enough to do without my services, but the three-day trip had been great fun and, at the end of it, Hirose offered to give me any help he could once I started my new piece of research.

But if I had a connection that would take me into the upper echelons of the ceramic art world – and an extremely useful connection it proved to be – I didn't actually know any famous potters. Akita offered to introduce me to ceramists he knew in Kyoto, but since he specialized in abstract art and since I was more interested in pottery that was, at least nominally, based on a functional tradition and, moreover, made in Kyushu, this offer of an introduction to new contacts in his network (though clearly exhibiting the kind of 'structural hole' that would add a new dimension to my study) seemed too remote from my interests to be taken up just yet. I therefore decided to start at the bottom of the aesthetic hierarchy in Kyushu where I lived and work my way up.

But *where* to start exactly? Since nobody in Onta itself participated in exhibitions any more,[2] the simplest answer seemed to be to go across to the neighbouring pottery community of Koishiwara (also called Sarayama) where I already knew half a dozen potters quite well from my previous period of fieldwork. While Sarayama Onta had been founded by a potter from Sarayama Koishiwara back in 1705, and while both had had rather similar methods of production until the 1960s, Koishiwara potters had for the most part decided to expand production to take advantage of their location within striking distance of both Fukuoka and Kita Kyushu cities, as well as to satisfy the booming tourist demand brought on by the popularity of the folk-art movement. As a result, unlike Onta's potters, they had discarded their traditional methods of clay preparation and cooperative kiln firing, thoroughly modernized production methods, and taken on apprentices, so that each household could pursue whatever marketing strategy suited its kiln operator best.

While some potters built sales outlets fronting the main road running through the village of Koishiwara (but not the hamlet of Sarayama itself), and catered primarily to tourist demand, others preferred to stay in Sarayama and produce work that was closer to the traditional ideal, but which nevertheless departed sufficiently from that ideal in style to make their pots seem more 'artistic'. These potters catered to a clientele which saw itself as more 'knowledgeable' and 'discerning' than the average tourist and which, for the most part, came across these potters' works in the exhibitions that they held in various department stores in the neighbouring cities of Kita Kyushu and Fukuoka, as well as those further off in Kumamoto, Oita and Nagasaki.

One potter, Jimbei Hagiwara, was particularly helpful right from the start of my research. Jimbei was a couple of years younger than me and had been adopted into one of the old Sarayama pottery households where he made 'traditional' wares with a 'contemporary' twist. Precisely because he was not born and brought up in the hamlet, Jimbei had a broader horizon and sphere of interests than some of his fellow potters and was genuinely interested in my research – if only because he himself had started on the bottom rung of the exhibition ladder a few years previously. Any initial enthusiasm in this, however, seemed to have worn off – mainly because he felt he wasn't getting anywhere much on the artistic ladder and didn't know why. He showed his pots once a year in different department stores dotted around Kyushu and, although he sold most of what he exhibited, it wasn't usually quite enough to meet the various expenses he incurred (from the cost of having all his bigger works properly boxed, to the money he spent on food, drink and the occasional hotel while he was away from home). He justified this by saying that at least his exhibitions attracted customers to his workshop in Sarayama. In other words, he was using one-man shows as a word-of-mouth marketing strategy.

But that was sales. What about the aesthetic appreciation of his work that exhibitions were designed to enhance? Here Jimbei felt totally lost, and was darkly pessimistic about his future as a 'ceramic artist'. The work he contributed to competitive exhibitions for Kyushu potters was usually accepted, all right. But he never won prizes or commendations (*shōreishō*) and when he contributed pots to national exhibitions, they were invariably rejected. Because he had no idea why this was so or what critics thought or felt when they looked at his pots, he'd recently joined an informal association of young potters, headed by a respected tea-ceremony potter in Agano, who occasionally arranged for one famous critic to fly down from Tokyo at potters' expense and comment on their work. This way, Jimbei hoped, he might begin to understand what it was that critics and curators and other people 'up there' were looking for. But he hadn't bargained for the fact that he would have to serve an 'apprenticeship' in the group he had joined before things happened. In many respects, as I was to find out later when I witnessed the judging of a major ceramics exhibition, the association's meetings were a kind of pre-selection process.[3] The critic in question was afforded an opportunity to see what was going on in pottery centres a long way from Tokyo, to link pottery styles with potters' faces, remember them, and then pick out certain works and have them scrutinized by his fellow panellists when called upon to jury a big ceramics or traditional craft exhibition.

What became clear fairly early on in my fieldwork, therefore, was that a lot of people seemed to be working in a vacuum. Potters like Jimbei had very little idea what it was that made their work 'beautiful', 'individual', 'meek', 'honest', and all those other words in the aesthetic vocabulary trundled out by critics in exhibition catalogues, lectures and occasional books. Critics themselves often had very little knowledge of what really went on at ground level, of what kinds of difficulties potters faced as a result of the exigencies of the materials, and thus production methods, that they used. Moreover, provided they had a sufficient supply of pots to exhibit, department-store representatives didn't want to know about either potters or critics, although they used both to their own ends as and when appropriate. The only thing that connected them all – potters, department stores and critics – was the work being produced. And, as I myself was learning through my own fieldwork experiences, it was only through this work that people made connections, formed networks and moved their way through the ceramic-art world. In short, I was in many ways following a *network of pots*, rather than a network of potters, critics, dealers, department stores or whoever. Making the link between things and people, on the one hand, and between people and aesthetic and other ideals, on the other, was proving to be the challenge in this particular piece of fieldwork.

When I arrived in Minamoto's gallery, I found half a dozen people sitting round drinking tea and eating bean cakes. Minamoto courteously introduced me to his wife, Masako, a plump woman of about my age, with an irresistible bubbling enthusiasm and straightforward manner that quickly put everyone at their ease. I was introduced, answered the usual questions about where I came from, what I was doing, where I lived, whether I was married, had a family and so on, and then found myself talking to my first serious pottery collector (I later learned that, besides placing pots all over every available space in his house, he hugged his favourite ones to him while in the bath).[4]

After half an hour or so, the customers left. None of them had bought anything, but, as I was to find out, Minamoto's gallery was a place where people gathered to talk, exchange information and gossip, and occasionally buy things. Masako ran this social-cum-business side of the gallery's activities (and, to continue from where we left off the previous chapter, it was virtually impossible to separate the two), while her husband, whom everyone called and referred to as Eisuke, spent a lot of his time driving around and visiting potters all over northern Kyushu, buying pots for his gallery (generally from those he knew his customers were interested in), and arranging a lot of exhibitions for both local department stores and others as far away as Hiroshima, Kobe and Osaka. In other words, he was the social link who followed the network of pots from their sites of production to where they were exhibited and sold and, in the process, developed around him a dense web of connections both up- and down-stream (as they say in marketing-speak).[5]

This much Eisuke told me fairly quickly as I interviewed him and, for the first time, I realized that I was having the world of ceramics explained to me in a simple, straightforward manner. At the same time, of course, I could see that he was watching me, paying attention to the kind of questions I asked, and gauging my reactions and follow-up questions to the answers he gave. Gradually, I circled round to my favourite enquiry about department stores and what was in it for them, and when I finally took the plunge about an hour into the interview, both he and Masako started to chuckle.

'I guess what they've been telling you is that they're "giving culture back to the people", or some such nonsense?' Eisuke asked rhetorically. When I nodded, slightly taken aback by such directness, he continued without batting an eyelid, 'It's all a load of lies, of course. But you know that.'

(Gulp!) Had I found the key that unlocked the door to that lovely garden Alice wanted to get into?

Masako broke in. 'The ceramic-art world's not what it seems on the surface, you know. There's an enormous difference between what we like to call "front" (*omote*) and "back" (*ura*) in Japanese.'

Eisuke continued, 'So you can't believe anything you hear from department stores, or critics, or potters. They're all afraid of the truth. And they certainly don't want a foreigner like you prying into their affairs. You'd upset their cosy little world if you knew what was *really* going on – especially if you wrote about it.'

So what *was* going on?

'Why don't we start by having dinner together?' suggested Eisuke. 'We can talk while we eat.'

And so we did – with 'eat' being the operative word because Eisuke, rather remarkably, didn't drink. And during our meal at a barbecue chicken *yakitoriya* restaurant, and then afterward back in the gallery, he and Masako began to tell me about the art world of Japanese ceramics. Eisuke was a real entrepreneur, who had spent quite a few years selling cups and trophies to whoever would buy them (golf clubs, schools, agricultural coops, city halls, you name it), and quite a few more years living off earnings he made from playing mahjong. He'd been in the pottery business three whole years and was heartily sick of the games people were playing and the part he himself was obliged to act if he was to make a living from his work as intermediary.

'You have to be an eight-faced beauty (*happō bijin*)', Masako explained with an infectious laugh. 'Do you know that expression? You've got to smile at everyone and seem like the same person, whatever angle people are looking at you from.'

'And it's really exhausting, keeping up appearances,' Eisuke continued, 'so you've actually done me a favour by coming to interview me, you know. You're the first person I feel I can talk to. You're a total outsider. You've got no vested interests – apart from getting information – so you're safe, if you see what I mean.'

And so they explained how department stores put on one-man shows in their art galleries to sustain customer interest for the big pottery exhibitions that they would hold two or three times a year. They pointed out that, yes, the big exhibitions were indeed cultural events, but that the two, three or eight thousand people who came to see them every week spent a lot of money elsewhere in the store and that this more than made up for the costs of the exhibitions themselves. If I wanted to follow that up, I'd need to go to Tokyo. That was the centre of things. Kyushu was peanuts by comparison.

They told me, too, about how one-man pottery shows had come to be judged by sales, since there were no adequate aesthetic criteria upon which all could agree. But the emphasis on sales figures meant that some well-placed potters inflated their turnover by talking their apprentices and former pupils into buying their work, in exchange for ensuring that *their* work was accepted by the jury in the next major competitive exhibition.

Then they recounted stories about how store representatives obliged potters to buy art objects at highly inflated prices as a way of reducing the actual cash stores would have to pay out at the end of an exhibition. If they dared to turn down such 'generous offers', potters would find suddenly that their next year's show at the store would be cancelled. Of course, this wasn't true of *all* potters, or *all* stores, but these were the kinds of goings-on that I'd need to find out about. I had to distinguish between gossip and hard facts and that wasn't going to be easy.

And so the 'interview' went on. By the time, I finally girded my loins to leave for home, it was one o'clock in the morning. I had been with the Minamotos for the best part of seven hours. My head was spinning with the information they had passed on to me, and I wasn't sure what to do next.

'Look,' said Eisuke, with his customary, but uncharacteristically refreshing, directness that I have only really come across since among entrepreneurial businessmen in Japan, 'why don't you become my "assistant"? That way you don't have to put on a suit every time you go to a department store. You can wear your jeans and trainers like me and go in by the back door carrying armloads of pots. I guarantee you'll hear stories that'll make the rest of your hair fall out.'

He lit yet another cigarette. 'And you can come with me in the car whenever I drive over to Arita or wherever, visiting kilns. That way you'll get to meet all the potters I know – from a fourteenth-generation holder of an "important intangible cultural property" who doesn't know how to make a pot, to rock-bottom craftsmen who know they are nothing but craftsmen – and a lot more besides who've got all sorts of artistic aspirations. And then you can begin to judge for yourself whether all you've heard this evening is glorious gossip, personal prejudice, or a reasonably accurate picture of the world of Japanese ceramics.'

And so I became Eisuke's 'assistant'. I wore my jeans and trainers, and carried pots up and down in the service lift on the day a store was closed and an exhibition was set up or dismantled. And I would hear those same men whom I had interviewed so formally in my suit and tie and who had spun me tales of Japanese department stores' return of culture to the people – these same men, also for the most part in casual clothes – telling the most outrageous tales about who had recently done or said what to whom, and how nobody gave a damn about, or even understood, the meaning of 'culture'. What I heard was a wonderful web of gossip and intrigue. But I also began to get important details like sales figures and store and dealer margins, and realized that there really wasn't that much money for any potter – and not just Jimbei – in a one-man show or exhibition. Not only did potters lose a week's work sitting in a windowless gallery, talking to casual and not-so-casual acquaintances as they consumed cup after cup of green tea. They usually had to pay for board and accommodation in a nearby hotel, since they lived too far away to commute, so that the sales that they made hardly covered their direct – let alone their indirect – expenses. Instead of financial reward, though, they got *kudos* – what Pierre Bourdieu has called 'cultural capital'.[6] They got it from the reputation of the store in which they were exhibiting and from the amount of sales they officially made. Occasionally, too, they'd get a percentage point or two from *who* had bought their pots, especially if it was a big-name corporate client. And, of course, they'd get more *kudos* from the news – if any – that they managed to generate in the local media. The ceramic-art world in Japan – like many an art world elsewhere in the world – thrived on a wholesome brew of information, flattery and gossip, the hard graft of making and keeping up connections, an honest attempt to produce good work, a frequent ambivalence about the role of commerce in 'art', and the ever-present hint of direct or indirect threat and/or bribery between certain actors in certain places on certain occasions.

Although I continued to carry out fieldwork among my friends in Koishiwara, where I also made pots and passed on to them a lot of the information I was getting, in the hope that it might dissuade them from pursuing the exhibition route (but what other choice did they have?), and although I frequently visited Tokyo and used my connections with Hirose and Akita to follow up leads in the capital, I spent a lot of time in the company of Eisuke whom I grew to like immensely. We talked for hours and hours during the long drives back and forth between Fukuoka and north Kyushu's pottery kilns, and we must have tried (and denigrated) the food of virtually every drive-in restaurant on each of our routes. I learned to put up, somehow, with his chain smoking, although he learned, too, to hold off from his next cigarette until after I'd finished eating and we'd ordered coffee. And as the days turned into weeks and the weeks into months, I finally began to get a clear picture of what was not just a 'world' but a whole 'field' of ceramic art (more of that in the next chapter).

It was on our way home from one of these long day-trips one beautiful late-autumn afternoon that Eisuke suddenly mused, à propos of nothing in particular, as we moved slowly along behind yet another large cement truck on the main road back to Fukuoka:

'You should hold your own show, you know. I mean, for the past four months you've been talking to all sorts of people, listening to their stories, and visiting potters and department stores and critics to get them to answer your questions. And we've joked together about how so-and-so did this or said that, and we've laughed at them in our cynical, knowing way. But you don't really know what it's like to hold your own show, do you? *You* haven't had to go through all the emotions other potters go through – making sure they've got enough good pots to exhibit, wondering who'll come and buy them, fighting the boredom of six days in a lifeless gallery with nothing to look at but the imperfections of their own work. Your own show would really give you a *feel* for what's going on. All that intellectual analysis of yours would move down *here*,' he said, tapping his solar plexus with one hand to indicate where Japanese often regard the 'real' self as residing.

I was appalled at Eisuke's idea – if only because I knew that there was no way that the pots I made would be anywhere near high enough a standard for an exhibition.

'Standard?' Eisuke raised an eyebrow. 'What standard? I thought we'd agreed there are no standards in the ceramic-art world. That's one of your conclusions, isn't it? Whatever standard there is consists of a strange mixture of aesthetic, commercial and social values, all of them as varied as the people involved. You've seen that. You can't use standards as an excuse now, you know.'

Eisuke was right. I said I'd think about it.

It was a combination, I think, of personal vanity and a sense of obligation toward those who were funding my research that made me fairly quickly come round to his suggestion. This was participant observation in its most acute and dangerous form: an opportunity to watch myself participating in my field of study and then weave these observations of my motivations, emotions, successes and failures into the general understanding I had already gained of the workings of the ceramic-art world.

Although there were all sorts of things that happened in the period leading up to, as well as during, my one-man show, it was the *planning* of it that illustrates rather well, I think, the positions people adopt and the strategies they pursue in any field of activity. Here there were three main challenges that needed to be met to create a suitable frame for the exhibition. First, we needed to find a location (that is, a department store). Secondly, we had to get the support of a backer (generally speaking, a newspaper) who would provide the show with much-needed publicity. And thirdly, there was the matter of timing. Ideally, we needed to put on the show at a time that would, for one reason or another, attract people's attention. These three challenges interlocked with one another in various ways and presented at least one Catch-22 situation: no department store would agree to provide a location for my show without media support, but no media organization would agree to back me without a location being fixed. Moreover, since both store and media organization lived off 'events', the timing of my show was actually rather important – in particular because I was a totally unknown quantity in the world of Japanese ceramics.

Eisuke characteristically went for the jugular by trying to solve both location and media support at the same time. The easy part here was tapping into personal connections. We both knew a senior desk manager, a Mr. Nagai, working in the local branch office of the national *Mainichi Newspaper* which, like its rivals, supported cultural activities in a big way. It made sense to approach him first, even though the *Mainichi* didn't have the kind of circulation in Fukuoka enjoyed by local newspapers like the *Nishi Nihon Shinbun*. So Eisuke telephoned Nagai who more or less immediately came over to the gallery to hear what was afoot. Having heard a rough outline of a plan for my exhibition and a request for any help his newspaper might be able to give, Nagai immediately asked about the venue of the show. Where was it to be held?

'Tamaya', said Eisuke without a moment's hesitation, naming one of Fukuoka's two biggest department stores. That seemed to satisfy Nagai who was clearly attracted by the news potential of an exhibition by a foreigner. But he didn't give immediate institutional support because, as he put it, 'I don't want personal connections to interfere with my newspaper's best interests.'

Of course, Eisuke had clearly thought about where my show might most beneficially be held. He had opted for Tamaya as his first choice because the store was family-owned and liked to think of itself as more 'cultured' than commercial. (This was a way of positioning itself vis-à-vis its main rival, Iwataya.) It was more likely than any other store, therefore, to provide my show with a venue.

But Eisuke hadn't been in touch with anyone at Tamaya when he told Nagai of where the show was to be held. So he very quickly arranged an appointment with a senior managing director of the store, and went to see him. After chatting about a rather successful exhibition he had arranged for Tamaya a few weeks earlier (just to remind the managing director of the dealer's competence and the store's indebtedness to him), Eisuke brought up and quickly sold him the idea of my pottery show. The notion of a show featuring an English academic-cum-potter linked, however tenuously, to the name of Bernard Leach was well worth pursuing. Did Eisuke have any thoughts about which newspaper might back the exhibition?

'The *Mainichi* is all for it', said the unflinching Eisuke, in the full knowledge that the newspaper had cooperated in such ventures with Tamaya before and that those employed in the two organizations got on rather well. The managing director was suitably impressed, but said that it would be good, too, if Eisuke could come up with a *reason* for my holding my show there. A department store didn't just put on cultural exhibitions for totally unknown people (however well connected they might be); it needed some justification, some newsworthy rationale, for doing so.

It was Masako who came up with the ingenious idea of putting on my one-man show during the week in which the annual Traditional Crafts Exhibition (*Dentō Kōgeiten*) was being held at Iwataya department store, Tamaya's arch-rival. Her logic was simple. All of Kyushu's potters would come into town to see the Traditional Crafts Exhibition and, since they had little else to do once they'd looked round and seen who was exhibiting what, they'd be bound to come along to my show – partly out of curiosity and partly to fill in the time before they went off to a pricey bar or two, frequented by young women who would giggle at their jokes, ply them with booze and occasionally allow a stray hand to stroke their thigh or other more private part of their anatomy. This in itself would be bound to please Tamaya. (I'm referring to the fact that potters would visit my show and not to their late night dalliances.) Not only would my show be newsworthy – how did an English-born craft potter compare with Japanese? It would attract visitors to the store which, year after year, lost a lot of business to its rival during the week of the exhibition and didn't know what to do about it.

And so, magically, location, media support and timing came together to enable the show to take place. Once he had heard Masako's idea, Tamaya's senior managing director almost clapped his hands in delight and agreed on the spot to my show being held in the store's fifth-floor gallery during the week of the Traditional Crafts Exhibition. Eisuke was then able to go back to Nagai and, having laid out all the detail, quickly persuaded him to agree to the *Mainichi Newspaper* supporting my show.

But at this point Nagai himself came up with a tactical suggestion. One of the problems with any art exhibition's being publicly supported by a major national newspaper was that, even though the show would be given a lot of publicity by the sponsoring newspaper, it would be ignored by all its rivals. This meant that only readers of one of the national dailies – the *Mainichi* or the *Asahi* or the *Yomiuri* – would to be likely to get to hear of a particular exhibition. Given his own newspaper's weak circulation in northern Kyushu, Nagai therefore suggested that I get a different 'official sponsor' for the show. He even knew where to find one. There was some kind of Anglo-Japanese Cultural Association, located in Kyushu University, that I could approach.

This time, I was the one who had to sell the show. 'It's no use my going,' Eisuke explained. 'These people are intellectuals. They're "cultured". They don't want to talk to a dealer like me. That'd put them off entirely. No, you go. It'll be simple. Just you see.'

And so I found myself one afternoon in a dingy office somewhere in Kyushu University, immensely glad that I was doing fieldwork and wasn't myself confined to a similar kind of space back in London, and talking to three men in grey suits and gold-rimmed spectacles who represented the Anglo-Japanese Cultural Association.

'What kind of pots do you make, Dr. Moeran?' The association's chairman asked politely.

This was serious. I was being addressed by my official title. And I'd been put on the spot. It was a question that helped me immensely later on during newspaper interviews and a late-night television appearance.

I found, for the first time, that I had to *say* something – and say something fast – about my pots, and so put into language what I had felt could never be properly expressed in words. And, just like some potters I'd heard, and like all the critics whose speeches I'd listened to at prize-giving ceremonies, informal meetings and art-museum tours, I began to spin a yarn – a rational[7] consisting of a rapidly-made series of connections between England and Japan, between Bernard Leach and Sōetsu Yanagi, between tradition and modernization, between handicraft and mechanized modes of production, between natural and artificial materials – you name it, I said it – and how all this gave rise to the *possibility* of an unselfconscious art. *That*, I finished with a flourish, was what my show would be about.

My three interlocutors smiled with pleasure and, nodding at one another enthusiastically, said that this was just the kind of activity their association wished to support. I had my official backer. But just to add a little icing to the cake, I took an opportunity to call on the Director of the British Council the next time I was in Tokyo. We'd known each other briefly more than a dozen years previously when we both lived in the Kansai area, so I decided to make use of this personal contact to ask if the British Council might be persuaded to sponsor my show.

'Of course, old boy,' came the immediate, effusive response. 'No trouble at all. Provided we don't have to give you money or anything like that. Hah, hah, hah!'

And so I got myself *two* prestigious names to sponsor my show and appear on the posters and invitations sent out all over Kyushu.

Comment

This establishment of an appropriate frame for my one-man show was crucial to its success – for success it was judged to be toward the end of February, once a hectic five days of interviews, sales pitches, brief chats with customers and lengthier ones with friends and acquaintances came to an end. Eisuke had dreamed up another novelty to attract people to my show, by arranging for me to make some porcelain pots in addition to the stoneware that I was already making at Hagiwara Jimbei's pottery in Koishiwara. 'Nobody makes both porcelain *and* stoneware,' he explained. 'It's either one or the other. This way we'll make sure *everyone* who's a potter turns up at your show.'

He was right in his forecast. We'd had something like a thousand people a day coming into the gallery. Not all the pots had sold, but enough had been so to quell – temporarily, at least –disparaging tongues in the ceramic-art world's corridors of gossip. Nagai, too, had been right in his strategy. Precisely because the *Mainichi Newspaper* was not sponsoring my show officially, most national and local dailies – including, of course, the *Mainichi* – devoted several column inches to it. Tamaya had been delighted by the show's popularity, since it gained from sales made elsewhere in the store. Nobody told me how much it made in this indirect manner, but it was enough to get the managing director down to the gallery once during the week, while the senior executive director of external sales and marketing passed by twice to congratulate us on the show's success. Would I perhaps be able to hold another show this time next year, *sensei* (a word that was used for eminent potters, as well as less eminent academics)?[8]

And I learned at first hand, as Eisuke had anticipated, the full gamut of emotions that an exhibiting 'artist' goes through during the course of displaying his work to a general public that is enthusiastic and sceptical, admiring and dismissive, virtually simultaneously. My own show taught me to see potters in a slightly different, more sympathetic perspective, as I realized how the exhibition frame established certain patterns of behaviour that couldn't be cast aside if I was to continue to operate my networks and connections in the ceramic-art world. Of course, I could allow myself occasional frame-breaking behaviour – like offering on TV to give away any pots that weren't sold, and running an ongoing written-bid auction of two pots on which Eisuke and I couldn't agree a price – precisely because I was *not* a long-term member of this world. Others – like Jimbei – were not so fortunate in the range of choices of action offered to them.

What I also learned was that the ceramic-art world was a little more than the sum of its 'networks of cooperating people' (as Howard Becker has nicely phrased it).[9] Rather, it constituted a field of individual actors, social networks and institutions, each of which had tactical positions (available and taken), discursive strategies and so on that together opened up a 'space of possibles' and permitted and constrained people to act in the way that they did. It is to an analysis of fields that I will now turn.

Notes

1. A detailed discussion of the contemporary Japanese art scene may be found in Thomas Havens, *Artist and Patron in Postwar Japan: Dance, music, theatre, and the visual arts, 1955–1980*, 1982.
2. Encouraged by an acquaintance at the heart of the Japanese Folk Art Move-

ment, Inoshige had in the early 1970s contributed a large lidded jar to the National Crafts Exhibition (*Dentō Kōgeiten*) and, to his own astonishment and his fellow potters' envy, had been awarded the Foreign Minister's Prize. This resulted in sufficient in-fighting within Sarayama to prevent him from taking the 'exhibition route' to success. (See Brian Moeran, *Folk Art Potters of Japan*, 1997 [1984], p. 168.)

3. At the same time, I also came to understand some of the formal criteria bought to bear, by one critic at least, in judging what made a pot 'good' or 'bad', 'beautiful' or 'ugly', 'art' or mere 'craft'.

4. Such behaviour is by no means eccentric among pottery collectors around the world.

5. In more formal terms, Eisuke might be described as an entrepreneur who had seen and seized an opportunity to link the two separate worlds of craft production and mass retailing, thereby illustrating Burt's argument about structural holes and the 'network entrepreneur'. This linking had been made possible by department stores' use of cultural artefacts as a way of fighting off price competition and repositioning themselves vis-à-vis supermarkets.

6. Pierre Bourdieu, *Distinction: A social critique of the judgement of taste*, 1984.

7. Howard Becker, *Art Worlds*, 1982, p. 4.

8. My one-man show also proved the general comment by informants that exhibitions didn't make money in themselves. After deducting expenses for materials and other production costs, as well as department-store and dealer percentages, from my total sales turnover, I was left with the sum of 'plus minus zero'. I did, however, have a *name* and it was that name that would have stood me in good stead if I'd decided to pursue a ceramic, rather than academic, career.

9. Becker, *Art Worlds*, p. 25.

–8–

The Art of Capitalizing

There were a number of important things that I relearned through my relationship with Minamoto Eisuke and the pottery exhibition that he gently pushed me into. One, of course, was the reminder of the importance of being able as fieldworker to get back stage in order to understand how and why the easily discernible front stage worked as it did. A second was how every social world has a primary frame of interaction, or 'social drama',[1] in which that social world is legitimized and sustained. As we have seen in earlier chapters, the primary frame in a rural community of potters was a drinking gathering, while in the advertising industry it was the presentation. In the ceramic-art world it was the exhibition. Exhibitions allowed potters to see the work of others living and working in the area; they put them in touch with other potters, dealers, even collectors and critics; they enabled them to be plugged into the latest fads and fashions and so into what was important in the ceramic-art world; and, less often, they encouraged dialogue with other potters about materials and techniques.[2]

A third thing I relearned was how, while moving through a trajectory from production to consumption, by way of distribution and appreciation, objects – in this case, pots; in a previous instance, advertising campaigns – formed a network of people around them. These people had their own individual networks, of course, so that the ceramic-art world consisted not only of 'an established network of cooperative links among participants',[3] but also of networks of ceramic art works. What I came to understand most clearly, though (although it took a little help from a French anthropologist-cum-sociologist to work it out), was the fact that all these interacting potters, critics, museums, collectors, galleries, dealers, department stores, retailers and buying public – not forgetting the art works themselves and what was said about and done with them – were inextricably caught up in a *field* of production.

The concept of 'field' (*champ* in French) has been most clearly enunciated by Pierre Bourdieu who developed it primarily in relation to forms of cultural production, such as the ceramic-art world I had been studying. The idea was developed over the years vis-à-vis what he saw as the limitations of structuralism and certain forms of Marxism, with their emphasis on how agency or practice was structured by *objective* social conditions, on the one hand, and of phenomenology and certain forms of interpretive sociology, anthropology and linguistic analysis,

151

which stressed the role of *subjective* individual experience and perceptions in the functioning of the social world, on the other.[4] Precisely because objectivism failed to cope with how individual conceptions and representations of the social world to some extent shaped social behaviour and that social world, and because subjectivism failed to see how consciousness was itself shaped by social institutions and organization generally, Bourdieu argued that we had to look at the 'objectivity of the subjective'.[5] As he neatly put it:

> It is so important, if one is to have a bit of freedom from the constraints of the field, to attempt to explore the theoretical box in which one is imprisoned.[6]

In an attempt to go beyond the idea of individual actors' free and unrestricted agency, on the one hand, and their constraint because of institutions of mechanistic determinism, on the other, he proceeded to introduce two concepts: habitus and field. *Habitus* was designed to account for the obvious creativity and inventiveness shown by individual actors in their everyday lives, while at the same time recognizing that their behaviour was to some degree regulated and orchestrated by the social environment in which they had been brought up and were living.[7] This environment predisposed, though it did not *oblige*, them to act in particular ways, so that habitus referred to a person's 'dispositions', which were both 'durable' in the sense that they were developed over his or her lifetime and 'transposable' because they were applied in all kinds of different spheres of activity. In many ways, therefore, habitus can be seen as a kind of 'a feel for the game'[8] – almost 'second nature' – in the sense that individuals did not necessarily calculate how they were going to act or react in a specific situation, but did not necessarily abide by the rules of the game either. It was thus both a structur*ing* and a structur*ed* structure[9] – an idea best illustrated, perhaps, by Rikizō's 'drunken' outburst during the Akiyasama gathering in Sarayama.

Clearly, people do not interact in a vacuum, but, as we have seen during the course of this book, operate in concrete social contexts, situations or frames that are governed by sets of objective social relations and so provide 'a kind of system of common reference'.

> Fields of cultural production propose to those who are involved in them a *space of possibles* that tends to orient their research, even without their knowing it, by defining the universe of problems, references, intellectual benchmarks (often constituted by the names of its leading figures), concepts in *–ism*, in short, all that one must have in the back of one's mind in order to be in the game.[10]

The 'space of possibles' to which Bourdieu referred (in this quotation, in the context of academia) itself arose out of a 'confrontation' between dispositions (habitus) and positions[11] – 'positions' being the roles available and the attendant 'ensemble of relations'[12] characterizing any field. Participants, he argued,[13] took up various positions in relation to one another and, whenever a new position was taken, the whole structure of the field was displaced, leading to a knock-on effect as those in other positions took up new positions in reaction to the change.[14] The fact that these new position-takings gave rise to further changes meant that the field as a whole was never stable or static, but always in flux as individual agents made their moves. Hence, his notion of a space of possibles. This argument is virtually identical to the case for the positioning of products and corporations made in advertising and marketing generally.

Bourdieu argued that these kinds of common reference emerged from many different but simultaneous, hierarchically-organized fields (artistic, cultural, economic, educational, intellectual, political, scientific and so on), each of which was relatively autonomous, functioned according to its own laws and relations of force (or power), operated in a particular structured space, and interacted with similarly functioning fields in what Bourdieu called 'structural homology'.[15] In other words, the structure of each field was determined by the relations it had with other fields, as well as by 'all relations among agents and institutions of diffusion or consecration'.[16] And to enter a field and play its game, an actor had to possess a minimum amount of what it takes (knowledge, skill, 'talent') to be accepted as a legitimate player.

What, then, were the knowledge, skill and talent that I possessed which enabled me to enter the field of ceramic art and hold my own one-man show? In the first place, thanks to my fieldwork research, I had come to learn about and know many of the major players in the region: from a highly respected thirteenth-generation overglaze enamel-ware potter to two more or less accepted academic critics located in Fukuoka, by way of the most powerful dealer in northern Kyushu. The fact that I also visited exhibitions in Tokyo, knew famous-name curators, and had even witnessed the jurying of a national exhibition, meant that my networks were sufficiently extended and unusual for local potters to want to tap into, if only to obtain the latest information and gossip from the capital. In other words, it was clear that I was au fait with current knowledge circulating in the field of ceramic art and it was on this basis that I was accepted as a legitimate player.

Skill and talent were rather different matters. I made it known that I had learned to make pots, while not officially undertaking an apprenticeship, at both Inoshige's and Jimbei's potteries. This was true, to the extent that I had worked there on and off as the mood took me during and between bouts of fieldwork over more than three years. However, so far as I know, nobody – other than Eisuke and potters in Onta and Koishi-wara – had seen any of my work. Given that three years (it used to be ten) is the absolute minimum period in which an apprentice potter learns his or her trade, it was therefore taken on trust that I possessed the necessary skill to enable me to put on a one-man show of my own. In fact, my pots were amateurish – primarily functional – and I did not have sufficient skills to make large decorative pieces of the kind frequently displayed in exhibitions.

There are all sorts of different interests at stake in a field, and participants invest in these and often compete for control of the resources of the field in which they operate. Such resources are sometimes material, sometimes social, sometimes ideological or symbolic, and together the way that they are distributed defines each field.[17] Bourdieu developed the concept of *capital* to describe and analyse these resources, and took into consideration the various forms of economic, educational, cultural, social[18] and symbolic capital that participants in a field tried to build up as part of their struggle for power, and then convert into another form that they lacked. In other words, people were always trying to capitalize on a particular situation and turn it to their advantage, depending on their position in a particular field of cultural production. Here two forms of capital were particularly important: *symbolic capital*, referring to 'the degree of accumulated prestige, celebrity, consecration or honour',[19] and *cultural capital*, or 'forms of cultural knowledge, competences or dispositions'.[20]

All in all, Bourdieu tried to incorporate three levels of social reality in his methodology.[21] One was the position of a cultural field within an overall 'field of power'. Another was the actual structure of a cultural field, made up, primarily, of the various positions occupied by actors competing for legitimacy. The third was the genesis and effect of participants' habitus.

As illustration of the relation between a cultural field and overall field of power, we need only recall the account of the studio set-up for the shooting of the hair-product poster. The hierarchy of power relations was made quite clear when the hair stylist insisted on having the photographer do one final set of photos after he had given orders for the set to be dismantled. As freelance employees (with their own regular assistants) hired for the day, both hair stylist and photographer argued more or less on an equal footing, although the latter may have been assisted by the fact that he was a man arguing with a woman. The art director, however, quickly made it clear that, as representative of an advertising agency employed by a client, he had hired both freelance personnel and was thus in overall charge of 'cultural production'. Moreover, when it came to extra costs incurred by the hair stylist's demand for a retake, the economic power of the advertiser was asserted.

If the studio frame was neatly divided into economic and cultural production, so, too, was the field of ceramic art. Potters, critics, gallery owners, department stores and newspaper organizations occupied positions related to one another and were themselves, as we shall see below, sub-structured into competing associations, institutions and personnel of one sort and another. All of these competed for legitimacy and used every strategy made available by the structure of the field to sustain or improve their positions in a market 'structured externally and internally by principles of discrimination, hierarchy and hegemony'.[22] The extent to which individual dispositions came into the formation of such strategies probably depended on individuals concerned. The fact that Jimbei Hagiwara, for example, was born outside Koishiwara, before being adopted as husband to the eldest daughter in a long-established pottery household there, almost certainly made it easier for him to pursue one-man shows and competitive exhibitions as an overall sales strategy, rather than toeing the tourist-art line adopted by many other Koishiwara pottery households.

In addition, Bourdieu was careful not to ignore the *works* produced in any field of cultural production and argued that there was a necessary 'homology between the space of creative works, the field of position-takings and the space of positions in the field of production'.[23] In other words, 'the "subject" of the production of the art-work – of its value but also of its meaning – is not the producer who actually creates the object in its materiality, but rather the entire set of agents engaged in the field.'[24] The overall 'aesthetic disposition' prevalent in a field or sub-field is created and sustained by the very way in which its participants function and act therein.[25]

> Given that the field of ceramic art was broadly divided into stoneware and porcelain, a division based on materials used and consequent technical differences in decorating and firing finished wares, and given that, as newcomer to the field with some knowledge thereof, but insufficient skills, I had to take up a position hitherto rarely, if ever, tried by potters who specialized in *either* porcelain *or* stoneware. Eisuke's suggestion that I make *both* porcelain *and* stoneware neatly reveals the validity of Bourdieu's argument about the homology between works, positions and position-taking. Moreover, my own 'aesthetic disposition', as expressed to members of the Anglo-Japanese Cultural Association, neatly reproduced one of the dominant aesthetic ideologies prevalent in the field of ceramic art during the period of my research. At the same time, by making both porcelain and stoneware, I was make a 'statement' to the effect that the barrier between 'traditional craft' and 'ceramic art' was 'false' and that my pots were, like myself as an initiate in the field, outside the Japanese negotiated discourse of beliefs about what did or did not constitute 'good' work.

And, having now – I think – transformed Bourdieu's complex theorizing into reasonably straightforward English, I want to spend the rest of this chapter looking more closely at how different, mutually transforming forms of capital were worked out among those occupying and challenging positions in the field of ceramic art: in other words, at how the different participants occupying competing positions capitalized on 'art'. In the next, and final, chapter, I will extend this discussion of 'field' beyond cultural production to take account of advertising and what more generally have been referred to as 'creative industries'.[26]

The Field of Ceramic Art

The field of ceramics in general may itself be defined 'by its position in the hierarchy of arts, which varies from one period and one country to another'.[27] In

Japan, the fact that a certain kind of pottery came to be made for the tea ceremony, itself developed from the middle of the sixteenth century as an aesthetic pursuit for feudal lords and other high-ranking samurai, has enabled ceramics as a whole, but especially 'traditional' wares, to move quite high in the hierarchy of arts, when compared with the level in – say – Greece or Great Britain (although, in the latter, there has been an ongoing 're-evaluation' of the role ceramics in the British artistic hierarchy during the past two decades). In other words, a combination of a highly developed aesthetic discourse, allied to other symbolic systems such as Zen Buddhist philosophy, as well as to an ongoing struggle for positions and political power among Japan's feudal lords, gave tea wares in particular, and ceramics in general, a great boost up the hierarchical scale of what constituted 'works of art'. Under such circumstances, it was not surprising to find perhaps that, during my research, all kinds of people – but especially critics, curators and dealers – made claims to their samurai ancestry, as a way of introducing or reinforcing, at least in their own minds, a tenuous correspondence between the social distinction of an audience that had existed historically for a particular kind of pottery, on the one hand, and the everyday clay objects that they handled during the course of their holding the positions they held then in the field of ceramic art.

Tea drinking began in China among Zen monks who used it as a way of not falling asleep during meditation, and later developed into a philosophy embracing calm and simplicity. Tea drinking (*cha-no-yu*) was then introduced in Japan and developed as a diversion of the military and wealthy merchant classes during the luxurious era of the latter half of the sixteenth century.

It was Sen no Rikyū who, under instruction from the *generalissimo*, Hideyoshi Toyotomi, revised tea ceremony rules and developed modern 'tea-ism', whose principles are harmony, reverence, purity and calm. Hideyoshi, being a fervent devotee of tea, as well as a shrewd ruler, 'was not slow to seize the opportunity offered by Cha-no-yu of encouraging the fashion for things of no intrinsic value among his vassals the great Daimyos, for since this value was created by his own connoisseur Rikyu and soon soared to a huge extent, he found it an easy matter to reward services to himself with Tea vessels instead of fiefs in many cases, an example which Tokugawa Ieyasu and his successors were naturally very pleased to follow'.[28] If this is true, then Hideyoshi's and Rikyu's names should probably be included in the *Guinness Book of Records* for having created, in the space of a very short time, premium and lasting value where virtually none previously existed.

Bourdieu argued that the structure of any field of cultural production is characterized by a fundamental opposition between the sub-field of restricted production and the sub-field of large-scale production.[29] Japanese ceramics does not in any way differ from this general rule. First, pottery kilns all over the country are distinguished between restricted (Hagi, Bizen, Karatsu, Agano, Onta) and large-scale

(Tokoname, Seto, Arita) production, although within the centres of large-scale production, restricted ceramic production can be found, and within the centres of restricted production, more and less restricted potters operate side by side (as in Koishiwara).

The opposition between restricted and large-scale production was accompanied by an aesthetic opposition between innovation and reproduction as markers of quality. Those working in the field of restricted production used the concept of innovation as a means of marking themselves and their works off as 'different' from others in the field, and usually adopted an aesthetic disposition that promulgated the importance, and encouraged the production, of 'one-off' wares. In the field of large-scale production, on the other hand, quality was established by the ability to reproduce in exact detail each and every stylistic and functional variety of pots manufactured. The concept of innovation was normally applied only to product innovations introduced by new or modified technology.[30]

The generally held tenet that, in restricted production, any work that does not replicate an existing or previous work is an innovation was apparent in the jury's decision at the Mainichi Japan Ceramics Exhibition in 1981 to award the grand prize to a large bowl contributed by overglaze-enamelware ceramic artist, Imaemon Imaizumi. This bowl, it was agreed by the judges, exhibited precisely the same form and overall design of many other such bowls produced over the decades by generations of Imaizumi family potters. However, instead of painting a plum red and dark green floral pattern on a mid-blue wash (*dami*) background, Imaemon had shown 'great innovativeness' by combining cherry pink flowers with pale green leaves on a grey wash background. In the jury's considered opinion, this apparently minor variation of design was 'stretching tradition to the limit'.

Secondly, within the field of restricted ceramic production, a general 'stylistic' opposition exists between two sub-fields: one devoted to 'traditional' and the other to 'contemporary' wares.

A struggle for legitimacy (in some respects heightened by Sōetsu Yanagi and his potter friends, Shōji Hamada, Kenkichi Tomimoto, Kanjirō Kawai and Bernard Leach in the 1920s and 1930s) resulted in the establishment and maintenance of two major sub-fields, one of 'traditional crafts' (*dentō kōgei*), the other of 'ceramic art' (*bijutsu tōgei*), each of which has its own association, national annual exhibition, and set of state-sponsored accolades. Each sub-field, too, embraces its own cultural producers (potters), composed of competing fractions consisting of dominant and subordinate positions whose power also lies in their regional proximity to the recognized centres of restricted ceramic production (Minō, Kyōto, Bizen, and so on). It subtends legitimizing critics who themselves base their competing renown and power on their ability to turn regional territories into artistic 'fiefs', whose potters become vassals by whom they are rewarded with gifts of pots and whom in turn they reward with recognition by the bestowal of prizes at carefully regulated national exhibitions.[31] Finally, each sub-field encompasses its institutions of display, with the 'traditional crafts' exhibition being held at Japan's most prestigious department store, Mitsukoshi, while 'ceramic art' is shown, along with the finer arts, in one of Tokyo's oldest museums of art. Cultural producers in both sub-fields, however, share department stores as their favoured venue for one-man shows, and these are ranked according to a prestige hierarchy that places big city stores higher than local city stores, and the capital, Tokyo, higher than all other cities, with its own stores – Mitsukoshi, Takashimaya, Isetan, Seibu, Matsuzakaya, Odakyū and so on – also ranked, all according to sales generated, but also to secondary characteristics applied: 'traditional', 'modern', 'contemporary', 'avant garde' and so forth.

This division between 'traditional craft' and 'ceramic art' to some – but by no means every – extent parallels the division in materials between stoneware and porcelain clay mentioned above. (Tea ceremony wares partly counter this general tendency.) The division is partly symbolic, partly technical (and therefore symbolic). It is based, on the one hand, on the valued-as-superior high temperature (approximately 1300 degrees) at which porcelain clay (which contains kaolin) needs to be fired, compared with the 1150–1200 degrees for stoneware; and, on the other, on a general cultural classificatory system that, in Japan as elsewhere, places porcelain with whiteness and purity, as opposed to the 'earthiness' of stoneware clay, which is thus correspondingly 'less pure'.

Although Eisuke's suggestion that I make and exhibit both stoneware and porcelain in combination revealed his instinctive feel for the game, he was careful to keep the two kinds of pot visually separate when it came to displaying them in the Tamaya department store gallery. Stoneware was arrayed on the left and porcelain on the right; the two only met in the middle of the display area at the far end of the gallery. Eisuke agreed that to mix them might have been pleasing aesthetically – it would allow people to compare similar forms and designs made with two different types of clay – but argued that, financially, it would have been little short of a disaster. 'People will keep looking from your stoneware to your porcelain and back again, comparing their relative merits, and never make up their minds to buy', he explained. Yet, although porcelain is generally able to command higher prices than stoneware, Eisuke insisted on a uniformity in pricing that went strictly by size. This strategy, too, was designed to make it easier for visitors to want to buy my pots.

That the work that I showed was not 'mine' was clear from the fact that it enabled new stylistic positions to be taken vis-à-vis art works in general. Thus, when decorating porcelain, I used some of the stoneware techniques that I had learned in the two Sarayamas. Similarly, one of my porcelain, as well as one of my stoneware, designs was later taken up by Jimbei Hagiwara and used for his functional stoneware, while another of my stoneware designs was likewise adopted by Kakuei Nakata (at whose kiln I had made my porcelain pots) for his porcelainware.

As a challenger in the field, as someone with almost no easily recognized and clas-sifiable credentials, and thus with little, if any, symbolic capital, I was actually in a position to *resist* the expectations of participants in the field. But this could happen only once. If I had agreed to Tamaya's suggestion to hold a second one-man show the following year, I would almost certainly have had to show greater craft skills and to move, if but slightly, toward the legitimating centre – albeit with the effect of my first show as a guide to the position taken in what would become the trajectory of my work.

Another major theme in Bourdieu's writings on cultural production is the concept of *dénégation* – variously translated as *negation, denial* and *disavowal*. Here those participating in a field of art pretend not to be doing what they are doing (although they also pretend to be doing what they are not doing). The particular focus of par-ticipants' collective disavowal tends to be 'economic' factors (as I learned time after time during my interviews with department store representatives who kept informing me that pottery and other art exhibitions were primarily aimed to give back 'culture' to their Japanese customers). As a result two opposed, but equally false, impressions emerge: disinterestedness and self-interest.[32]

In some ways, on the surface at least, it was I who came closest to disavowing com-mercial interest and profit during my exhibition, because it didn't matter whether my show made money or not. It was an experiment on Eisuke's and my part, to pitch me into the game and see what happened. I was assured that I wouldn't have to pay out any-thing from my own pocket. But, there again, although I may blithely *think* (or try to *delude* myself) that financial concerns were irrelevant, this was not so – as can be seen in my proud proclamation that the show grossed a little over $17,000 in five days, although I can then disavow this by adding that, after Eisuke and Tamaya had taken their margins (50 per cent all told) and I had paid expenses covering the boxing of pots, as well as the costs of materials and firing (more than $8,000 in all), I was left with 'plus minus zero'. As a newcomer I had the greatest interest in projecting a disavowal of self-interest![33]

But what about the others involved? Eisuke needed to make *some* sales to satisfy both official and unofficial backers – Tamaya department store and the *Mainichi News-paper* – even though each professed to be involved because the idea of the show was 'fun' (*omoshiroi*). If nothing else, then, Eisuke hoped to provide himself with enough money to cover his petrol and cigarette expenses (his nominal margin was 20 per cent of sales), even though he, too, repeatedly said that it wasn't the money that mattered in this particular show. Although Tamaya professed a certain nonchalant disregard for income in its impression management before the show (its margin was fixed at 30 per cent), the fact that its managing director and senior external sales director visited the gallery a number of times revealed that the show's ability to draw customers was having a positive economic effect on the store's overall daily turnover. It was on this basis that the show was deemed by them to be a 'success', and Eisuke gained, if nothing else, social capital as initiator of the exhibition.

The issue of disavowal brings us face to face with the fact that the producers, public mediators and marketers of ceramic art – like the makers and marketers of art all over the world – were (and, of course, still are)

> Adversaries in collusion, who each abide by the same law which demands the repression of direct manifestations of personal interest, at least in its overtly 'economic' form, and which has every appearance of transcendence although it is only the product of the cross-censorship weighing more or less equally on each of those who impose it on all others.[34]

Each of these adversaries *has* to have both of the others to operate successfully in the field, since it is the existence of the third party that both divides and unites them all[35] – something that is also found in the field of advertising where clients, agencies and media organizations also incessantly collide and collude. In her analysis of the French art world, for example, Raymonde Moulin[36] points out that painters used to deny that market constraints impinged on their creative freedom and tended to assert their independence at all times from the social world in which they operated. Yet they consciously employed various strategies to attract the attention of other painters, dealers, critics and collectors. These could be *self-promoting* (attending dinner parties with critics, collectors and important dealers), *daredevil* (including eccentric behaviour and unusual dressing), or *charismatic* (where the daredevil approach was adopted in extreme so that people came to see a particular painter's behaviour as inner-directed and therefore charismatic). In this way, painters were experts in practical sociology,[37] but they had always to be *seen* to be responding to intrinsic creative needs rather than to social demands.[38]

> Similar strategies are adopted by dealers, critics and collectors. For instance, dealers need to win over critics. A critic comes to a gallery show and is impressed, and a painter's work is immediately worth more than before.[39] Dealers also have to win over important collectors and make them into allies, for it is through selected collectors that a dealer starts 'the propaganda machine' on behalf of a particular 'artist'. So he makes concessions in order to ensure that a painting goes where he wants it to go because a discerning collector's decision to buy a painter's work confirms the dealer's judgement and taste. As Arnold Hauser puts it: 'The artist creates the form of the works, the mediators their legend.'[40]
>
> Although money is never avowed as the aim of collecting, a collector is regarded as a 'connoisseur' according to the amount of profit he earns from buying and selling his collection.[41] Collectors buy low and sell high. They also buy enough paintings to be able to influence the market, so that every collector is potentially a dealer, too.[42] A collector who owns a number of paintings by a particular painter can drive up the price for that painter's work in public auction sales, and so enhance the value of his collection.[43]

So what are the relations between potters, critics, retailers and general public? How do these adversaries in fact collude in the ceramic-art world? What roles do they adopt as gatekeepers?

Let me start with an example of a potter colluding against his public, as well as against other potters who might challenge his position. Once during my fieldwork, the association of Agano potters of which Jimbei Hagiwara was a member decided to pay a respectful visit to the kiln of a Mr. Tsuchiya, an extremely well-known tea-ceremony potter working in Hagi, near the western tip of the main island of Honshū. Jimbei and I drove there together, met up with other members of the association, and went to meet the great man. First, of course, we had to take part in a tea ceremony performance and, in the customarily ritualized, hushed and heavy atmosphere that accompanies such theatrical frames, did our best to admire appropriately the tea utensils – including, of course, Tsuchiya's own tea bowl – that we had used, and the view through the open wooden shutter to the standard garden with miniature *bonsai* trees, moss, pond, mud-walled outhouse with thatched roof, and subtle autumn colours.

One of the ways in which the quality of a pot is assessed is by turning it upside down and examining its foot rim. This gives an indication of a potter's turning vis-à-vis 'throwing' or forming technique. This attention to a pot's foot rim has at least one interesting consequence. Nowadays almost all exhibition pots, but especially tea-ceremony pots, are boxed, and collectors keep their prized works in these boxes, taking them out only when they wish to use them. The longer a pot remains in a box, the more likely its foot rim is to leave a mark therein. Consequently, when handed an 'antique' and attempting to verify its authenticity, aficionados will deliberately examine the box, together with the calligraphy and seal on its lid, before untying the ribbon, taking out the antique, and without observation placing it upside down on the tatami mat on which they are kneeling. They will then examine very closely the mark left by its foot rim in the box. By matching box mark with actual foot rim, an expert is in this way able to say that a pot is 'authentic'.

Boxing a pot, and inscribing a box, increases a pot's value immensely. For this purpose, famous tea masters are hemmed in by dealers who persuade them to give tea bowls a 'name' ('Floating Moon', 'Autumn Breeze') and who, after handing over an appropriate fee, sell them for five to ten times their original asking price. At one point, when I thought that I might, after all, have to sell my Bernard Leach 'Pilgrim' plate, I contacted a dealer who insisted that I have it boxed and signed by Bernard's widow, Janet (whose signature thus authenticated the work). The box itself was made, I was told, by Japan's best box maker and cost me ¥20,000 ($200 at the time). The signature cost nothing, other than the price of the petrol for a very long drive from Kyushu to Kanazawa. The plate itself, initially purchased for £100 (approximately $150), then valued before boxing at ¥200,000 ($2,000), was now ready to be sold for ¥1 million ($10,000).

In my own one-man show, I, too, was required to have boxes made for my pots, which I was then required to 'sign'. Eisuke argued – and buyers confirmed – that my 'calligraphy' was sufficiently 'unusual' to give each pot 'added character'.

Tsuchiya then took us to a quiet and 'rustic' workshop where he proceeded to sit down at a kick wheel and demonstrate the art of making tea bowls. Dressed in loose-fitting jacket and *monpē* baggy farmer's trousers, he was suitably modest throughout in this exercise in impression management. As he worked, he told us more about his philosophy of pottery-making: how it was crucially important to use natural materials throughout – from forming and shaping tools to glaze materials and a kiln that was fired with wood; how a kick-wheel was so much better than an electric or other mechanized form of wheel, since it allowed the spirit of the body to enter into the pot being made; and so on and so forth.[44] And, as he spoke, he carefully made three or four tea bowls which he proceeded to cut round the lip to produce an (albeit artificially induced) 'natural look', before, much to the astonishment of the assembled group of admirers, crumpling the form up in his hands and tossing it into the clay pit in the corner of his workshop. This elicited the appropriate question. How many of the many tea bowls he made was he actually satisfied with?

As Tsuchiya gave his answer (three out of one hundred), Jimbei – who was not interested in tea wares – and I quietly stepped out through the door of the potter's workshop and walked toward his climbing kiln, with stacks and stacks of precisely chopped logs of wood lining one side. The accumulated dust and humidity, however, quickly made it clear that this kiln had not been fired for a very long time. We looked at each other, said little, and walked back, trying a closed door on one side of the corridor as we went. It opened and, putting our heads round the door, we saw a second, much more functional, workshop, replete with three electric wheels and an electric kiln, plus various bags of mass-manufactured chemical glaze ingredients. So this was how Tsuchiya *really* made his pots!

The disavowal here took place through the aesthetic philosophy that we had been listening to – one which, from his practised manner of speaking, he clearly repeated to the many aficionados (critics, collectors, tea-ceremony specialists, and 'disciples' like ourselves) who came to visit his pottery. It was crucially important to create this atmosphere of extremely restricted production because Tsuchiya was charging at least $15,000 for every tea bowl he sold. As with haute couture dresses, certain vintage bottles of wine, or a dead celebrity's memorabilia, there was no strictly economic relation between this retail sales price, on the one hand, and the minimal cost of materials and production, on the other, although the former was probably quite reasonable if each tea bowl were to be seen as 'a product of a vast operation of *social alchemy* jointly conducted, with equal conviction and very unequal profits, by all the agents involved in the field of production'.[45] If members of his public had become aware of the fact that Tsuchiya could, if he wished, churn out two hundred tea bowls a day, still discard several dozen he wasn't satisfied with, glaze the rest with ready mixed glaze materials and load and fire his electric kiln twice a week, they would never have been prepared to pay the symbolic price he demanded for his work. And Tsuchiya himself, of course, would never have been in the running for a 'national treasureship'.

There is always the possibility that Tsuchiya may have been passing off as his own work tea bowls that were in fact made by one of his apprentices or assistants. (Why else would he have *three* electric wheels in his 'other' workshop?) This brings to mind the famous, or infamous, tale of the discovery, soon after the end of the Pacific War, of a large and ancient, Einin Period (1293-1298), ash-glazed jar. Two coincidences accompanied its discovery during the construction of a country road. First, the pot somehow escaped being broken by the bulldozer whose driver unearthed it. Secondly, a dealer happened to be standing in a nearby field and was able to whisk the jar away, no questions asked. The jar's rarity led to a well-known ceramic artist, Tōkurō Katō, writing about it at some length in his *Dictionary of Japanese Ceramics* (*Tōki Daijiten*), published in 1954, and he even used a photograph of the Einin Jar to grace the book's dust jacket.

Eventually the renowned critic, Fujio Koyama, who was considered *the* expert on traditional Japanese ceramics at the time, got to hear of the jar's existence. Having seen the pot, he pronounced it 'authentic' and, since he was then working for the state's Agency of Cultural Affairs (*Bunkashō*), declared that it should be officially designated an important national treasure. This came to pass in 1959.[46]

At the time of the announcement, Tōkurō Katō, who was one of Koyama's close friends, contacted a major daily newspaper and publicly announced that the Einin Jar had been made by none other than himself. This created a furore that was further inflamed when Tōkurō's son, Mineo, contradicted his father by claiming that it was *he*, and not his father, who had made the pot. He proceeded to prove his point by giving demonstrations in a Tokyo department store, throwing jars identical in shape to that which was causing so much embarrassment to the authorities. A panel of 'experts' quickly concluded that the jar was a fake and Koyama was obliged to resign from his position.

There is a double irony that turns this piece of folklore into comic tragedy. Koyama had until then been one of Katō's closest friends, but the affair put an end to that friendship. Moreover, Mineo became so angry with his father that he took his wife's name (Okabe) and, it is said, never spoke to Tōkurō again.[47]

The ceramic art world was extremely ambivalent about money.[48] As a general rule, most potters and critics believed that money 'destroyed' good work. Potters who were obviously 'commercial' or 'too' commercial were condemned (as were critics who were seen to be 'on the take') – an ideological position that even Eisuke, in an unguarded moment, occasionally adhered to when talking about a particular potter. On the other hand, by having an agent who would regularly take over the marketing of their works, potters gained in prestige.[49] Indeed, money itself contributed to potters' prestige, since turnover from one-man shows was a means of gauging 'artistic success'. There were various generally-agreed levels of such success – ranging through approximately five steps, from $20,000 income from a week's show at the bottom, to upwards of $1 million at the top – so that exhibitions thus established and sustained what Caves refers to as the *A list/B list* property by which talent in creative industries in general is ranked.[50] In other words, shows – precisely because of all the unseen costs militating against economic profit per se (boxing, obligatory art-object purchases, accommodation, entertainment, work days lost, and so on)[51] – encouraged the accumulation of symbolic capital, defined by Bourdieu as: 'economic or political capital that is disavowed, misrecognized and thereby recognized, hence legitimate, a "credit" which, under certain conditions, and always in the long run, guarantees "economic" profits'.[52]

In many ways, critics were in the best position to disavow economic interests since, ideally at least, their focus of interest was on the work itself and nothing else (although, in fact, all critics tended to link the quality of pots with the character of the potters who made them – a 'character' that reflected the moral and aesthetic disposition of the field as a whole). As is customary in other fields of art in other societies,[53] critics regularly allowed economic transactions to cloud the 'independence' of their assessment of works, but made full use of disavowal to enhance their reputations (symbolic capital) while lining their pockets (economic capital), although 'it is not always easy to ascertain after the event how far certain stages on the path to Parnassus have been paid for, so to speak, with false coins'.[54]

> Potters who aimed to move up the exhibition ladder and artistic hierarchy needed the support of critics who could, and for a sum would, write recommendations (*suisenbun*) on their behalf (for posting at the entrance to a one-man show and using on invitation cards), select their pots in competitive exhibitions, and award the occasional prize.[55] In this way, they sanctioned a potter's reputation and effected attendant economic consequences in terms of the increased prices that an exhibiting or award-winning potter could acceptably charge.[56] The fact that they would also mention potters' names when called upon – as they frequently were at the time of my research – to write or edit books about Japanese ceramics also contributed to the building of reputations.
>
> Critics would visit potters from time to time and, in exchange for services promised or rendered, or even as a means of attracting their attention in the first place, potters would occasionally give critics samples of their work. It would be in a critic's economic interest, therefore, to devote critical praise to such a potter, since by so doing he would inevitably increase the value of the work that was now in his possession. Moreover, such praise would itself redound to his cultural capital as critic, since the increasing value of the work of the artist praised, coupled with the critic's own accumulated collection of that artist's work, prompted collectors (and, of course, other critics who were themselves in the same game) to comment favourably on his foresight and aesthetic sensibility in 'discovering' the potter in question. In this way, an increase in cultural capital would inevitably redound favourably on a critic's overall symbolic capital.

To what extent payola – defined as 'a bribe paid in order to influence a gatekeeper's choice among competing creative products'[57] – was extensively practised is unclear. Rumours and gossip of underhand dealings, however, abounded – thereby underlining the insecurity felt by participants in the field regarding such issues as 'standards', 'skills', 'talent' and 'quality'.

One classic instance of such gossip surrounded a well-known Karatsu potter – let us call him Boroemon – who at the time of my research was said to have spent ¥30 million ($300,000) 'bribing' those concerned in and around the Japan Art Association to award him the coveted and prestigious honour of Award of Cultural Merit (*Bunka Kunshō*). As my many informants gleefully observed, Boroemon's manipulations had so far not met with success, although they were prepared for what they perceived to be 'the inevitable' one day. Their glee centred on the fact that, although practising a traditional form of stoneware pottery for which Karatsu is famous, Boroemon had consciously taken the position of *not* participating in the Traditional Crafts Association's activities (where a number of other long-established '*-emon* potters' operated), but had instead strategically opted for 'pure art'.

If rumour is to be believed, Boroemon was not the only potter then or previously (or, probably, even now) who tried to bribe his way to prestige. By general consent, potters at the lower levels of forces and struggles in the field of ceramic art reckoned that ¥30 million was a not unreasonable investment to make on the part of an artist aiming for the highest accolade. Award of a 'national treasureship' or 'cultural merit' automatically permitted an exponential increase in prices for works. Consequently, the investment could be recouped within a year or two. Thereafter was pure profit. It may have been to counter this expectation of accompanying commercial success that the relevant committees tended to bestow the ultimate honours in their power only on the *very* aged.

What the critic's activities reveal is that a clear distinction needs to be made between 'the apparent producer' (in this case, the potter) and the 'discoverer' of the apparent producer, or creator.[58] As the above example makes clear, the critic was in the best position to take on this task, but it might also be a potter or a dealer who 'consecrated' an 'up-and-coming ceramic artist' (*kore kara no tōgeika*). For example, a senior already 'consecrated' and established artist, working within the frame of one of the two ceramics associations mentioned earlier, might easily 'promote' the work of his favourite former apprentice (and might just as easily denounce it) and, through the activities of the association in question, raise him, by means of exhibition inclusions, prizes and appointments, to the upper echelons of 'potter power'.

One thing I learned during the preparations leading up to my one-man show was that it had to be properly framed with all the customary trappings. These included, beside boxing pots, the writing of the mandatory *suisenbun* recommendation. Given that Eisuke was aiming to attract a large number of potters to the show, he decided that it might be better to have one of their number, rather than a critic, write the necessary paragraph or two. However, given the factionalism rife in the field and given the perpetual and unceasing flow of gossip surrounding all those participating in the field of ceramic art, it was very difficult to find a potter whose name and reputation were sufficiently respected by all to achieve the task of attracting them to my show. In the end, we agreed to approach Imaemon Imaizumi, thirteenth generation producer of Nabeshima overglazed enamel ware, and now 'national treasure', and asked him if he would be so kind as to write a 'recommendation' on my behalf. We were fortunate. Being a responsive, kind and gentle man, Imaemon agreed – possibly because he felt in some way obligated toward me, since I had previously translated a book published about his pottery style from Japanese into English and had helped him with some other minor translation work for display in the gallery at his home in Arita.

Critics, however, were not the only 'discoverers' of 'artists'. Indeed, perhaps more regularly than critics, dealers or gallery owners were also in a position to consecrate artists (as is well known from stories of French Impressionism),[59] for whose work they acted as 'guarantors'.[60] At the same time, however, dealers would also rely on the opinion of already consecrated potters when it came to deciding whose work they should buy and display, since the latter were likely to be aware of innovations in their own field.[61]

Eisuke's 'gallery' consisted of his 'stable' of potters, a couple of academic critics on whom he could call to validate their work, his regular clientele and buyers off the street, besides his wife and himself.[62] He would 'introduce' to his gallery's regular clientele the work of various isolated potters whom he had heard about or chanced upon during his frequent drives around the north Kyushu countryside, thus joining otherwise separate roles as patron and tastemaker.[63] Here three considerations were paramount: one was the tastes of his buyers, which he had come to know over time, and to which he knew he could probably match a particular ceramic style; another was his own 'feel' for what would sell, regardless of whether a particular collector would or would not be interested in the pots he put on display. A third consideration, which was – and is – somewhat paradoxical in a field whose members laud the 'eternity' of art and the unchanging nature of 'beauty', was novelty. A new name, a new face, a new style of pottery – these were what drove the ceramic-art world which flourished on a balance between the new and the old, the fashionable and that which was 'beyond fashion', and therefore between the commercial and the symbolic. Such 'discoveries', of course, added to Eisuke's reputation for having a 'good eye', and so increased his symbolic capital, making him seem less 'commercial' and more 'artistic' (there being an inevitable and necessary causal effect between the two). As he was well aware, the ultimate denunciation would be that, as a dealer, he was calculatingly mercenary. Disinterestedness, therefore, was everything.[64]

And all this was possible because of the field itself, described by Bourdieu as 'the locus of the accumulated social energy which the agents and institutions help to reproduce through the struggles in which they try to appropriate it and into which they put what they have acquired from it in previous struggles'.[65] It was in these ongoing and continuous struggles among people in different positions that the value of works of ceramic art, together with the beliefs underpinning that value, was generated and negotiated. All were engaged in the art of capitalizing on ceramic art.

Notes

1. Victor Turner, *Dramas, Fields and Metaphors*, 1974.
2. Cf. Richard Caves, *Creative Industries: Contracts between art and commerce*, 2000, p. 26.
3. Howard Becker, *Art Worlds*, pp. 34–5.
4. Randal Johnson, 'Editor's Introduction: Pierre Bourdieu on art, literature and culture', pp. 1–28 in P. Bourdieu, *The Field of Cultural Production*, 1993, p. 3.
5. Pierre Bourdieu, *The Logic of Practice*, 1990a, pp. 135–41.
6. Pierre Bourdieu, *The Field of Cultural Production: Essays on art and literature*, 1993, p. 184.
7. Bourdieu, *The Logic of Practice*, p. 53.
8. Bourdieu, *The Field of Cultural Production*, p. 189.
9. Johnson, 'Editor's Introduction', p. 5.
10. Bourdieu, *The Field of Cultural Production*, p. 176.
11. Ibid., p. 61.
12. Ibid., p. 119.
13. Ibid., p. 58.
14. Walter Powell (in *Getting into Print*, 1986, pp. 45–6), and following James Thompson (*Organizations in Action*, 1967), points out how every publishing company in the field must stake out for itself a domain 'in terms of goods or services produced, client population, geographical location, and services rendered'. No two companies can occupy the same domain and each company's ability to stake out a domain must be recognized and accepted by others in the field.
15. Bourdieu, *The Field of Cultural Production*, p. 84.
16. Ibid., p. 133.
17. Ibid., p. 30.
18. James Coleman (in 'Social capital in the creation of human capital', 1988) defines social capital as the ability of people to work together for common purposes in groups and organizations (quoted in Fukuyama *Trust*, 1995, p. 33). Francis Fukuyama adds, arguably, that 'social capital . . . rests on cultural roots' (ibid.). My suggestion here is that the economic field is more important than 'culture' per se.

19. Pierre Bourdieu, *In Other Words: Essays towards a reflexive sociology*, 1990b, p. 22.

20. Johnson, 'Editor's Introduction', p. 7.

21. Ibid., p. 14.

22. Stuart Plattner, *High Art Down Home: An economic ethnography of a local art market*, 1996, p. 194.

23. Bourdieu, *The Field of Cultural Production*, p. 182.

24. Ibid., p. 261.

25. Ibid., p. 257; Becker, *Art Worlds*, p. 138.

26. Caves, *Creative Industries*.

27. Bourdieu, *The Field of Cultural Production*, p. 47.

28. A. L. Sadler, *Cha-no-yu: The Japanese tea ceremony*, 1934, p. 71.

29. Bourdieu, *The Field of Cultural Production*, p. 53.

30. Caves, *Creative Industries*, p. 202.

31. Thus, it used to be said that one Tokyo museum curator 'owned' Hagi, and that another critic was in the process of 'conquering' Agano and other potteries in northern Kyushu. Such taking of positions was preceded, or simultaneously accompanied, by the curator's and critic's acquisition and display of 'knowledge' associated with the potteries in question.

32. Bourdieu, *The Field of Cultural Production*, p. 74.

33. Ibid., p. 82.

34. Ibid., pp. 79–80.

35. Georg Simmel, *Grundfragen der Soziologie*, 1917, p. 68, quoted in Arnold Hauser, *The Sociology of Art*, 1982, p. 452.

36. Raymonde Moulin, *The French Art Market: A sociological view*, 1987.

37. As Hauser says in *The Sociology of Art* (p. 214), 'The artist only becomes an artist when he enters into interpersonal relationships.'

38. Moulin, *The French Art Market*, pp. 126–31; cf. also Hauser, *The Sociology of Art*, p. 397.

39. The same happens in New York when a critic or curator goes to an artist's party! (Karl Meyer, *The Art Museum: Power, money, ethics*, 1979).

40. Hauser, *The Sociology of Art*, p. 468.

41. Stuart Plattner (in *High Art Down Home*, p. 167) reports that 'people in the art world joke that when collectors get together they talk about their passion for art, whereas artists talk about money'.

42. Meyer, *The Art Museum*, p. 181.

43. Moulin, *The French Art Market*, p. 88.

44. Given that what Tsuchiya had to say was very close to the folk art philosophy of Sōetsu Yanagi (himself accused of borrowing his ideals from the tea ceremony), we might recall another comment from Pierre Bourdieu (in *The Field of Cultural Production*, p. 83): 'The dominant are drawn towards silence,

discretion and secrecy, and their orthodox discourse . . . is never more than the explicit affirmation of self-evident principles which go without saying and would be better unsaid.'

45. Bourdieu, *The Field of Cultural Production*, p. 81.
46. In this respect, Koyama might be compared to the publishing and press critic who 'in spite of his apparent independence, even his dictatorship – assumes the function of a handyman. He belongs to the establishment and fulfils, as the guardian of *idées reçues*, a vital task in the preservation of the dominant system' (in Hauser, *The Sociology of Art*, p. 485).
47. Brian Moeran, 'Japanese ceramics and the discourse of "tradition",' 1990b, pp. 214–5.
48. Hauser himself reflects this ambivalence when he writes (*The Sociology of Art*, p. 516) that 'the assumption of an analogy between value and price in the area of art would be the worst example of that objectivization which robs a state of affairs of its meaning'.
49. Cf. Hauser, *The Sociology of Art*, p. 509.
50. Caves, *Creative Industries*, pp. 7–8. For more on this, see the following chapter.
51. It will be recalled in this context that some potters felt obliged to command their (former) apprentices to buy their work, in order to boost flagging sales at a show. Similarly, the importance of 'best-seller' lists in the publishing business has in the past encouraged the authors of a 'best-selling' business book to buy up 50,000 copies of their own work in order to keep it on the *New York Times* best-seller list (Caves, *Creative Industries*, pp. 152–3).
52. Bourdieu, *The Field of Cultural Production*, p. 75.
53. Moulin, *The French Art Market*, p. 76; Caves, *Creative Industries*, pp. 194–5.
54. Levin Schucking, *The Sociology of Literary Taste*, 1974 [1944], p. 57.
55. Prizes did not confer as much financial gain as, for example, an Oscar in the film industry which can add from $5–$30 million to US box-office takings for a film (Caves, *Creative Industries*, p. 198).
56. Moulin, *The French Art Market*, p. 77.
57. Caves, *Creative Industries*, p. 286.
58. Bourdieu, *The Field of Cultural Production*, p. 78.
59. Ambroise Vollard *Recollections of a Picture Dealer*, 1978 [1936].
60. Moulin, *The French Art Market*, pp. 37–65.
61. Caves, *Creative Industries*, p. 32.
62. Becker, *Art Worlds*, pp. 110-11.
63. Cf. Meyer, *The Art Museum*, p. 166.
64. Eisuke thus more or less accorded with Hauser's description (in his *The Sociology of Art*, p. 516) of a dealer as one who 'administers to the public not merely by organizing buyers into groups, defining directions of taste, creating

fashions, channelling the consumer's receptivity, but also by taking over – in relationship to the artist – the role of the patron and the person giving the commission'.

65. Bourdieu, *The Field of Cultural Production*, pp. 78–9.

–9–

Creative Fields

Now that I have shown how *individuals* take up positions vis-à-vis one another, as well as vis-à-vis institutions in the field (of ceramic art), I want, in this last chapter, to extend the concept of 'field' to different kinds of activities and to take as my main focus the positions and position-takings of large-scale *organizations* and their structured components vis-à-vis others in the field.

Bourdieu developed the idea of 'field' in relation to cultural production, and applied it in particular to art and literature. As a result, perhaps, the concept has been seen to have a limited validity. This is unfortunate because it is clearly applicable to other kinds of business activity where 'economy' and 'culture' clash. The London stock exchange (divided into its different parts – Government stock, Mines, Oils and Industries), with its panoply of stockbrokers, jobbers, investment analysts, private and corporate investors, as well as old-boy networks, plus all kinds of related institutions from the Stock Exchange Council to the Bank of England, by way of the Treasury, would be one example. Another would be the toy industry, with its trade exhibitions, retail chains, and manufacturers like LEGO analysing markets, dreaming up product-range ideas, arranging media tie-ups, building theme stores and parks, and all the while concentrating intensely on branding, branding, branding as a means of differentiating itself, its products, its employees, and its customers from competing manufacturers.

Economic Properties of Creative Production

In fact, the toy industry may in many respects be classified as a 'creative industry' and it is on the field of creative industries – in particular, advertising – that I want to focus in this chapter. Any industry that relies on the creative element of *design* as an important component in the manufacture and sale of its products is likely to find itself having to deal with the not necessarily harmonious combination of culture and economy demands. People working in design – whether of a LEGO brick, a ghetto blaster, a car interior, a soft-drinks bottle and accompanying bottle opener, or my computer mouse – tend to work with functional and aesthetic ideas of one sort or another, while those charged with product development and sales probably have at least one eye firmly fixed on costs that may prevent designers from putting their ideal plan into effect.

Certain industries – and I am thinking of ones like fashion, film, music, publishing and other media and entertainment industries – are characterized by a number of general features (including design) that make them resemble the art and literary fields of cultural production and thus seem perfect candidates for field analysis. These features have been analysed at length by the economist Richard Caves who suggests that they include seven basic economic properties.[1] These I will link here to the fields of advertising and fashion-magazine publishing.

First, there is the *nobody knows* property of cultural production in which demand is uncertain. Until a particular product or work is placed before a consumer, it is not at all certain how he or she will react to it.[2] This is because creative industries produce what are called 'experience goods' – like concerts, fashion clothing, films, perfumes, television commercials and so on. Of course, market research can be, and is, used to find out if they will 'work', but even so its results are not always accurate. Thus success – whether of a fashion magazine, theatrical production or Hollywood film – is unpredictable.[3]

Unpredictability – of individual temperament, of employees' positions, of the winning and maintaining of accounts, of advertisers' corporate strategies, and of the economy as a whole – characterizes the Japanese advertising industry. Even though market research is conducted, and some idea can be gained about whether a particular product or image meets with potential consumers' expectations, nobody knows until that product hits the supermarket shelves or the ad the news stands. Those concerned tend to go on 'gut feelings', cross their fingers and hope for the best – or, at least, that the worst will not happen. A similar situation exists in the publication of women's fashion magazines whose sales are predictably unpredictable from month to month, in spite of certain 'overall tendencies'.

It is in an attempt to overcome this unpredictability of 'tastes' that advertising personnel massage their networks, since it is these interpersonal connections that establish some sort of ordered structure in which all concerned may operate. Nevertheless, even here, differing expectations about norms of behaviour in such social interaction lead to misunderstandings – as Yano's rueful account of his golfing weekend demonstrates. Moreover, corporate decisions regarding the deployment of individual employees also add to the unpredictable nature of interpersonal relations – an unpredictability that encourages even *more* personal connections to be made between individuals working for companies doing business with one another.

The *nobody knows* property rife in the field of advertising thus creates its own field of forces and struggles, involving individuals within and between firms, as well as among firms generally. It is, as we will see later on, exacerbated by the fact that no advertiser in Japan gives *all* of its account to a single advertising agency, but instead distributes it among a number of different agencies, none of which is in possession of all the information required to arrive at a complete understanding of its client's overall marketing and sales strategy. This means that it is unable to produce the 'perfect' advertising campaign, unless it obtains the information it seeks from media organizations, which place other advertising campaigns for the same client made by different agencies and thus get to hear some of what others know but the agency in question does not know. The *nobody knows* property thus enables, too, a field of power. It is in an assertion of their power that advertising clients rarely, if ever, immediately accept an agency's campaign proposal made at a competitive presentation, but instead demand that the selected organization 'go back to the drawing board' – a drawing board for which they have provided hitherto only primary colour crayons.

Second, there is the *art for art's sake* property which arises from the fact that creative workers care about and take pride in the work they produce. All creative industries are distinguished by the fact that they employ 'creative' and what Caves calls 'humdrum' personnel. Thus, we find structural oppositions between director and producer, editor and publisher, computer geek and software salesman, designer and engineer, copywriter and account planner, and so on and so forth in all sorts of different fields of work. The exact nature of these oppositions, however, differs from one society to another, as well as from industry to industry, and may incorporate a 'sliding scale' of creativity.

In every advertising industry, humdrum and creative personnel clearly compete with each other. Marketers constantly have to remind their creative teams that advertising is there to sell products, and that clever headlines, alluring images and 'creative' ideas do not fulfil their proper purpose unless they are firmly rooted in market analysis. Creatives, for their part, often alight on ideas – a phrase, an image, the perfect celebrity endorser – that they then have to justify to their account planner and marketing team. When I hit upon the tagline, *It's in the Name*, for Frontier, for example, I had to explain to the senior account executive in charge of the presentation *why* I thought it was appropriate. To do so, I took a number of Frontier's competitors' taglines, together with the two that the client had supplied (*The Art/Pulse of Entertainment*), compared them by means of syntagmatic and paradigmatic structures first proposed by the linguist, Ferdinand de Saussure, and showed how *It's in the Name* stood out from all the others, with the possible exception of Sony's *The One and Only*. But this kind of analysis did not *precede* the 'invention' of the tagline. Rather, advertising works by a process of postrationalization, as creative and humdrum personnel seek to reconcile their different attitudes to the job in hand.[4]

In Europe and the United States, where an ideology of 'individualism', 'creative artist' and 'talent' or 'genius' prevails, it is often the case that the field of advertising will appear to give more weight to the demands of 'creativity', and thus symbolic capital;[5] or at least to accept that economic capital is *not* the bottom line (as it is supposed to be in a field of large-scale production). In Japan, on the other hand, where – in ideological terms – people more generally value interpersonal connections and regard 'creative ideas' as emerging from social interaction as a whole, 'creativity' and those who do 'creative' work are given far less weight, and the field comes to be dominated by economic capital. This is not to say that there is no argument about the relative merits of 'line' (profit) and 'staff' (cost) employees. Much social interaction within an agency revolves around getting the 'right chemistry' to enable account teams to function effectively, and that means ensuring mutual respect for the relative forms of capital each participant brings to a task. But, unlike in Europe and the United States, the field of advertising in Japan is not, and has not been, dominated by CEOs who – like David Ogilvy and others – are or were copywriters and other creative personnel, rather than humdrum businessmen. Masao Inagaki, former CEO and now chairman of ADK, for example, has been first and foremost sales-oriented.

In the field of fashion magazines, publishers arrange themselves 'against' editors, in the sense that the former are concerned with advertisers and the money that advertising brings in to cover production and distribution costs and, hopefully, make a profit, while the latter focus their attention on writing and producing the cultural content of a magazine. In this respect, editors are the 'creative' ones. However, when it comes to subcontracting photographers, hair stylists, make-up artists, models and others involved in the production of fashion and beauty photography, editorial staff find themselves in the commercial driving seat having to ensure that schedules are met, costs not overrun, and so on. They are now the humdrum staff arranged 'against' external creative personnel.

The fact that creative personnel cannot be pinned down beforehand about the aesthetic choices that go into their work gives rise to some uncertainty about how exactly an 'inner vision' will materialize in a product. This adds to the *nobody knows* effect.

Account teams – made up of one or more members of an agency's different account services, media buying, marketing and creative divisions – spend a lot of time arguing among themselves about what is the 'best' form to be taken by the advertising campaign on which they are working. Different conflicts may emerge at different stages of the campaign's preparation. For example, in the preparation of a contact-lens campaign, a copywriter was convinced that the phrase 'corneal physiology' (*kakumaki seiri*) provided by the client in its product information, was sufficiently vague and unusual to be used as a headline to attract the targeted audience of young women in their late teens to late 20s. He had to be reminded several times by the marketing team that its research showed that young women were not interested in the technology underpinning the manufacture of contact lenses and were primarily concerned with a user benefit – comfort. Thus 'corneal physiology' would not be the most appropriate headline to use in this campaign.

Later on, in negotiations with the client, when the account team had fixed on the headline 'soft hard' (*yawaraka hard*) as most appropriate in meeting the marketing team's insistence on appealing to consumer desires, the product manager argued that the earlier headline of 'corneal physiology' was more appropriate, since it reflected his company's technological breakthrough and superiority over its competitors. This time, it was the copywriter who vigorously defended the new headline of 'soft hard'; young women consumers were not interested in product benefit, so much as user benefit. In this exchange, the account executive in charge felt obliged to sit slightly on the client's side of the ideological fence[6] and, in the end, prevailed upon the copywriter to include 'corneal physiology' as a subheading in the campaign's print advertisements.

In this copy-led campaign, there were numerous difficulties in putting together a series of visual images that would match the headline, avoid certain restrictions relating to medical products (among which contact lenses were included), find a suitable celebrity endorser who would appeal to young women consumers (rather than either the young male creative team or the 55-year-old male product manager), and please the client. At one stage, the art director persuaded the product manager that it would make sense to include a green, rather than the then standard blue, 'lens cut' at the bottom of the advertisement. His reasoning was, on the one hand, that green was 'ecological' and so conformed to a mini-fad for 'ecological fashion' at the time and, on the other, that green would differentiate the client's product from all other contact lenses currently advertised. The product manager, having accepted this argument, then argued long and hard over what he regarded as the 'muddy' (*dorokusai*) hue of the actual green finally selected by the art director who, for his part, had to explain how his choice of green was not 'muddy' but 'bright' (*tōmeikan no aru*) and matched the overall 'tone' of the sepia-tinted photograph of the selected celebrity to produce a 'soft-hard' image. This difference of 'aesthetic' opinion ended up in a stalemate, but the *art for art's sake* property prevailed when the art director's choice was included in the finished advertisement.[7]

Third, there is what is known as the *motley crew* property. Many products put out by creative industries require all sorts of different expertise. These diverse skills have to be co-ordinated in such a manner that every step along the way to completion contains all the necessary elements doing their necessary job. Creative products must conform to preconceived ideas of what is appropriate in the context and must also exhibit an acceptable level of proficiency.

An advertising campaign depends in its production upon the different sets of expertise brought by different members of an agency's account team: overall planning and client liaison work by one or more account executives; analysis of competing products and advertising campaigns, consumer tastes, corporate strategies, and so on by marketing staff; transformation of marketing data and analysis into linguistic and visual ideas by copywriter, art director and other creative personnel; selection of appropriate media outlets and calculation of media time and space costs by a media buyer. These tasks are carried out both jointly – as in the initial orientation – and independently – as with market analysis or the creative search for the magic phrase or image that will set the campaign alight. Often they will involve some, but not other, groups of personnel as the various sets of data are discussed, mulled over, disputed, reviewed and fitted to advertising products. Thus meetings of the 'account team' may consist of just account executive and media buyer; or of copywriter and art director alone; or of account executive, marketing team and client; or of account executive, marketing and creative personnel; and so on, depending on the stage at which the development of the campaign as a whole has reached.

When it comes to a presentation, the client does not expect its selected agency to provide a complete and utterly professional set of finished print advertisements and/or television commercials, since it will not have paid for studio production with attendant cast. Instead, an agency's account team provides – albeit expensive – 'mock-ups' of ads which include illustrated or photographic visual images, headlines, sub-heads, logo and tagline, but meaningless, repeated phrases (*parts of parrots preserved in parcels of pickled pirates parts of parrots preserved in parcels of pickled pirates parts of parrots preserved*, or Japanese equivalent) that constitute 'dummy' body copy. This meets the criterion of acceptable proficiency.

Once a client has given the go-ahead for production of a campaign, the creative team bring in yet more personnel – celebrity, celebrity manager, models, model agency, photographer, fashion stylist, hair stylist, make-up artist, studio and related assistants, followed by sound engineer, special sound effect specialist, film editor and so on – to add to and strengthen the motley crew property.[8] All these personnel need to be properly coordinated by the art director who has produced a 'final' image on which they base their work. But each tends at once to bring to bear the *art for art's sake* property on this image, thereby affecting the final product. Thus the photographer will alter slightly the angle of the camera in order to highlight some aspect of the celebrity's features that he believes reinforces the image aimed at by the art director. Similarly, the hair stylist will take advantage of the weight of a model's hair to suggest a revision in style, and the specialist in sound effects will find just the 'right' combination of plinks and plonks to give the accompanying television commercial a 'soft-hard' feel. Somehow, the art director has to keep control of these creative interpolations by his motley crew and show a finished product that the client can still recognize from the 'drawing board' mock-ups.

Fourth, there is the *infinite variety* property. This refers both to 'the universe of possibilities from which the artist chooses' and to 'the array of actual creative products' available to consumers.[9] Precisely because products are differentiated – and yet, though not identical, quite similar – consumers have trouble agreeing in general about which is 'better' as a whole. This is complicated by the fact that they tend to make their comparisons along a number of different dimensions.

Infinite variety is at the very heart of advertising and forms the basic principle on which the industry thrives. As a property, it prevails in three interlocking spheres of institutions, people and products. As a principle, it determines the positions taken and struggled for in the field.

Briefly, the system of production, distribution, representation and consumption of goods and services characterizing contemporary capitalism and the 'circuit of culture'[10] obliges manufacturing and other corporations to set themselves off from one another by means of logos, corporate cultures, mission statements, CEO personalities and so on; marketing consultants to propose new and 'different' ways to market products and brands (as well as corporations); advertising agencies to find 'unique' ways to illustrate, explain, image and sell those goods; and consumers to buy and use them as part of their own separate processes of economic, social and symbolic differentiation.

It is not only consumers who have trouble in agreeing about what is 'better' or 'worse'. In the production of fashion magazines, senior editors often cannot decide which photograph of a model – or which photograph of two different models – should grace the cover of a title's next edition. The model's pose, the materials, cut and colours of the clothes she wears, the texture of her skin, the colour of her eyes and hair, together with its length and style, as well as the background to the photograph (studio or location, street or beach), all contribute to an overall image whose effect must be matched by appropriate headlines in appropriate colour, font, type size, spacing, grid distribution and so on. Since it is the cover photograph that 'sells' the magazine, and since editors are continually conscious and apprehensive of what or whom competing titles might select for their cover photos (the same supermodel or celebrity would be a 'disaster'), two potential covers may be run side by side right to the last minute before printing, when the publisher's opinion may also be sought in the final selection process. Thus four different teams of people are involved in a cover – two on the production side (Fashion and Art), and two more on the selection side (Editorial and Publishing) – each bringing to bear a wide variety of criteria (from an aesthetics of form to potential sales) in deciding which image is 'the best'.

Fifth, there is what is known as the *A list/B list* property which arises from the fact that cultural products differ in the quality of skills they display (although, inevitably, other criteria are brought to bear in the assessment).[11] Consequently, art worlds negotiate a ranking of artists, screenwriters, photographers, solo pianists, potters and so on, as well as of related institutions like galleries, studios, department stores, museums and so forth.

Magazines are generally ranked by their ability to bring in advertising, as is made clear by the fact that even publications with healthy circulations may 'fold' because of lack of advertising. Fashion magazines are ranked higher as a category than magazines devoted to hobbies, news, travel and so on, because of the brand names of their advertisers, the quality of the advertisements they carry, and the accompanying quality of paper and print that they use. Among the dozen or so fashion magazines published in the United States, titles like *Vogue* and *Harper's Bazaar* are ranked well above *Allure*, *Glamour* and *Mademoiselle*, with *Marie Claire, Elle* and *InStyle* occupying an intermediary position in the status hierarchy. The jostling for positions in the *A/B lists* is effected through sales, which well-known advertisers a magazine attracts, and the quality of its photography (especially fashion photography) and related personnel.

These personnel – especially fashion photographers and models, but also hair stylists and make-up artists – keep portfolios of their work. Those on the *B list* in particular hawk their portfolios around the offices of magazine fashion and beauty departments, in the hope that they may be selected for a photo shoot or story (which will be added to their portfolios). Models also visit magazines with their portfolios, but they simultaneously spend a lot of time among photographers, hoping that the latter might select them for a particular job since a 'new face' can make a photographer (as

Janice Dickinson did Mike Reinhardt) and move him from *B* to *A list*.[12] Alternatively, they may link up with model agents (as Linda Evangelista did with Gérald Marie) and, via connections with a renowned photographer (in this case, Peter Lindbergh), become famous enough to 'make' a model agency (Elite) (which is part of another, related ranking hierarchy).[13] In all these cases, it is *who* a particular model or photographer is that, as in art, gives the product (a fashion photograph or advertising campaign) a provenance that itself contributes to the *A list/B list* properties in an inextricably entwined combination of social, symbolic and economic capital.

As we saw in the previous chapter, this ranking of talent occupies a lot of the conversations taking place among those concerned in a creative field.

In the field of advertising, as the previous examples imply, the *A list/B list* property functions in a number of different sub-fields. First, advertisers are ranked, primarily on the amount (that is, the economic sum) of advertising they place with media every year, but also on the product they advertise (a car or toothpaste, haute couture or panty-liners) and their own corporate ranking (itself often based on turnover and market share) in the field of business in which they operate (Toyota or Suzuki, Sony or Sanyo). Secondly, agencies are ranked, primarily according to turnover, so that the Top 10 constitute the *A List* and the rest *B* and other lists, although other perceived qualities are also taken into account and applied as 'characteristics' to individual agencies: 'power' to Dentsu, 'intelligence' to Hakuhodo, 'human resources' to Asatsu, and, at one stage, 'creativity' to McCann Erickson. Thirdly, media organizations are ranked, both by turnover (*Yomiuri* over *Sankei* newspapers, Fuji over MegaTon TV networks) and by 'intellectual content' (Asahi over Yomiuri and Fuji).

Accounts, too, are given their *A list/B list* rankings and so take on the same kind of provenance as art objects. (Remember how pots are boxed, named, signed and sealed.) Agencies and other participants in the field rank accounts as 'desirable' according to the prestige of the corporation awarding the account, since such prestige rubs off onto the agencies concerned. Hence their favoured use of the phrase 'blue chip' accounts. An advertiser's status itself depends in large part on the commodity or service it produces. In the field of foreign cars in Japan, for example, Mercedes-Benz ranks above BMW which itself outranks Audi, Volkswagen and Volvo. When Asatsu won the Mercedes-Benz account in the late 1980s, a number of eyebrows were raised since, at the time, the agency was positioned in the lower ranks of Japan's top 10 agencies, while Mercedes-Benz was *the* luxury car imported into the country. When the agency lost the account some years later, there was a knock-on effect that redistributed the advertising accounts of the top three European car manufacturers among the top three Japanese advertising agencies: Mercedes-Benz-Dentsu; BMW-Hakuhodo; and Audi-Asatsu (ADK).

Because advertising agencies have to cooperate so closely with celebrities and creative artists of all types, and because the *A list/B list* property has an important effect on consumer perceptions of products advertised, agency personnel need to be constantly up to date with gossip and information affecting the rise and fall in prestige of those assigned to *A* and *B lists*. This means keeping abreast of the demeanour and mis-demeanours of all the artistic personnel with whom they may already have, or in future wish to have, professional dealings, since these can have a knock-on effect vis-à-vis products advertised. Hence, when Shintarō Katsu, an actor renowned for playing the part of a blind swordsman in films and television dramas, was arrested at Honolulu airport for possession of (a very small amount of) drugs, the advertiser Kirin Beer – clearly frightened of what it perceived to be a potential negative public reaction to its product and corporate image – ordered its agency, Hakuhodo, to pull a series of just-completed commercials starring Katsu before they were even run on television. Pepsi Cola faced a similar problem when the singer Michael Jackson was first accused of child molestation. Estée Lauder, for its part, decided not to replace newly contracted model, Elizabeth Hurley, following revelations that her actor boyfriend, Hugh Grant, had been involved with a 'divine' prostitute in Los Angeles.

Sixth, there is the *time flies* property. As we have already noted, creative activities often involve complex teams (the *motley crew* property) whose members have to co-ordinate their activities temporally.

A fashion magazine in Japan hits the shelves of retail outlets some 30 and 40 days before the issue date. Thus the January issue of *Elle Japon*, for example, will be pub-lished on November 27 the previous year (and so be able to carry plenty of Christmas-related advertising and editorial matter). In order to meet that deadline, editorial staff need to have an initial 'brainstorming' meeting to discuss the overall contents of the issue in the middle of September. The Editor-in-Chief and her Deputy Editors then follow up with their own selection process a few days later, before distributing edito-rial tasks to their team, as well as directing the fashion and beauty editors to pursue par-ticular paths. Each of these liaises with the Art Department, which advises on layout, copy, headlines and word counts, and sets a deadline for submission of material.

In the meantime, the Advertising Sales Department has been gathering orders from clients for ads for the January edition, and, in consultation with the Editor-in-Chief, begins to outline a rough plan of the magazine, showing which pages are to be taken by advertising, and which by editorial matter. In order to ease the problems caused by the *time flies* property, every magazine will adopt a fairly standard format that includes fixing first, the *number* of pages devoted to a particular part of the magazine (twelve pages of two-page ad spreads before Contents and Masthead pages, for example, or the 52-page 'fashion well' uninterrupted by advertising); secondly, the *content* of pages (*Opinion, In Vogue, Ellements* and so on) that follow the Contents and Masthead pages and give a magazine its 'brand property'; and thirdly, a regular division of editorial *flow* into Features, Fashion, Beauty, Health and so on.

The latter are themselves usually standardized sub-sections. The American version of *Marie Claire*, for example, regularly includes Reportage, Investigation, Campaign, First Person, Exclusive and Relationships under the heading Features. The sub-heading of Relationships itself contains regular themes: Couples, Dating, Intimacy, Love Life and Men Confess. This makes the magazine easily recognized by the reader of *Marie*

Claire. More importantly, it assists editorial staff overcome the *time flies* problem by enabling them to produce material according to a previously established and accepted formula.[14]

This means that those who can meet a certain production schedule are likely to get the nod over those who are not sure if they can, or who are already engaged for part of the time, even though the latter may be preferred candidates for the activity in question. Temporal co-ordination brings with it a potential hold-up problem, as someone refuses or is unable to work at a particular time, and this may affect production expenses and revenue.

Apart from summarizing the impermanence of advertising campaigns once they have been produced, the *time flies* property applies to all aspects of an agency's work, from client orientation to competitive presentation five to six weeks later. This means everything from co-ordinating its motley crew of account team and production personnel, on the one hand, to timing a campaign's placement in different media according to its client's marketing aims, on the other.

Account teams are put together through the connections an account executive has internally among colleagues, but he may be obliged to use a freelance copywriter or art director if no 'suitable' candidate can be found closer to home. Similarly, a creative team may feel that a particular celebrity – let us say, a tennis star – would be ideal to endorse a particular product, but then finds itself unable to use her because the production of the campaign coincides with the middle of the professional tennis season. Since a hold-up would not be tolerated by the client, the team has no choice but to rethink its strategy of celebrity endorsement.

The final placement of advertising campaigns may also be important to the client. Chocolate manufacturers, for example, want to ensure that their ads are placed in the January, February and March issues of magazines (depending on issue publication dates), in order to coincide with Valentine's Day gifting customs. A supermarket or department store demands that its announcement of the following week's special offers or art exhibition be placed in the weekend edition of a newspaper (something that, because of its regularity, is not hard to arrange). Manufacturers in general may be extremely particular about the timing of a new-product campaign which has to coincide with its launch date. Even when media are fully booked, they will generally adapt their advertising schedules to allow for such special temporal circumstances, at the risk, however, of infuriating an already scheduled advertiser which is 'bumped off' the schedule until an appropriate slot opens. This can in fact lead to a series of reshuffles over time as the advertiser concerned claims its right not to be kept waiting and demands immediate (i.e. the following day) restitution in the schedule, thereby displacing another advertiser who then demands, etcetera, etcetera.

Seventh, there is the *ars longa* principle. Because many creative products (though not their performance) last over time and permit composers, writers, and so on to collect money for copyright, creative industries have to ensure that rents are collected from and/or paid to those concerned as appropriate. This may have certain organizational implications, like the emergence and use of specialist agents, for example.

> The *ars longa* principle is one that is often pertinent in the use of advertising images, so that all agencies keep in touch with an assortment of managers, agents and other personnel representing celebrities, photographers, models, dance troupes and so on, to whom rents are paid. With advertising endorsements, celebrities – and sometimes more famous models – are required to sign contracts stipulating the exact nature of the work undertaken and exclusion clauses covering everything from endorsing rival companies' products to nudity.
>
> The other area of *ars longa* with which advertising agencies frequently deal is patents. On one occasion, at an internal meeting following a speculative presentation to an existing client for a new sports drink, Yano and his team agreed that the client's brand manager appeared sufficiently interested in the idea for them to register the proposed brand name, *Marathon*, with the appropriate Patents Office. In its continued work with animation cartoons, Asatsu has been involved in the patenting and merchandising rights of all kinds of character merchandise, from which the agency itself sometimes collects rents.
>
> Sometimes, an agency's work for a client will itself generate *ars longa* characteristics and necessitate organizational change. For example, as a result of its work on behalf of a Young Musicians Summer School, involving an annual concert under the direction of an internationally renowned conductor and spin-off CD, Asatsu established its own separate office devoted entirely to this task. In this way, over time, the agency developed a number of subsidiary companies around it, specializing in everything from publishing to music, by way of direct marketing and special sports events.

Finally, in addition to the seven properties outlined by Caves, we may add what I shall call the *double consumer* property. As the distinction between creative and humdrum personnel implies, many creative industries find themselves addressing at least two different audiences during the course of cultural production. One of these audiences is the targeted consumers of the product; the other is the individual or organization providing the money for the creative product.

> In the creation of an advertising campaign, every agency finds itself addressing two audiences: one, the targeted consumers of the product advertised; the other, the advertising client for whom the campaign is being created. The account executive in charge of the campaign needs to ensure, therefore, that the campaign both meets marketing criteria regarding end-consumers and satisfies members of the corporation financing the campaign. During preparations for a new contact lens campaign, an account team at Asatsu found itself also having to take into account the interests of a third audience group: medical specialists who were in a position to recommend the advertised contact

lens to consumers. The fact that the latter were for the most part young women aged between 18 and 25 years, while the former were middle-aged men, meant that the creative team found itself severely limited in both the language and visuals that it could make use of in the campaign.

The problem of differing interests of advertising sponsors and consuming public, and how these affect cultural content, has been touched on in previous discussion of fashion magazines, and extends to media productions in general. Sponsors have been known to go to absurd lengths to ensure that there is no hint of a rival's name in a film script, for example – as when Chrysler once insisted on removal of an offending phrase 'ford the river'. By corollary, placement brokers work in conjunction with script writers to construct stories, or *fabulae*, conducive to the thematization of products.[15]

In many creative industries, a third audience consists of the creative professionals working therein. Thus fashion photographers, hair stylists, make-up artists and so on pay particular attention to the fashion photographs that appear in monthly magazines, and use them to build their own portfolios, as well as to admire, criticize and adapt where appropriate the ideas of others in the sub-field in which they work.

Advertising Field

As we have seen in the various fieldwork stories told in earlier chapters, the field of advertising production consists mainly of advertising agencies and their clients, as well as market-research consultants, production companies, and studios and agencies of various kinds related to the world of entertainment (photographers, musicians, models, fashion and hair stylists, make-up artists and so on). It also includes, as the third main player in the field, media organizations like newspaper and magazine publishers, radio and television stations. All of these together participate in what Bourdieu has nicely referred to as a 'cultural value stock exchange'.[16]

At the same time, it can be seen that the field of advertising extends into and brings together related fields of media, fashion, film and music. It is also linked to other fields of advertising, media, entertainment and so on, in different parts of the world (in the United States, Britain, Japan and so on): in terms of personnel (for example, supermodels and photographers); institutions (global agencies like J. Walter Thompson and Saatchi & Saatchi, and global advertisers like Chanel and Coca Cola); and products (global advertising campaigns and all sorts of borrowed images and advertising styles). In this respect Japan's field of advertising constitutes a *field of fields*.[17]

The distribution of positions available to and adopted by participants in these fields include choices between commercial and highbrow, documentary and infotainment, the market and creativity, consecrated and untried, and so on. For example, advertising agencies in Japan (and elsewhere) approach particular sponsors and media organizations who are known to be well disposed toward one kind of television programme or another kind of cultural event, and so encourage institutional homology around certain cultural forms. By its very position in the field, a distillery is more likely to support a sporting event than an animated cartoon film for children, which would appeal more to a toy manufacturer while the visit of a Russian ballet troupe would not.

Fashion magazines exemplify the structural homology in the distribution of positions in the field. Because they devote most of their editorial pages to fashion and beauty, magazines attract advertisers from the fashion and beauty industries, and because they attract these advertisers, magazines continue to focus on women's fashion and beauty, even though external societal changes may have affected the social role of women and people's perceptions thereof. The introduction of health as a new editorial category in women's magazines during the 1990s reflects such a societal change.

Occasionally, like an advertising agency, a magazine will follow its advertising client abroad. *Marie Claire*, for example, launched a Turkish edition of its title when one of its major advertisers and then stakeholders, L'Oréal, advised those concerned that it wished to open up the market for its beauty products in Turkey. There is thus a close connection between market and cultural product.

Bourdieu's argument about positions, position-takings, a field of forces and field of struggles is exemplified in the field of advertisements.[18] As we are all acutely aware, companies of all kinds make use of advertising to bring to the notice of their consuming publics (or 'target audiences') various aspects of the work in which they are engaged. Thus, an automobile manufacturer will advertise an updated version of a popular family car, a supermarket its special offers of the week, and cosmetics firm the launching of a 'new' body lotion. With every advertising campaign (complete with language and visuals), a subtle change is wrought. The car advertisement may hark back to an earlier ad by the same or rival automobile manufacturer; a supermarket special offer may be phrased as a variation on a famous *haiku* poem by Bashō; the body-lotion campaign will almost certain use a famous model, who is not allowed by contract to endorse products for competing cosmetics or related forms, and whose face therefore establishes the cosmetics firm for which she is advertising in contrast to all other competing companies (whose models are similarly constrained by contract from endorsing the products of rival firms), while simultaneously linking that advertiser with other companies in related and different fields of production (fashion and fashion accessories, jewellery, automobiles, health foods, beauty treatment centres and so on) for whom she is also acting as product endorser. Every campaign thus marks a (subtle) shift in positions, both synchronically across all simultaneously appearing advertising campaigns (especially within the same field and in neighbouring, often interrelated, fields), and diachronically over time, revealing a trajectory of past advertising campaigns conducted by the advertiser in question (think, *Absolut*), as well as of those of its competitors. The position that an advertiser and its agency take every time they prepare to launch a new advertising campaign, therefore, depends on all the campaigns that have appeared previously, as well as on those currently on offer through the various media available. Of course, a change in the media – such as the introduction of the internet – has a similar effect on positions and position-takings, as does a particular advertiser's decision to opt for a hitherto untried media form or content.

At the same time as mediating between different fields, an advertising agency operates within its own field, offering packages that it knows will not or cannot be offered by rival agencies. By accepting that it is 'right' for a particular package, an advertising client consolidates the position that it has already taken by means of other campaigns and sponsorship 'opportunities' in the field of media production, and in this way converts its economic into cultural capital. For example, a petro-chemicals company, anxious to regain social credibility after an oil spill, may well be persuaded to sponsor a series of television documentaries on the environment. Its decision will at least in part be influenced by the fact that the series is to be aired by a television network known to be 'serious' and offered to it by an advertising agency also commonly admired for being 'intelligent' – two characteristics that support its perceived identity as a 'socially responsible' corporation.[19] In other words, in the field of advertising and world of business generally, all firms are concerned about whom they interact with and want to ensure that they place themselves in the 'right' corporate environment.

Let me give a more concrete example of how a particular field may function with regard to positions and position-takings. The advertising agency Asatsu (now ADK) was founded in March 1956, four years after the Japanese government had issued its first television licence and three years before the country's first television network was established. Because Asatsu was a latecomer in the advertising field, it had to find a way of getting round the stranglehold then exerted by the large, firmly entrenched agencies which had been in business since the end of the nineteenth century and which had, as a result, built up seemingly impregnable networks of personal contacts among those responsible for the sale of advertising space in the main medium of newspapers. There was often no way that it could directly approach media organizations which refused to deal with new, untried agencies. As a result, it had to purchase newspaper advertising space for its clients through an already established 'monopoly agency' (*senzoku dairiten*) like Dentsu. This cut into its profits.

The obvious potential and increasing popularity of the new medium of television provided the upstart agency with the opportunity it sought, since at that time commercial television stations were desperate for programme ideas that would attract both sponsors and audiences. Moreover, established agencies were for the most part reluctant to invest in a new medium when they were living comfortably enough off the old ones. This reluctance permitted a new position to be taken in the field of advertising.

At the very beginning, the agency's CEO, Masao Inagaki, made use of his personal contacts and networks developed during previous employment in the publishing industry to go into magazine advertising in a big way. He and his colleagues in Asatsu then had the smart strategic idea of forging a link between the old print medium of magazines and the new visual medium of television by transforming printed comics into animation films. In 1964, it televised the *manga* series, *Eightman*, which immediately drew more than 30 per cent audience ratings. Then, two years later, it brought another part of the publishing industry onto the scene when it televised the book *Super Jetter*, and simultaneously arranged for serial rights of the story to be published as a children's comic magazine. Next, it transformed a drama about baseball, *Kyojin no Hoshi*, into an animation series that drew the highest annual ratings for all television programmes during the next three years. By 1973, the agency was creating its own animation series – for example, *Majinger Z*, which fuelled a long-term 'robot boom' among young children in Japan – and these it was able to sell to publishing houses to be printed in comic magazines. The high-tech robot cat, *Doraemon*, is Asatsu's long-running, all-time hit.[20]

> Bourdieu himself asked: 'what is the degree of conscious strategy, cynical calculation, in the objective strategies which observation brings to light and which ensure the correspondence between positions and dispositions?'[21] To this question, as he recognized, there is no simple answer. Individual actors' unconscious dispositions come into play in the formulation of strategies such as the one described here – some are more reckless or careful 'by nature' than others – but this does not necessarily mean that 'because positions arise quasi-mechanically – that is, almost independently of the agents' consciousness and wills – from the relationship between positions, they take relatively invariant forms'.[22] This is to give too much emphasis to structure and not enough to agency. As Asatsu's venture into cartoon programming shows, in large-scale fields of (cultural) production, at least, actors *do* consciously calculate their strategies. This is what the field of forces in business is all about.

The advertising agency's success in the field was not limited to media products, but extended to other organizations involved in the financing and production of such products. In establishing a niche market for itself in television and magazine publishing, Asatsu was able to enter into business relationships both with major corporations anxious to sponsor its animation programmes and with television stations keen to put on popular new programmes. The latter, through their own business networks of sponsoring corporations, then introduced the agency to first class (or 'first stream' [*ichiryū*]) sponsors with which it was virtually impossible to do business at the time because of Asatsu's low position in the field of forces that characterized Japan's hierarchy of corporate prestige.[23] Moreover, since television stations in Japan are closely linked to newspapers in terms of investment capital, personnel and news supply,[24] they also helped Asatsu make and sustain contacts with advertising departments in affiliated newspaper organizations, and in this way broke down the monopoly on newspaper-space-buying hitherto held by the large and well-established agencies.

This example illustrates well the strategic possibilities that characterize the field of advertising in Japan. By the simple strategy of transforming different print media into television programmes, and vice versa, Asatsu was able to link the two partly separated fields of publishing and television, on the one hand and, on the other, to make use of connections developed therein to enter into other related fields. Moreover, it also initiated long-term partnerships, with toy manufacturers in particular, and in some cases profited from merchandising rights associated with its programmes. Such partnerships have in large part depended on the cultivation of personal networks among those representing the organizations involved.

Three superimposed layers of production are at work here. First, there is the media product itself – the television programmes, cartoon strips, books and advertising campaigns (print ads and TV commercials) in which Asatsu is involved. Secondly, there are the individual players or actors who are involved in the production of the advertising work (the account executives, copywriters, art directors, market analysts and so on). And thirdly, there are the institutions – in particular, advertising corporations, media organizations and agencies – that constitute the structured field of advertising production, all of whom are constantly (re)positioning themselves strategically vis-à-vis others in the field. Together they fashion, create, manipulate and maintain an intricate web of symbolic, cultural, social, educational and economic capital discussed by Bourdieu. The field of advertising (as well as other related fields) contains within it, but goes beyond, the 'population' of organizations and individual people linked therein by their interaction.[25] It is the field as a whole – the positions of which it is constituted and the positions taken by actors in the field – that together condition the ways in which advertising forms and messages are produced, as well as the *social trajectories* of participants in the field.

A fashion photographer's trajectory only makes sense in the world of the fashion magazines to which he or she contributes – in the United States, *W, Allure*, Glamour, *InStyle, Marie Claire, Elle, Harper's Bazaar* and, at the top of the prestige hierarchy, *Vogue*. Similarly, a fashion model's trajectory is judged by her ability to grace the covers of select hierarchically ordered magazines, which may include general-interest news weeklies like *Time* and *Newsweek*, as well as the more specialized fashion and beauty titles. Neither photographers nor models are paid very large sums of money for the jobs they perform[26] – itself slightly remarkable, given the fact that it is the fashion photographs that sell fashion magazines and covers that sell all magazines.[27]

At the same time, however, while appearing to conform to the symbolic capital developed and sustained by magazine titles, these personal trajectories are often converted into economic capital as models and photographers find themselves hired for comparatively large sums of money to participate in commercial advertising campaigns. Moreover, the symbolic capital developed over the years by a magazine like

Vogue will inevitably, in spite of falling sales, still attract advertisers who are sufficiently mesmerized both by *Vogue*'s symbolic cachet and by the cultural capital of its high-class, educated and affluent readers to pay the premium prices for advertising space demanded by the magazine.

In many ways, the structure of any field depends on the way in which money circulates among participants.

> The field of fashion magazines interacts with related fields of advertising, publishing, fashion, beauty and photography. Somewhat similarly to an advertising agency, a (fashion) magazine may be defined as 'a publishing firm with a staff that performs different tasks for which different types of actors within the magazine are responsible'.[28] The main opposition at play is between publishing and editorial work: publishing being connected with the attraction and inclusion of advertising in a magazine; and editorial work with the creation of interesting articles, stories, features, pictures and infotainment for the benefit of readers who are specifically sold to, and targeted by, advertisers. Since the cover price of a fashion magazine cannot begin to cover its costs, it has no choice but to rely on advertising income. This leads to a strained relationship between 'editorial independence' and publishers' attempts to please their advertisers. As a result, it is often difficult to judge whether an 'editorial' page is in fact just that, or yet another covert piece of promotion for a favoured advertising client.[29]

The driving force in both formal and informal relations in the field of Japanese advertising is the system of accounts – the sums of money that enable advertising and media organizations to function in the first place. This system of distributing money among the various participants in the field of advertising has an effect on the distribution of positions both *within* an agency and *between* an agency and other organizations. Unusually, as mentioned earlier, advertisers in Japan do not allocate the whole of their account to a single agency, as they have tended to do in Europe and the United States of America. Instead, they split their accounts – by medium, by product line, even on occasion by agency (with one doing marketing; another creative; a third media buying, and so on). In this way, they provide two, three, or more agencies (just how many are contracted depends on the size of the client company and its advertising budget) with smaller sums of money than is the case, say, in the USA.

> Foreign advertisers in Japan are continually surprised by, and complain about, the way in which Japanese companies, without apparent fear of confidentiality being abused, split their advertising accounts. When Mercedes-Benz Japan first awarded its account to Asatsu, for example, it expressed considerable and vociferous concern over the fact that the newly appointed agency also handled several accounts of a rival Japanese automobile manufacturer, Mitsubishi Motors. How could there not be a conflict of interests? In spite of the agency's reassurances, Mercedes-Benz apparently at one point

requested that Asatsu ditch its Japanese client, even though Mitsubishi was, at the time, the agency's largest and longest-held single account and even though Mercedes-Benz and Mitsubishi Motors were soon to enter into a technology development partnership. When this tactic failed, the European car manufacturer insisted that its account be run from an independent office entirely separate from the building in which the Mitsubishi account was handled. Similar stories abound.

Because they involve not just advertising itself, but sales strategies, corporate imaging, media and other forms of promotion, accounts tend to determine the functional units (each consisting of numerous positions) – Sales, Marketing, Promotions, Media Buying – into which every agency is structured *internally*. At the same time, the broad nature of an account makes cross-divisional co-operation (in other words, networks and connections) essential within an agency. Moreover, precisely because Japanese corporate advertisers prefer to split their accounts and to distribute them as comparatively small sums of money among a number of different agencies, agencies need to operate numerous small organizational units – action sets or project teams of client groups and account teams – to handle them. Finally, by their successes and failures, accounts contribute in large part to employees' ability to take positions and rise up through the ranks to senior management. In this way, they affect an agency's promotional system and formal organizational structure.

Given the conventional belief that Japanese corporate hierarchy depends more on seniority than on individual talent, it came as somewhat of a surprise to find during fieldwork research in Asatsu that almost all senior managerial staff had risen to their positions on the basis of their success in first attracting prestigious clients to the agency and in then developing their accounts into large and profitable business activities. (By corollary, if, by perceived incompetence, a manager lost an important account, either he resigned, or he moved company of his own accord, or he was effectively sidelined.)

The number of such successes also influenced the hierarchical side of the agency's organizational structure. (The cross-department account teams contributed importantly to a horizontal and balancing matrix structure.) The more successes were rewarded, the more new horizontal levels had to be created between the top and bottom tiers of organization, and occasional new vertical units created to accommodate the agency's lateral strategic successes. Over the years these developed from a simple Department-Division-Board of Directors structure based on five functional divisions, to a more complex Group-Section-Department-Division-Office-Board of Directors structure with nine functional offices.

Externally, the system of split accounts favours advertisers in that they have a competitive lever with which to control those working in the agencies contracted. As we have noted earlier in this chapter, advertisers are the only ones who have an overall view of their advertising and marketing strategy; their contracted agencies are limited to but partial views, which can make their work extremely difficult, time-consuming, even wasteful (if, for example, an agency's creative team were to come up with a campaign idea that had in fact already been devised and completed, but not yet aired, by another agency for a related product manufactured by the same advertising client). In other words, the split-account system creates a field of struggles that itself sustains a system of hierarchical power relations between advertisers and agencies. But it does also favour agencies to the extent that, if they lose an account, the financial implications are not such that – as with an American agency that loses a large account – their overall stability is threatened.[30] In other words, lay-offs do not usually occur as a result of an account being lost – so that the split-account system also indirectly supports a general ideal espoused and partially practised by large corporations in Japan (including Asatsu): the so-called system of 'permanent' employment. In this way, the field of advertising overlaps with the more general field of corporate business organization.

In addition, precisely because accounts are split, agencies' account executives are always tempted to get a larger slice of the advertising cake than they have already been given. There are two aspects to this. On the one hand, an advertising agency is prepared to carry out low-level, less obviously visible, aspects of advertising and promotion on behalf of a large, well-known client, in the hope and expectation that it will eventually gain access to more lucrative, above-the-line contracts (for television advertising, for example). The split-account system in this way encourages an advertising agency to expand its activities into all aspects of Japan's consumer and other markets.

As a means of overcoming built-in restrictions to the making of 'real money' in the advertising field, based primarily on the length of establishment of participating players, Asatsu, like any other advertising agency, needed to adopt a strategy, or series of strategies, that would enable it to gain access to the 'tasty' (*oishii*) forms of media buying. One, as we have seen, was to challenge the orthodox traditions of agency-*media* relations by opening up a new space for advertising. Another was to challenge a *client*'s accepted ongoing relations with its space- or time-buying agency. This it did by undertaking all kinds of financially unrewarding tasks, in the hope that the client – through ongoing connections established and nurtured between account executive and manager concerned – would persuade itself that the new agency might actually provide a better service in other parts of its advertising activities, including media buying. Thus Asatsu would take on, for example, the job of designing and setting up standardized sales counters at all the retail outlets of a major cosmetics firm which spent an enormous amount of money on television commercials, as well as in newspaper and magazine advertising. This was a careful strategic move calculated to show the cosmetics client the agency's willingness to do a lot of hard work for comparatively little financial reward and thus to impress on it its potential to carry out other tasks closer to the heart of advertising per se. Thus, little by little, the agency was able to take on one different account after another, moving from retail-space design to arrangement of an annual sales convention and thence from small to much larger cosmetics accounts where Asatsu was asked to handle media-buying (but not creative) activities.

This calculated strategy was not *only* with financial reward in mind. The agency's client was an extremely prestigious and respected firm in Japan's – and, indeed, the world's – corporate hierarchy. By being awarded an account by such a top-ranking client, therefore, Asatsu stood to increase its own prestige within the agency status rankings. Even in this field of large-scale production, therefore, we find that agency managers and employees are always trying to ensure that their economic capital is matched by their clients' symbolic capital. In other words, money alone is insufficient to guarantee power in the field of Japanese (or other) advertising.

On the other hand, this market mechanism of financing the work of advertising agencies encourages, as we have seen, informal contacts between account executives and their counterparts in client companies (like Yano's golfing weekend). This is because it is the personal relationship, rather than a more professional approach to executing an account, which ultimately determines whether an account stays with a particular agency, is increased, decreased, multiplied, or withdrawn. Indeed, such personal relations are often carried over into the contents of the advertisements themselves, where certain images may be suggested by an agency precisely because they are known to appeal to the private taste of the client's product manager.[31] In other words, the very number of accounts – and the competition that they generate among agencies, media, production companies and other organizations in the advertising industry – makes interpersonal relations an even more important factor in Japanese business relations than they already are in other advertising industries where accounts are not split.

During preparations for its competitive presentation to Frontier, the agency's account team found itself having to face the problem of which of three corporate taglines it should adopt in its proposed campaign. The two standard phrases introduced at Frontier's orientation with the agency were *The Art of Entertainment* and *The Pulse of Entertainment*. For various reasons, neither of these taglines was thought to be very good, but at the same time both were thought to be far superior to a third phrase elicited from his opposite number by the account executive and said to be a tagline much favoured by Frontier's senior decision-making executive: *The Light of Joy and Creativity*. In spite of its obvious lack of appeal, the account team time and time again came back to discussing its possible adoption, on the grounds that the Frontier executive who favoured it ultimately was to decide which of the two agencies competing in the presentation was to be awarded the account.

Fortunately a form of common sense prevailed and *The Pulse of Entertainment* was chosen, although backed up by my own suggestion of *It's in the Name* as a credible alternative. Frontier eventually selected *The Art of Entertainment* as its tagline, but admitted that everyone present had liked *It's in the Name*. Unfortunately, however, this tagline was seen to be a little too close to Sony's *The One and Only*, as well as being 'a little – ten to twenty years – ahead of its time'.

Notes

1. Richard Caves, *Creative Industries*, 2000, pp. 2–9.
2. Cf. also Howard Becker, *Art Worlds*, 1982, pp. 122–3.
3. Such unpredictability is by no means limited to creative industries – as followers of stock-exchange indices will be uncomfortably aware.
4. Brian Moeran, 'Imagining and imaging the other', 2003b, pp. 100-1.
5. Cf. Robert Jackall and Janice Hirota, *Image Makers: Advertising, public relations, and the ethos of advocacy*, 2000, pp. 95–9.
6. Ibid., p. 93.
7. Brian Moeran, *A Japanese Advertising Agency*, 1996, p. 159.
8. Cf. Michael Arlen, *Thirty Seconds*, 1981.
9. Caves, *Creative Industries*, p. 6.
10. Paul du Gay et al., *Doing Cultural Studies: The story of the Sony Walkman*, 1997.
11. The *A List/B List* property is used to measure *all* companies in Japan by all kinds of different criteria – corporate turnover, profit, number of employees, CEOs' university backgrounds, and so on – in regular business economy annuals published in the format of *sumō* wrestling-competition announcements. Given this and another incidence footnoted earlier of a property occurring outside the sphere of creative industries, I should say here that I am not entirely convinced that all the properties distinguished by Caves are in fact exclusive to creative industries and that, as as result, they need some refining.
12. The fact that a photographer can 'make' a model encourages liaisons of various kinds between them (like David Bailey and Jean Shrimpton, for example, or Victor Skrebneski and Cindy Crawford).
13. Michael Gross, *Model: The ugly business of beautiful women*, 1995, pp. 28, 190, 356, 456, 481.
14. Cf. Becker who, in *Art Worlds*, p. 128, comments on how distribution systems produce standardization of culture-industry products.
15. Ernest Sternberg, *The Economy of Icons: How business manufactures meaning*, 1999, p. 91.
16. Pierre Bourdieu, *The Field of Cultural Production*, 1993, p. 137.
17. Cf. Ulf Hannerz, 'The global ecumene as a network of networks', 1992.
18. Bourdieu, *The Field of Cultural Production*, p. 30.
19. Cf. Michael Gerlach, *Alliance Capitalism*, 1992, p. 87, on the perceived characteristics of corporate groups in Japan.
20. By the mid-1990s, Doraemon book sales amounted to 110 million copies,

while its 17 films had been seen in cinemas by more than 60 million people. The weekly television programme handled by the Agency has been running in Japan for thirty years and may now be found on television screens in many other parts of Asia (cf. Saya Shiraishi, 'Japan's soft power: Doraemon goes overseas', in P. Katzenstein and T. Shiraishi (eds) *Network Power: Japan and Asia*, 1997). Merchandising connected with the cat can be found on clothes, stationery and household goods – even on a school bus. Royalties connected with such merchandising came to US$153 million between 1979 and 1994 (Frederik Schodt, *Dreamland Japan: Writings on modern manga*, 1996, p. 217). In some of this the agency has had a share of the profits.

21. Bourdieu, *The Field of Cultural Production*, p. 72.
22. Ibid., p. 59.
23. Or, in Rodney Clark's phrase, 'status gradation of industry' (*The Japanese Company*, 1979).
24. D. Eleanore Westney, 'Mass media as business organisations: A U.S.-Japan comparison', in S. Pharr and E. Krauss (eds), *Media and Politics in Japan*, 1996, p. 60.
25. This is where Bourdieu (*The Field of Cultural Production*, pp. 34–5) says that he differs from Howard Becker (*Art Worlds*) because, in his analysis of 'art worlds', the latter limited his discussion more to a network of cooperative links among participants therein. My own reading of *Art Worlds*, however, suggests that Becker (p. 36) is extremely aware of the way in which an art world extends into a more general social field which itself needs to be taken into account and analysed.
26. Patrick Aspers, *Markets in Fashion*, 2001, p. 17.
27. Janice Winship, *Inside Women's Magazines*, 1987.
28. Aspers, *Markets in Fashion*, p. 92.
29. Ellen McCracken, *Decoding Women's Magazines: From Mademoiselle to Ms.*, 1993.
30. It will be recalled from an earlier chapter that Edward Lorenz ('Neither friends nor strangers', 1991) describes a rather similar set of relationships and social outcomes between client firms and subcontractors in the French engineering industry located around Lyons.
31. Michael Schudson, *Advertising: The uneasy persuasion*, 1984, p. 44; Moeran, *A Japanese Advertising Agency*, p. 89.

Conclusion: The Business of Ethnography

So there you have it. I've said what I set out to say, plus a bit more as I discovered one or two unanticipated things en route through these chapters. But that's what writing is all about. Words, like things, have a life of their own, too.

The argument has been simple and the tales, I hope, telling. There is little more to do than reprise the former for the sake of those too lazy or busy to read the rest of the book, and then to add a few words about fieldwork and ethnography as part of my overall take on what the direction in which I believe what might broadly be called business studies, advertising and marketing should head.

Reprise

The argument is this. Social life is largely – not exclusively, but largely – formed around things of one sort or another. These things are sometimes what people start out with (wood for the carpenter, a table for the customer). At other times they are introduced to support already existing behaviour and interaction (like royal regalia, or the shell bracelets of *kula* fame). At yet others they are used to transform people's perceptions of things themselves (Dali's urinal or Magritte's Brie cheese).

Things are more and less tangible. Pots and magazines, for example, we can pick up and examine. Their glazes and glossy paper are smooth to the touch; we can even smell the glue used to bind a magazine's pages together. Advertising, bank and consumer accounts, however, are less tactile. Like certificates of one sort and another (life insurance policies, stocks and shares, graduation diplomas) or computer programs, they demand certain interpretive processes to make sense of them. Some things – works of art or (academic) books – are tactile enough, but their main purpose in life is to encourage communication. Things give people ideas of one sort and another. They lead to shared beliefs. Always and inevitably, they bring some people together and exclude others. The social exchanges that take place through things are often strategic.

If, in our lives – whether as anthropologist, sociologist, tourist, or new employee – we focus on a particular thing, we quickly find it connects a whole network of people. It doesn't matter how mundane it is.[1] In this book I've traced some of the ways in which pots, ads and fashion magazines do the same sort of thing: how people go about making and selling them; the different sets of ideas other people

193

have about the things themselves and how one *should* go about making and selling them; the beliefs they all put into them; the games they all play as they interact with one another, as well as with the pots, ads or fashion magazines, or whatever.

The things I've chosen are, perhaps, a little out of the ordinary. They are not cheque books, pills or cans of beer. And the stories I've told to illustrate my argument have almost all taken place in Japan. But, so far as the argument itself is concerned, it doesn't matter *what* things we study, or *where* we study them. We will still find ourselves embraced by a social world of one sort or another. And it is the thing (together with its surrounding technology) and not a set of national cultural dispositions (for want of a better phrase) that usually inflects the form the social world around it takes. This is why small-type coastal whalers in Japan, Norway, Iceland and the Arctic region communicate with one another so easily. It's also why those working in advertising industries in the United States and Britain can pick up so quickly on the nuances and practices of Japanese advertising. There *are* cultural differences, of course, but for the most part they come *second* in people's fabrication, use and understandings of things.

From this, I moved on to argue that there are three social phenomena that we should keep an eye out for and analyse carefully in our study of things and the ways people interact with them. The first of these is frames. Frames consist of physical settings like an office, a gallery, a lecture hall or a guest room in which certain kinds of activity – work of some kind, an art or craft display, the dissemination, reception and discussion of ideas, or drinking exchanges and inebriation – take place. They consist primarily of the co-ordinates of space, time and purpose for which participants have gathered. Another word I might have used for them is social settings. It is in these social settings that we can see what is important to people in the social worlds in which they participate. Not surprisingly, therefore, every social world tends to have one or two primary frames in which most – if not all – its beliefs and practices come to the fore: drinking in a rural community, for example; department-store exhibitions for potters; competitive presentations for advertising agencies; studio and location shoots for fashion magazines and related personnel.

The second is networks. How people link up with one another and move along networks in order to achieve what they want to achieve and get where they want to get is also very instructive. We see how people create, flaunt, exchange and transform different kinds of – in particular, economic, social and symbolic – capital in order to take advantage of their networks and their positions in the field as a whole. It's not as easy, though, to follow networks as it is to analyse frames. They extend on and on, seemingly endlessly – so much so that participants themselves often don't know where they lead to beyond the first few links in the human chain. And they ramify in all sorts of different and unanticipated directions. But still, I said, it's worth looking at *connections* because it is through connections that most of our worlds revolve. This is particularly true of business. And precisely because business involves individual people and the companies they work for, I also suggested that we need to look at how connections made between individuals can be transformed into strategic alliances between corporations and other organizations.

And the third is fields. Fields are more abstract. If frames are most appropriate for a micro-level of sociological analysis, and networks for an intermediate level, fields are very much at the macro-end of the theoretical continuum. It is only by closely examining both frames and connections, by taking into account both individual participants and institutional players that we can begin to understand the workings of the field in which they take up positions and to which they are subject. I suppose if I were an economist I might have called a field a market. But for most economists, unlike anthropologists,[2] markets don't encompass the social embeddedness of economic actions in the way that fields do. A field is therefore conceptually larger than and embraces within it the particular market in which its actors are also involved.

In using these three concepts of frames, networks and fields, I have made slight adaptations to how they have been used and analysed previously. Whereas Erving Goffman used frame to analyse the organization of *experience*, I have applied it to *social* organization and structure. With networks, I have tried to link early anthropological work, focusing on how individual actors use networks to cut across enduring groups and institutions, to more recent studies in economic sociology, which focus more on the interrelations between personal connections and organizational alliances, and on how the existence of the one assists in and sustains the formation of the other. And with fields, I have extended Bourdieu's argument about cultural production to creative industries more generally, and added that it is probably applicable in large part to *all* fields where (industrial) design is an important element in the production of things.

Throughout the book, I have been concerned to bring out from the accompanying fieldwork data the relational dimensions of action and meaning, and the strategic nature of the social exchanges I describe and analyse. Against the grain of a lot of current anthropological writing, I have provided you with some radical social contextualization: real food for abstract thought.

Fieldwork

Fieldwork – with its periods of 'particularly heightened activity'[3] and 'inherent story-like character'[4] – has been the driving force behind the theoretical argument presented here. Tales from the field have been used to illustrate the general argument, push it forward a little at a time, and intimate how, as an anthropologist, I acquired the necessary cultural knowledge to make sense of the social situations that I encountered.[5] In this respect, the different kinds of fieldwork conducted over the course of more than a dozen years lived in different parts of Japan have been a long social process of learning about and coming to terms with Japanese culture. It is through frame- and network-grounded fieldwork, I have suggested, that we can begin to get to grips with and understand what is going on in different corners of our social lives.

And, although I'm a social anthropologist and although I firmly believe that fieldwork is the stuff of anthropology as a discipline, I have been anxious not to make a fetish out of it as a methodology. One reason for this is that I'm not sure about the heuristic value fieldwork has as a *method* in the first place – which may be why I've allowed you to glimpse me in my *yukata*, moving to the slow rhythm of the *bon odori* ancestral dance, my shadow etched by the light of the fireflies. Sure, there are things that you do and things that you don't do in the field. And, as the story about Rikizō taking issue with me clearly shows, there are things that you learn to put off until it's safe to do them. In this respect, tales from the field become a manual of etiquette, with the kind of dos and don'ts dealt with in the *Dear E. Jean* pages of one of my favourite fashion magazines.[6]

You learn, too, to use information already gleaned to glean more information – although you may need to be circumspect about letting on how much you actually know about the people you're studying when you talk to them. They'll often try to bring you in on *their* side of the story and play you off against their rivals. In these respects, there's a methodological building-up of research data from one interview to the next, in the same way that participating in frames and following connections gradually brings to light the structure of the field as a whole. There's a delicate balancing act to be done here as you walk the tightrope slung over competing groups, factions and networks of people.

But there's an awful lot that's unplanned and which, if you were to stick to some idea of fieldwork 'method', you wouldn't be able to cope with in the raw. In this sense, Ivan Karp and Martha Kendall are right to talk of 'the myth of fieldwork methods'.[7] As Danny Miller likes to tell his students, 'consistent methodology is bad methodology'.[8] Fieldwork needs an immense amount of flexibility and you need always to be able to adapt to unexpected situations, although you (and I) need to be careful not to dismiss the idea of method entirely. There are 'tricks of the trade', for a start, to help you along.[9] The best one I know is the 'Close the notebook' trick. When someone starts telling you some *really* interesting stuff that is definitely back and not front stage, and when that informant seems, maybe, slightly hesitant about whether he or she's doing the right thing, then you very deliberately close your notebook and put it away in your pocket so that he or she knows you're no longer taking notes.[10] And when somebody is *only* telling you front-stage stuff and seems embarrassed, for whatever reason, by your presence, you can do the same. In the first instance, your informant can carry on saying what he or she wants to say without fear of being recorded. In the second, there's a good chance that he or she'll suddenly open up to reveal things that the notebook inhibited him or her from saying. All you have to do is try to remember the gems that then litter the conversation. If nothing else, it's a good way to train your memory.

But this trick of the trade itself invites another: what I like to call 'Case the joint'. Like a thief before a burglary, you always need to check out the area round where you're going to conduct an interview. On the assumption that something might well happen to make you close your notebook (and you can see from these examples that, for better and for worse, I am one of those fieldworkers who prefer not to use tape recorders), you should make sure you know where to run to in order to get down everything you haven't been able to record – and write up in fuller detail what you *have* recorded while it's still fresh in your mind. So, the trick is to find a café or restaurant or reasonably quiet bar – even a car[11] – where you can sit, think through, recall and, these days, type up on a laptop computer the interview you've just completed.

But, as I said above, there probably aren't *that* many objectively useful and practical tips for the participant observer, for whom fieldwork is primarily a combination of understanding and causal explanation[12] and – as this book shows – a movement from observation (where method helps) to participation (where it doesn't) and thence to interpretation (where it might). This is probably why it is theorists and not fieldworkers who occupy the high-status positions within the field of anthropology and sociology. After all, 'fieldworkers are notorious analytic bricoleurs, sniffing out and sifting through current theory for leads as to how fieldwork materials might be conceptualized'.[13]

And yet, these days, fieldwork, or – as it is often confusingly called by those who are neither sociologists nor anthropologists – ethnography, appears to be a fashionable way to conduct research in modern organizations, marketing and related forms of business. As John Van Maanen has noted:

> There is, in fact, some reason to believe that fieldworkers are the leading edge of a movement to reorient and redirect theoretical, methodological, and empirical aims and practices in all the social sciences except, perhaps, the dismal one.[14]

This makes a fieldworker like myself immediately want to preen his feathers in a self-important manner, but perhaps the idea itself is not so surprising. As Timothy Malefyt and I have pointed out elsewhere,[15] in certain fundamental respects – though not in others – fieldwork bears a marked resemblance to advertising and marketing-research methods. Moreover, it can clearly contribute to more nuanced understandings of how business organizations in general function – something that has been around in the field of Japanese anthropology for some decades now,[16] but is only more recently being rediscovered in that of organization studies and anthropology more generally.[17]

So the meaning of 'fieldwork' as a *name* for the core activity of anthropology may be said to have changed. Where once it referred to idyllic surroundings set, if not in actual fields, at least in a rural environment full of palm trees and beaches, it then had to be used to describe the concrete jungle to which urban anthropologists turned their attention.[18] Maybe it was this perceived anomaly – together with the fact that rural communities were either becoming increasingly depopulated as their members sought work in urban areas, or were themselves increasingly sucked into the (sub)urban sprawl – that caused people to reflect upon the nature of fieldwork and the ways in which they wrote about it. But the material presented in this book brings sense back to the very word, 'fieldwork'. It is in precisely the fact that it helps the participant observer understand and analyse a *field* of social relations – consisting of all the individuals, organizations, networks, institutions, positions and dispositions, formal and informal structures, beliefs and ideals, power and struggles of which it is composed – that the meaning of fieldwork can be said to lie.

How the fieldworker arrives at such an understanding of a complex field, though, is less easy to pinpoint. What I have suggested is that we generally engage in two very different kinds of fieldwork activity. One is the traditional, situated form of participant-observation where a fieldworker finds a village, school, office, or some such concrete setting, plumps him- or herself down and stays more or less put there for the next twelve months, asking questions, watching what's going on, keeping a diary, thinking up more questions, drawing genealogies, tables, charts and pictures generally, taking part in things as much as he or she's able or allowed, wondering if there are any more questions to ask, and so on and so forth. This *locus classicus* of anthropological fieldwork I have referred to as *frame-based fieldwork* in which the fieldworker is more or less *anchored* in a particular social group and setting. This was the kind of fieldwork I carried out in the pottery community of Sarayama (although I did find myself being drawn further afield because of the pottery's incorporation in a Japanese, and European and North American, arts-and-crafts movement). The frame was also partly there – in the form of several floors in five different office blocks scattered around the bottom end of the Ginza – when I studied the advertising agency, Asatsu.

The other kind of fieldwork is much less solidly anchored, since it involves the fieldworker's following a *flow* of social interaction along networks of people and things. This is what I have called *network-based fieldwork*. Here there is no fixed point to settle down and study. Rather, there are – as in networks themselves – nodes where people come together and particular activities take place. These nodes are themselves frames of one sort or another – a gallery exhibition, studio fashion shoot, competitive presentation, pottery workshop, and so on – where connections glue themselves together for greater or shorter lengths of time before moving on in their various directions.

This distinction between anchored frame- and flowing network-based kinds of fieldwork echoes Roland Barthes' distinction between anchorage and relay in his analysis of a Panzani food ad,[19] and the extension thereof in my own discussion of women's-magazine production,[20] where editorial staff try to lead their readers effortlessly from one topic to another while advertisers try to halt those same readers in their tracks and pay attention to the product advertised. Sometimes, as in good old-fashioned rural studies, fieldwork is primarily frame-based. At other times, as Hannerz argues for urban anthropology,[21] and as I discovered in my study of ceramic art in Japan, it is networks that dominate fieldwork research. At yet other times, as in my research in the advertising agency, fieldwork exhibits a matrix structure of networks and frames. These, so far as I can tell, are 'the classic conditions of fieldwork' which are *never* going to be altered by 'unexpected contexts, shifting constituencies, and changing agendas that anthropologists find themselves encountering'.[22]

It is thus somewhat naive of those claiming to be themselves fieldworkers to argue – or, rather, preach – that 'new and more complicated research locations are giving rise to shifts in the character of both fieldwork and fieldworker'.[23] Fieldworkers are *always* going to have to communicate with the people they study, whether new problems appear and new techniques are developed, or not.[24] The fact that, nowadays, anthropologists choose new kinds of research projects that are closer to home, 'differently problematized and innovatively conducted',[25] doesn't alter the fact that the object of our study – social organization and its surrounding cultural phenomena – has not changed fundamentally. People still act in frames, whether these are office meetings, family dinners or internet chat sites. They still use networks and take advantage of connections whenever they can – some more than others, maybe, but still they do so. And they still tend to find themselves in organizational structures of one kind or another, and spend a lot of time and energy first working out, and then trying to get round, rules of appropriate behaviour therein. And, precisely because of its basis in experience, fieldwork remains – and will remain – 'organizationally and technologically the most personalized and primitive'[26] kind of research method practised by anthropologists, sociologists, advertisers, marketers and others for whom, in one way or another, participant observation matters.

Ethnography

Properly speaking, as I have said, ethnography is the writing down of fieldwork material in such a way that it is 'empirical enough to be credible and analytical enough to be interesting'.[27] This involves certain skills that set the ethnographer somewhat apart from the fieldworker (even though the two are often one and the same person). After all, most of us practise fieldwork in one sense or another – which is what makes it 'the paradigmatic way of studying the social world'.[28] Most of us most of the time try to work out, subconsciously at least, why people act and react the ways they do, why things are as they are, how they might be improved, and so on and so forth. We engage in corridor conversations, share meals or drinks, participate in meetings of one sort or another, network with business or other colleagues, assimilate information, try to make sense of ambiguous signals and messages, and learn ourselves how to act appropriately in the environment in which we find ourselves.[29] And the more we engage in such activities, the more we learn, and the more we're able to move smoothly through the traps and snares that inevitably beset the field of forces in which we find ourselves. Fieldwork's the business of everyday life.

Writing it all down, though, or even trying to explain things verbally, in such a manner that others can readily understand us, is much more problematic. There is now much written about writing ethnography – notably by those who do not themselves write much ethnography – and what they have had to say is known well enough by those for whom I am writing here not to need further rehearsing.[30] (And for those readers outside this narrow field, it doesn't really matter.) As this book has shown, fieldwork accounts include plenty of stories – told either by those one is studying among themselves, or about the experiences of the participant observer in the field. Just *how* these stories are related, however, becomes an academic issue. Is 'one' to become detached and document the native's point of view, before interpreting everything with grand omniscience? Or am 'I' to slip into confessional mode, and show my biases, character flaws and bad habits as I reveal the shocks and surprises that overtook me at various points of the participative experience? Or should I write down a series of impressions designed to open up the back stage of fieldwork practice, so that it is the doing that becomes the focus of my readers' attention?

All three of these ways of writing fieldwork – formal (what's done), confessional (who's doing it) and impressionist (actual doing) tales[31] – are to be found in this book, although there is much more emphasis on the last than the first, and plenty of confessions have been made – from the ironic self-portrait to an assumed empathy with my well-informed informants, by way of the usual dose of luck, being there at the right time, and so on.[32]

But enough of confessions. I have made use of dramatic recall to draw my readers into unfamiliar worlds, and fragmented knowledge to illustrate the learning processes that go on in the field. I have given characterization to the supporting cast of my 'informants' – Rikizō, Inoshige, Yano, Eisuke and others – and thereby allowed them to seem like a 'natural' part of the fields in which they operate.[33] And I have used various stylistic techniques to create a sense of 'closeness' to my readers, and to control an illusion that 'you, dear readers' are also 'there' with me in the field. This is the art of impression management as well as of the impressionist tale.

At the same time, though, I have, I hope, in large part fulfilled John Van Maanen's criteria of 'a minimally acceptable table of contents for an account of fieldwork' where he says authors must discuss:

> Their pre-understandings of the studied field as well as their own interests in that scene; their modes of entry, sustained participation or presence, and exit procedures;[34] the responses of others on the scene to their presence (and vice versa); the nature of their relationship with various categories of informants; and their modes of data collection, storage, retrieval, and analysis.[35]

I'm not sure that much more needs to be said. I could go on, of course, citing in-vogue academic celebrities here, one or two venerable ancestors there, gradually building up page after page of dense prose and closely annotated text. But I have an uncomfortable feeling that I wouldn't be able to add very much – if anything – to all that has been said before. And anyway, as generations of students already know from long-suffering experience, we ageing academics tend to drone on and on and take others in the field – and, more worryingly, ourselves – much too seriously. I'd be much better advised to call it a day.

So be it. Or as they say in Japanese, *sayōnara*.

But is that it? Can I honestly say that a manuscript is at an end simply because the writing thereof has come to a stop? What is this 'end' exactly? What happens to this manuscript now that it has been completed? A whole new set of strategic exchanges starts at this point. Presumably – because I'm a sort-of-scholar working in an academic field which requires these days that I show my educational capital by publishing essays, articles in learned journals, monographs and so on – I will send it off to a publisher. But what kind of publisher? General, university or vanity press? First, second or third rate in the *A list/B list* prestige hierarchy? Whoever it is will have the manuscript reviewed by another scholar 'in the field', who will probably recommend certain changes of a more or less substantial nature. These will then be reflected upon and, partially at least, incorporated in a revised version of this same (though now slightly different) manuscript, which will then be accepted for publication, with contract issued, signed and countersigned, and accompanying vague promises of a paperback edition (*if* the hardback printing of probably not much more than 200 copies sells out fairly promptly, blah-blah-blah).

The manuscript will then go through those processes of production – copy-editing, cover design, inclusion of the title (which itself may be changed at the last minute) in the publisher's catalogue and list of 'forthcoming titles'– that transform it into a *book*. This book is then printed (once slotted into a printer's schedule and woe betide the author if he is late in submitting required material), given a dust jacket with illustration or other design, title, author's name on the front and single paragraph contents appetiser on the back – with, hopefully, a phrase or two of PR(aise) from leading lights in the discipline, and perhaps outside it, who have been inveigled into endorsing the new tome, generally as a result of personal connections of one sort or another, but possibly by an inducement in the form of cash, or free books, supplied by the publisher for services rendered.

And then there are the proofs to read and the bloody Index to complete.

And now the book-as-commodity, rather than manuscript-as-thought-process, is distributed into the wider world of the academic (or, by some fluke of circumstance, more general entertainment) field where it will first be read and reviewed in scholarly journals by colleagues who – as a result of impressions formed, and intellectual or personal loyalties developed, in other frames of academic activity (conferences, university membership, already published works) – may or may not have an axe to grind vis-à-vis its contents and/or its author, or who may need to feel that he or she has a great opportunity to impress *his or her* colleagues by her critical stance in the review in question . . .

Which, in turn, may or may not affect the desire of others to find this book on library or bookstore shelves, may or may not encourage them to open it and read (parts of) the Introduction and a chapter here or there – in short, become 'readers'. (What book, after all, has contents powerful and intriguing enough to attract concentrated reading of more than a few dozen pages? I am reminded of those seemingly endless two-hour lectures that, as a professor, I am obliged to give to an audience of students whose attention span, it is well known, is only 20 minutes at the very most.) And, as a result of this cursory dipping into the book's pages, or merely into a review thereof, these 'readers' will then disseminate by word of mouth the information that this book is 'good', or 'bad', or merely 'indifferent', and so rank its author accordingly in the fashion hierarchy of provisional celebrity-hood that now characterizes the academic industry.

All of which may itself lead to invitations to the author to be a visiting scholar at prestigious or less prestigious academic institutions and to give plenary-session speeches, invited lectures, or panel presentations at more or less well-known conferences, in the company or not of other celebrity names – opportunities for yet more strategic exchanges.

At which time, there may be invitations to, or opportunities for, the author to explain, justify, or rephrase the arguments first made in his book, and to respond to criticisms made thereof by colleagues who, in this game of distinction (a basic marketing principle), need to make *their* mark within the frame of their own department, discipline, and/or university . . .

And so may complete other manuscripts framed by the contents of this book, which, once accepted for publication, may be referred to me (with accompanying inducement) by the publisher who requests that I myself re-frame this new book with a back-cover blurb or even, if deemed appropriate (I would have to be *very* famous), Foreword . . .

Which may provide me with the opportunity to establish and reinforce a network of scholars who, if the network itself is dense and strong enough, together develop into a 'school' of thought that will, by its very presence and by the activities of its members (publications in refereed journals, strategic appearances at selected and important conferences) make an impression on the intellectual practices of those operating within a disciplinary field . . .

And, as a result, reframe that field.

Notes

1. A discarded Coke bottle, for instance, acted as the single focus of action – and merchandising star – for dozens and dozens of people in the film *The Gods Must Be Crazy*.
2. James Carrier (ed.), *Meanings of the Market*, 1997.
3. C.W. Watson (ed.), *Being There: Fieldwork in anthropology*, 1999, p. 2.
4. John Van Maanen, *Tales of the Field*, 1988, p. 8.
5. Kirsten Hastrup and Peter Hervik (eds), *Social Experience and Anthropological Knowledge*, 1994, pp. 1–12.
6. Cf. Van Maanen, *Tales of the Field*, p. 80.
7. Ivan Karp and Martha Kendall, 'Reflexivity in field work', in P. Secord (ed.), *Explaining Human Behavior, Human Action and Social Structure*, 1982, p. 251.
8. Daniel Miller, 'Advertising, production and consumption as cultural economy', 2003, p. 77.
9. Howard Becker, *Tricks of the Trade*, 1998.
10. Malcolm Chapman makes a similar point in his 'Social anthropology and business studies: some considerations of method', 2001, p. 28.
11. Hortense Powdermaker, *Stranger and Friend: The way of an anthropologist*, 1967, pp. 157–8, 215.
12. Burawoy, 'Introduction', *Ethnography Unbound*, 1991, p. 3.
13. This can be said, alas, of almost the entirety of anthropological writing about Japan. As a result, some of the most interesting material has been written by

those not in the field: for example, Lévi-Strauss on Heian Period cousin marriage, Maurice Bloch on death rituals, cosmogony and the state, and Roland Barthes' semiotic interpretation of aspects of contemporary Japanese culture. See also Van Maanen, *Tales of the Field*, p. 66.

14. Van Maanen, *Tales of the Field*, p. 125.
15. Timothy de Waal Malefyt and Brian Moeran, *Advertising Cultures*, 2003, pp. 12–17.
16. For example, Ronald Dore, *British Factory–Japanese Factory*, 1973; Thomas Rohlen, *For Harmony and Strength*, 1974; and Rodney Clark, *The Japanese Company*, 1979.
17. I say 'rediscovered' because, as mentioned earlier, there was quite a lot of early sociological fieldwork in business and professional organizations of one sort or another, from the 1920s and 1930s studies of the Western Electricity Hawthorne Plant in western Chicago and Cicero to the post-war ethnographies of the Chicago School of sociology under the guidance, principally, of Everett Hughes. Anthropologists have made their contributions over the years, notably June Nash among others, but the fact that they have focused on organizations within their own, rather than another, culture and studied 'up' among professionals and elites, rather than 'down' among villagers and hobos, has tended to marginalize them from the central activities of the discipline as a whole. (See Helen Schwartzman, *Ethnography in Organizations*, 1993, and also for example Susan Wright (ed.), *The Anthropology of Organizations*, 1994, and Tony Watson, *In Search of Management*, 2001.)
18. Powdermaker, *Stranger and Friend*, 1967.
19. Roland Barthes, *Image–Music–Text*, 1977, pp. 38–41.
20. Brian Moeran, *A Japanese Advertising Agency*, 1996, pp. 227–9.
21. Ulf Hannerz, *Exploring the City*, 1980, Chapter 5.
22. George Marcus, 'Critical anthropology now', 1999, p. 4.
23. Ibid., p. 7.
24. Powdermaker, *Stranger and Friend*, p. 286.
25. Ibid., p. 7.
26. J. Lofland, 'Styles of reporting qualitative field research', 1974, quoted in Van Maanen, *Tales of the Field*, p. 24.
27. Van Maanen, *Tales of the Field*, p. 29.
28. Burawoy, 'Introduction', *Ethnography Unbound*, 1991, p. 3.
29. Watson, *In Search of Management*, p. 8.
30. For the sake of the citation index, the seminal work is James Clifford and George Marcus (eds), *Writing Culture*, 1986.
31. Van Maanen, *Tales of the Field*, Chapters 3, 4 and 5.
32. Let me quickly make it clear that, whatever the impression given by the stories told, I couldn't possibly 'melt into' my surroundings in Japan, even

though I may for a while 'forget my self'. For a start, I'm Caucasian, whose skin texture, hair (what's left of it), colour of the eyes, and general bodily proportions make me immediately different from those Japanese with whom I interact. I tend, too, to speak my mind (as my friend Mariko discovered when she told me how 'insignificant' the food was that she had prepared for me). Such forthrightness doesn't necessarily help in a society where people tend to prefer indirect modes of communication. And at my height – a full six foot four-and-a-half inches or 1.97 metres tall – I can hardly masquerade as the proverbial 'fly on the wall' taking notes unobserved. The idea of assimilation becomes absurd here.

33. Van Maanen, *Tales of the Field*, pp. 73–81.
34. Exit procedures have not been discussed in detail, although one such was my own one-man pottery show devised by Minamoto Eisuke. The two frame-based fieldwork periods (in Sarayama and Asatsu) were undertaken on the understanding that, initially, they would last for a particular period of time. In each case, this period was extended: from one to two years in Sarayama, and from three months to a year in Asats?. People generally knew that an end was in sight, although they quite often, and rather sweetly, expressed surprise that I should actually pack up my things and leave.
35. Van Maanen, *Tales of the Field*, pp. 93–4.

Bibliography

Appadurai, Arjun (ed.) (1986) *The Social Life of Things*. Cambridge: Cambridge University Press.

Arlen, Michael (1981) *Thirty Seconds*. Harmondsworth: Penguin.

Arrow, Kenneth (1974) *The Limits of Organization*. New York: Norton.

Aspers, Patrick (2001) *Markets in Fashion: A Phenomenological Approach*. Stockholm: City University Press.

Atsumi, Reiko (1979) 'Tsukiai – obligatory personal relationships of Japanese white-collar company Employees', *Human Organization* 38(1): 63–70.

Bachnik, Jane (1989) '*Omote/ura*: indexes and the organization of self and society in Japan', pp. 239–62 in C. Calhoun (ed.) *Comparative Social Research* 11. Greenwich, CT: JAI Press.

—— and Charles Quinn (eds) (1994) *Situated Meaning: Inside and Outside in Japanese Self, Society, and Language*. Princeton, NJ: Princeton University Press.

Baker, Wayne E. (1987) 'The network organization in theory and practice', pp. 397–429 in W. Richard Scott (ed.) *Organizations: Rational, Natural, and Open Systems* (2nd edn). Englewood Cliffs, NJ: Prentice-Hall.

Barnes, John (1969) 'Networks and political processes', pp. 51–76 in J. Clyde Mitchell (ed.) *Social Networks in Urban Situations*. Manchester: Manchester University Press.

Barthes, Roland (1977) *Image–Music–Text*. London: Fontana.

—— (1983) *Empire of Signs*. London: Jonathan Cape.

Bateson, Gregory (1972) *Steps to an Ecology of the Mind*. New York: Ballantine.

Becker, Howard (1982) *Art Worlds*. Berkeley and Los Angeles: University of California Press.

—— (1986) *Writing for Social Scientists*. Chicago: University of Chicago Press.

—— (1998) *Tricks of the Trade*. Chicago: University of Chicago Press.

Beetham, Margaret (1996) *A Magazine of Her Own*. London: Routledge.

Befu, Harumi (1980) 'The group model of Japanese society and an alternative', *Rice University Studies* 66(1): 169–87.

—— (1989) 'A theory of social exchange as applied to Japan', pp. 39–66 in Yoshio Sugimoto and Ross Mouer (eds) *Constructs for Understanding Japan*. London: Kegan Paul International.

Benedict, Ruth (1946) *The Chrysanthemum and the Sword*. Boston: Houghton Mifflin.

Bengtsson, Karsten (2003) 'Netværksteorier blomstrer i USA', *Universitetsavisen* 14: 9.

Berger, Bennett (1986) 'Foreword', pp. xi-xviii in E. Goffman, *Frame Analysis*. Boston: Northeastern University Press.

Bloch, Maurice (1992) *Prey Into Hunter: The Politics of Religious Experience*. Cambridge: Cambridge University Press.

Blumer, Herbert (1986) *Symbolic Interactionism: Perspective and Method*. Berkeley and Los Angeles: University of California Press.

Bott, Elizabeth (1957) *Family and Social Network*. London: Tavistock.

Bouchet, Dominique (2003) 'Kulturforskelle – en styrke', pp. 33–47 in P. Milner, T. Morsing and K. Overø (eds) *Mit Europa*. Copenhagen: Linhardt og Ringhof.

Bourdieu, Pierre (1984) *Distinction: A Social Critique of the Judgement of Taste*. London: RKP.

—— (1990a) *The Logic of Practice*. Cambridge: Polity.

—— (1990b) *In Other Words: Essays Towards a Reflexive Sociology*. Cambridge: Polity.

—— (1993) *The Field of Cultural Production: Essays on Art and Literature*, edited by R. Johnson. Cambridge: Polity.

Burawoy, Michael (1991) 'Introduction', pp. 1–7 in M. Burawoy et al., *Ethnography Unbound: Power and Resistance in the Modern Metropolis*. Berkeley and Los Angeles: University of California Press.

Burt, Ronald (1983) *Corporate Profits and Cooptation: Networks of Market Constraints and Directorate Ties in the American Economy*. New York: Academic Press.

—— (1992a) *Structural Holes: The Social Structure of Competition*. Cambridge, MA: Harvard University Press.

—— (1992b) 'The social structure of competition', pp. 57–91 in N. Nohria and R. Eccles (eds) *Networks and Organizations: Structure, Form and Action*. Boston, MA: Harvard Business School Press.

—— (2000) [1993] 'The network entrepreneur', pp. 281–307 in R. Swedberg (ed.) *Entrepreneurship: The Social Science View*. Oxford: Oxford University Press.

Carrier, James (ed.) (1997) *Meanings of the Market*. Oxford: Berg.

Castells, Manuel (2000) [1996] *The Rise of the Network Society*, 2nd edn. Oxford: Basil Blackwell.

Caves, Richard (2000) *Creative Industries: Contracts Between Art and Commerce*. Cambridge, MA: Harvard University Press.

Chapman, Malcolm (2001) 'Social anthropology and business studies: some considerations of method', pp. 19–33 in D. Gellner and E. Hirsch (eds) *Inside Organizations: Anthropologists at Work*. Oxford: Berg.

Clark, Eric (1989) *The Want Makers – Lifting the Lid Off the Advertising Industry: How They Make You Want to Buy*. New York: Viking.

Clarke, Rodney (1979) *The Japanese Company*. New Haven, CT: Yale University Press.

Clifford, James and George Marcus (eds) (1986) *Writing Culture*. Berkeley and Los Angeles: University of California Press.

Cohen, Abner (1974) *Two-Dimensional Man: An Essay on the Anthropology of Power and Symbolism in Complex Society*. London: Routledge & Kegan Paul.

Dale, Peter (1986) *The Myth of Japanese Uniqueness*. London: Croom Helm.

Danto, Arthur (1981) *The Transfiguration of the Commonplace*. Cambridge, MA: Harvard University Press.

Deighton, Len (1988) *Spy Hook*. London: Hutchinson.

DiMaggio, Paul and Walter Powell (1983) 'The iron cage revisited: institutional isomorphism and collective rationality in organizational fields', *American Sociological Review* 48: 147–60.

Doi, Takeo (1973) *The Anatomy of Dependence*. Tokyo: Kodansha International.

Dore, Ronald (1973) *British Factory–Japanese Factory*. Berkeley and Los Angeles: University of California Press.

—— (1983) 'Goodwill and the spirit of market capitalism', *British Journal of Sociology* 34: 459–82.

—— (2000) *Stock Market Capitalism: Welfare Capitalism – Japan and Germany versus the Anglo-Saxons*. Oxford: Oxford University Press.

Du Gay, Paul, Stuart Hall, Linda Janes, Hugh Mackay and Keith Negus (1997) *Doing Cultural Studies: The Story of the Sony Walkman*. London: Open University/Sage.

Frake, Charles (1964) 'How to ask for a drink in Subanun', *American Anthropologist* LXVI (6): 127–32.

Frances, Jennifer, Rosalind Levavic, Jeremy Mitchell and Grahame Thompson (1991) 'Introduction', pp. 1–23 in G. Thompson, J. Frances, R. Levavic and J. Mitchell (eds) *Markets, Hierarchies and Networks: The Coordination of Social Life*. London: Open University/Sage.

Fukuyama, Francis (1995) *Trust: The Social Virtues and the Creation of Prosperity*. Harmondsworth: Penguin.

Geertz, Clifford (1973) *The Interpretation of Cultures*. New York: Basic.

Gellner, David and Eric Hirsch (eds) (2001) *Inside Organizations: Anthropologists at Work*. Oxford: Berg.

Gerlach, Michael (1992) *Alliance Capitalism: The Social Organization of Japanese Business*. Berkeley and Los Angeles: University of California Press.

—— and James Lincoln (1992) 'The organization of business networks in the United States and Japan', pp. 491–520 in N. Nohria and R. Eccles (eds)

Networks and Organizations: Structure, Form and Action. Boston, MA: Harvard Business School Press.

Gimpel, René (1966) *Diary of an Art Dealer*. New York: Farrar, Straus and Giroux.

Godbout, Jacques (1988) *The World of the Gift*, in collaboration with Alain Callé. Montreal and Kingston: McGill-Queen's University Press.

Goffman, Erving (1959) *The Presentation of Self in Everyday Life*, New York: Anchor.

—— (1986) [1974] *Frame Analysis: An Essay on the Organization of Experience*. Boston: Northeastern University Press.

Granovetter, Mark (1974) *Getting a Job: A Study of Contacts and Careers*. Cambridge, MA: Harvard University Press.

—— (1985) 'Economic actions and social structure: the problem of embeddedness', *American Journal of Sociology* 91(3): 481–510.

Gross, Michael (1995) *Model: The Ugly Business of Beautiful Women*. New York: Warner Books.

Gulati, Ranjay and Martin Gargiulo (1999) 'Where do interorganizational networks come from?' *American Journal of Sociology* 104(5): 1439–93.

Hannerz, Ulf (1980) *Exploring the City: Inquiries Toward an Urban Anthropology*. New York: Columbia University Press.

—— (1992) 'The global ecumene as a network of networks', pp. 34–56 in A. Kuper (ed.) *Conceptualizing Society*. London and New York: Routledge.

Hastrup, Kirsten and Peter Hervik (eds) (1994) *Social Experience and Anthropological Knowledge*. London and New York: Routledge.

Hauser, Arnold (1982) *The Sociology of Art*. London: Routledge & Kegan Paul.

Havens, Thomas (1982) *Artist and Patron in Postwar Japan: Dance, Music, Theatre, and the Visual Arts, 1955–1980*. Princeton, NJ: Princeton University Press.

Heimer, Carol (1992) 'Doing your job *and* helping your friends: universalistic norms about obligations to particular others in networks', pp. 143–164 in N. Nohria and R. Eccles (eds) *Networks and Organizations: Structure, Form and Action*. Boston, MA: Harvard Business School Press.

Hendry, Joy (1993) *Wrapping Culture: Politeness, Presentation, and Power in Japan and Other Societies*. Oxford: Oxford University Press.

Ibarra, Herminia (1992) 'Structural alignments, individual strategies, and managerial action: elements toward a network theory of getting things done', pp. 165–88 in N. Nohria and R. Eccles (eds) *Networks and Organizations: Structure, Form and Action*. Boston, MA: Harvard Business School Press.

Jackall, Robert and Janice Hirota (2000) *Image Makers: Advertising, Public Relations, and the Ethos of Advocacy*. Chicago: University of Chicago Press.

Johnson, Chalmers (1980) '*Omote* (explicit) and *ura* (implicit): translating Japanese political terms', *Journal of Japanese Studies* 6(1): 89–115.

Johnson, Randal (1993) 'Editor's Introduction: Pierre Bourdieu on art, literature and culture', pp. 1–28 in his P. Bourdieu, *The Field of Cultural Production*. Cambridge: Polity.

Johnston, Russell and Paul Lawrence (1991) 'Beyond vertical integration: the rise of the value-added partnership', pp. 193–202 in G. Thompson et al. (eds) *Markets, Hierarchies and Networks: The Coordination of Social Life*. London: Open University/Sage.

Kalland, Arne and Brian Moeran (1992) *Japanese Whaling: End of an Era?* London: Curzon.

Kanter, Rosabeth Moss (1993) [1977] *Men and Women of the Corporation*. New York: Basic.

—— and Robert Eccles (1992) 'Making network research relevant to practice', pp. 521–7 in N. Nitin and R. Eccles (eds) *Networks and Organizations: Structure, Form and Action*. Boston, MA: Harvard Business School Press.

Karp, Ivan and Martha Kendall (1982) 'Reflexivity in field work', in P. Secord (ed.) *Explaining Human Behavior, Human Action and Social Structure*. Beverly Hills, CA: Sage.

Kipnis, Andrew (1997) *Producing Guanxi: Sentiment, Self, and Subculture in a North China Village*. Durham, NC and London: Duke University Press.

Knoke, David and James Kublinski (1991) 'Network analysis: basic concepts', pp. 173–82 in G. Thompson et al. (eds) *Markets, Hierarchies and Networks: The Coordination of Social Life*. London: Open University/Sage.

Kumon, Shumpei (1992) 'Japan as a network society', pp. 109–41 in S. Kumon and H. Rosovsky (eds) *The Political Economy of Japan*, Volume 3, *Cultural and Social Dynamics*. Stanford: Stanford University Press.

Kuper, Adam (2001) 'Fraternity and endogamy: the house of Rothschild', *Social Anthropology* 9(3): 273–88.

Lakoff, George and Mark Johnson (1980) *Metaphors We Live By*. Chicago: University of Chicago Press.

Lebra, Takie Sugiyama (1992) 'The spatial layout of hierarchy: residential style of the modern Japanese nobility', pp. 49–78 in her edited *Japanese Social Organization*. Honolulu: University of Hawai'i Press.

Lévi-Strauss, Claude (1985) 'Cross-readings', pp. 79–87 in his *The View from Afar*. New York: Basic.

Lincoln, James, Michael Gerlach and C. Ahmadjian (1996) 'Keiretsu networks and corporate performance in Japan', *American Sociological Review* 61: 67–88.

Lofland, J. (1974) 'Styles of reporting qualitative field research', *American Sociologist* 9: 101–11.

Lorenz, Edward (1991) 'Neither friends nor strangers: informal networks of subcontracting in French industry', pp. 183–92 in G. Thompson et al. (eds)

Markets, Hierarchies and Networks: The Coordination of Social Life. London: Open University/Sage.

Lupton, T. and S. Wilson (1959) 'Background and connections of top decision-makers', *Manchester School*: 30-51.

McCracken, Ellen (1993) *Decoding Women's Magazines: From Mademoiselle to Ms*. Basingstoke: Macmillan.

McKay, Jenny (2000) *The Magazines Handbook*. London: Routledge.

Malefyt, Timothy (2003) 'Models, metaphors and client relations: the negotiated meanings of advertising', pp. 139–64 in T. Malefyt and B. Moeran (eds) *Advertising Cultures*. Oxford: Berg.

—— and Brian Moeran (eds) (2003) *Advertising Cultures*. Oxford: Berg.

Marcus, George (1998) *Ethnography Through Thick and Thin*. Princeton: Princeton University Press.

—— (1999) 'Critical anthropology now: An introduction', pp. 3–28 in his edited *Critical Anthropology Now: Unexpected Contexts, Shifting Constituencies, Changing Agendas*. Santa Fe, NM: School of American Research Press.

—— and Michael Fisher (1986) *Anthropology as Cultural Critique*. Chicago: University of Chicago Press.

Martin, Samuel (1964) 'Speech levels in Japan and Korea', pp. 407–15 in D. Hymes (ed.) *Language in Culture and Society*. New York: Harper and Row.

Mayer, Adrian (1966) 'The significance of quasi-groups in the study of complex societies', pp. 97–122 in M. Banton (ed.) *The Social Organisation of Complex Societies*, ASA Monographs 4. London: Tavistock.

Meyer, Karl (1979) *The Art Museum: Power, Money, Ethics*. New York: William Morrow.

Miller, Daniel (2003) 'Advertising, production and consumption as cultural economy', pp. 75–90 in T. Malefyt and B. Moeran (eds) *Advertising Cultures*. Oxford: Berg.

Mintzberg, Henry (1973) *The Nature of Managerial Work*. New York: Harper and Row.

Mitchell, J. Clyde (1969) 'The concept and use of social networks', in his edited *Social Networks in Urban Situations*. Manchester: Manchester University Press.

Mitchell, Marilyn (1998) *Employing Qualitative Methods in the Private Sector*. Qualitative Research Methods Series 42. Newbury Park: Sage.

Moeran, Brian (1986) 'One over the seven: *sake* drinking in a Japanese pottery community', pp. 226–42 in J. Hendry and J. Webber (eds) *Interpreting Japanese Society*. Oxford: JASO Occasional Papers. (Reprinted in J. Hendry (ed.) (1998) *Interpreting Japanese Society: Anthropological Approaches*, 2nd edn. London: Routledge.)

—— (1988) *London Daigaku no Nihongo Gakka*. Tokyo: Jōhō Centre.

—— (1990a) 'Making an exhibition of oneself: the anthropologist as potter in Japan', pp. 117–39 in E. Ben Ari, B. Moeran and J. Valentine (eds) *Unwrapping Japan*. Manchester: Manchester University Press.

—— (1990b) 'Japanese ceramics and the discourse of "tradition"', *Journal of Design History* 3(4): 213–225.

—— (1993) 'A tournament of value: strategies of presentation in Japanese advertising', *Ethnos* Volume 54, Numbers 1–2: 73–93.

—— (1996) *A Japanese Advertising Agency: An Anthropology of Media and Markets*. London: Curzon.

—— (1997) *Folk Art Potters of Japan: Beyond an Anthropology of Aesthetics*. London: Curzon.

—— (1998) [1985] *A Far Valley: Four Years in a Japanese Community*. Tokyo: Kodansha International (originally published as *Ōkubo Diary: Portrait of a Japanese Valley*. Stanford, CA: Stanford University Press).

—— (2000) 'The split account system and Japan's advertising industry', *International Journal of Advertising* 19(2): 185–200.

—— (2003a) 'Fields, networks and frames: advertising social organization in Japan', *Global Networks* 3(3): 371–86.

—— (2003b) 'Imagining and imaging the other: Japanese advertising international', pp. 91–112 in T. Malefyt and B. Moeran (eds) *Advertising Cultures*. Oxford: Berg.

Mouer, Ross and Yoshio Sugimoto (1986) *Images of Japanese Society*. London: Kegan Paul International.

Moulin, Raymonde (1987) *The French Art Market: A Sociological View*. New Brunswick, NJ and London: Rutgers University Press.

Myers, Fred (ed.) (2001) *The Empire of Things: Regimes of Value and Material Culture*. Santa Fe, NM: School of American Research Press.

Nakane, Chie (1967a) *Kinship and Economic Organization in Rural Japan*. London: Athlone.

—— (1967b) *Tate Shakai no Ningen Kankei*. Tokyo: Kōdansha Gendai Shinsho.

—— (1970) *Japanese Society*. Berkeley and Los Angeles: University of California Press.

—— (1978) *Tate Shakai no Rikigaku*. Tōkyō: Kōdansha Gendai Shinsho.

Nitin, Nohria (1992) 'Is a network perspective a useful way of studying organizations?' pp. 1–22 in N. Nitin and R. Eccles (eds) *Networks and Organizations: Structure, Form and Action*. Boston, MA: Harvard Business School Press.

Plattner, Stuart (1996) *High Art Down Home: An Economic Ethnography of a Local Art Market*. Chicago: University of Chicago Press.

Powdermaker, Hortense (1967) *Stranger and Friend: The Way of an Anthropologist*. London: Secker & Warburg.

Powell, Walter (1986) *Getting into Print*. Chicago: University of Chicago Press.

Rohlen, Thomas (1974) *For Harmony and Strength*. Berkeley and Los Angeles: University of California Press.

Sadler, A. L. (1934) *Cha-no-yu: the Japanese Tea Ceremony*. London: Kegan Paul, Trench, Trubner.

Sahlins, Marshall (1965) 'On the sociology of primitive exchange', pp. 139–236 in M. Banton (ed.) *The Relevance of Models for Social Anthropology*. London: Tavistock.

Salaman, Graeme (1997) 'Culturing production', pp. 235–84 in P. du Gay (ed.) *Production of Culture/Cultures of Production*. London: Sage/Open University.

Sampson, Anthony (1965) *Anatomy of Britain Today*. London: Hodder & Stoughton.

Satō Tomoyasu (1981) *Keibatsu: Nihon No New Establishment*. Tokyo: Rippū Shobō.

Schodt, Frederik (1996) *Dreamland Japan: Writings on Modern Manga*. Berkeley: Stonebridge Press.

Schucking, Levin (1974) [1944] *The Sociology of Literary Taste*. Chicago: University of Chicago Press.

Schudson, Michael (1984) *Advertising: The Uneasy Persuasion*. New York: Basic.

Schwartzman, Helen (1993) *Ethnography in Organizations*. Qualitative Research Methods Series 27. Newbury Park: Sage.

Shiraishi, Saya (1997) 'Japan's soft power: Doraemon goes overseas', pp. 234–72 in P. Katzenstein and T. Shiraishi (eds) *Network Power: Japan and Asia*. Ithaca, NY: Cornell University Press.

Smith, Charles (1989) *Auctions: The Social Construction of Value*. Berkeley and Los Angeles: University of California Press.

Srinivas, M.N. and André Beteille (1964) 'Networks in Indian social structure', *Man* 64: 165–8.

Sternberg, Ernest (1999) *The Economy of Icons: How Business Manufactures Meaning*. Westport, CT: Praeger.

Thompson, James (1967) *Organizations in Action*. New York: McGraw-Hill.

Turner, Victor (1974) *Dramas, Fields, and Metaphors: Symbolic Action in Human Society*. Ithaca, NY and London: Cornell University Press.

Useem, Michael (1979) 'The social organization of the American business elite and participation of corporation directors in the governance of American institutions', *American Sociological Review* 44: 553–72.

Van Maanen, John (1988) *Tales of the Field*. Chicago: Chicago University Press.

Van Wolferen, Karel (1989) *The Enigma of Japanese Power*. London: Macmillan.

Vollard, Ambroise (1978) [1936] *Recollections of a Picture Dealer*. New York: Dover.

Watson, C.W. (ed.) (1999) *Being There: Fieldwork in Anthropology*. London: Pluto.

Watson, Tony (2001) *In Search of Management: Culture, Chaos and Control in Managerial Work*. London: Thomson.

Weiner, Annette (1994) 'Cultural difference and the density of objects', *American Ethnologist* 21(2): 391–403.

Westney, D. Eleanore (1996) 'Mass media as business organisations: A U.S.–Japan comparison', pp. 47–88 in S. Pharr and E. Krauss (eds), *Media and Politics in Japan*. Honolulu: University of Hawai'i Press.

Whyte, W.F. (1984) *Learning from the Field*. Beverly Hills, CA: Sage.

Wilk, Richard (1996) *Economies and Cultures: Foundations of Economic Anthropology*. Boulder, CO: Westview.

—— (2002) 'When good theories go bad: theory in economic anthropology and consumer research', pp. 239–50 in J. Ensminger (ed.) *Theory in Economic Anthropology*. Walnut Creek, CA: AltaMira.

Wilson, Thomas (ed.) (forthcoming) *Drinking Culture: Alcohol and the Expression of Identity, Class and Nation*. Oxford: Berg.

Winship, Janice (1987) *Inside Women's Magazines*. London: Pandora.

Wright, Susan (ed.) (1994) *Anthropology of Organizations*. London and New York: Routledge.

Wrong, Dennis (1961) 'The oversocialized conception of man in modern sociology', *American Sociological Review* 26(2): 183–93.

Yang, Mayfair Mei-hui (1994) *Gifts, Favors and Banquets: The Art of Social Relationships in China*. Ithaca, NY: Cornell University Press.

Index